T0305217

England's Discontents

England's Discontents

Political Cultures and National Identities

Mike Wayne

First published 2018 by Pluto Press
345 Archway Road, London N6 5AA

www.plutobooks.com

British Library Cataloguing in Publication Data
A catalogue record for this book is available from the British Library

ISBN 978 0 7453 9932 4 Hardback
ISBN 978 0 7453 9933 1 Paperback
ISBN 978 1 7868 0321 4 PDF eBook
ISBN 978 1 7868 0323 8 Kindle eBook
ISBN 978 1 7868 0322 1 EPUB eBook

This book is printed on paper suitable for recycling and made from fully managed and
sustained forest sources. Logging, pulping and manufacturing processes are expected to
conform to the environmental standards of the country of origin.

Typeset by Swales & Willis

Simultaneously printed in the United Kingdom and United States of America

Printed and bound by CPI Group (UK) Ltd, Croydon, CR0 4YY

Contents

Introduction

The national question is today returning to the political agenda in a rebalancing of priorities after a period in which radical politics was largely defined by a transnational, anti-globalisation focus. With the collapse in the 1990s of nation-state regimes claiming to be communist, and with capitalism operating on an increasingly transnational basis, transnational political movements targeting multinational institutions, such as at the summit meetings of the big powers or transnational corporations, indicated a shift in political energies consonant with the moment. Yet the Arab Spring and the Egyptian Revolution of 2011 in particular, returned us joltingly to the question of political power at the national level. Here all the classic tropes of the revolutionary situation returned – a popular revolt against a hated government embodied in a particular figure (Mubarak), a violent oppressive state meeting popular resistance that then fractures the army, the role of external nation-states allied with the oppressive state and its national oligarchy, an alliance of popular forces overcoming to some extent prior divisions and, perhaps most pressingly and what was least satisfactorily resolved in the Egyptian case: what would the political organisational forms and objectives be that could displace the status quo? In short, power and the legitimacy of power and counter-power on the terrain of the nation-state were starkly posed.

The Egyptian Revolution, whose symbolic centre had been the occupation of Tahrir square in Cairo, in turn spawned the Occupy movement in Spain, North America, Britain and elsewhere. Although this was a synchronous international movement, this was also the beginning of each movement turning towards its own national context and state to demand change. Thus we saw the rising popularity of once-marginal parties such as Syriza in Greece, the formation of new political parties such as Podemos in Spain or newly vibrant forces emerge on the Left within the old established parties, such as Bernie Sanders's 2016 run at the Democratic Presidential candidate in the US or the bolt-from-the-blue success of Jeremy Corbyn in becoming leader of the Labour Party in 2015. This return to the national stage for political contestation is a tacit recognition that governmental power gives access to at least some branches of state power and state power remains a significant prize in the struggle for a better world. This is not to say that the transnational arena in which nation-states are situated is not criss-crossed by very powerful economic and institutional forces that are operating above the nation-state. Yet these forces and organisations struggle to achieve anywhere near as much legitimacy and democratic credibility as the nation-state has accumulated, despite continuing deficiencies, over several hundred years.

Despite the international context of nation-state development and therefore the commonalities which similar social and economic structures produce, the national question is a question of the *specificity* of national development in each case. In the British context there has been an extensive debate about the historical formation of Britishness and how that determines our present condition. In this debate, what has loomed large has been the early development of agrarian capitalism in England especially and how that may have cemented the economic, political and symbolic power of an agrarian elite that in turn gave an inflection and centrality to ruralism, undemocratic state institutions and an anti-democratic, anti-meritocratic ideology in the British imaginary. The historical development of the Industrial Revolution, another world first, then adds a new set of social and cultural forces to the mix, themselves split between those attached to industrial capital and those that made up the industrial workforce. The complex relationships between these new social agents and practices and the older ones associated with agrarian capitalism produce in turn a wide range of interpretations and debates concerning these relations and their actual and desired relative weight and importance in the formation of Britishness as a composite outcome of all these relationships. This reflexive commentary on historical developments becomes in turn a part of the historical process. And this is all overlaid again by the development of the empire whose legacy and long-term effects, economic, political and cultural, are still active and contested in our contemporary scene. All this before we even consider how this complex of forces, including the rise of the middle class, entered into and were transformed again by the twentieth century.

So a return to the national question in a British context, means a return to debates about the specific history of national *identities* that form the composite notion of Britishness. *Identities* in part because in the British case, this is a supranational unit made up of both regional and national identities (England, Wales and Scotland, but also Northern Ireland and before 1922 the entirety of Ireland). *Identities* because (as the case of Ireland already alerts us to) imperial power projection meant that Britishness was entangled globally with territories around the world and then subsequently inward migration brought significant numbers of people from the former colonies into Britain, especially after the Second World War. *Identities* also because different classes and alliances between classes have struggled to shape Britishness in their own collective image. And *identities* because contesting political cultures have developed as the key organisational forces that have brought together regions, nations, ethnicities and classes and given them particular accents, narratives and political and cultural representation. The term 'political cultures' refers to recognisable value systems that seek representation at the level of the state but which have their roots in a capillary-like network of social, economic and cultural relationships far broader than formal institutions of political power (i.e. parliament and parties).

Everything above already indicates that I do not approach national identities in the classic manner of the British or English authors who enumerate an arbitrary list of discrete characteristics (e.g. modest and self-effacing, emotionally reticent, individualistic, polite, practical, etc., etc.). Such approaches to the question of identity lack both a sense of historical change and formation (they become unchanging essences) and a sense of 'structure' or the structuring forces that gives rise to the empirical characteristics. They also often conceal how a particular (upper class) identity has come to stand in for the national. In this empirical approach we move from a rather haphazard and apparently subjective list of traits to a universal: *this* amounts to *the* British identity, when we should be looking for structured but composite formations that alter historically as the outcome of political struggles, which are always ultimately contests of power over resources and recognition or esteem.

It is de rigeur to stress the plurality and hybridity of national identities in contemporary cultural studies. It has become a standard trope in the study of culture and undoubtedly speaks to very important truths about identity in general, whether we are thinking about identity in relation to the individual, the social group or national identity/ies. What has been termed the 'linguistic turn', beginning with the theoretical revolution of structuralism in the late 1950s, developed a new model of identity. Structuralism taught us that identity, and meaning in general, was always *relational*. Not a word, a meaning or identity could signify something without differentiating itself from other words, identities or meanings. Intelligibility of meaning was always ghosted by the difference of a signifying unit from other signifying units in complex relationships. Scaled up to the question of national identity, Britishness, for example, was defined by its relations of difference with other national identities (American or German national identities for instance) rather than its own inner essence.

As structuralism passed into post-structuralism, so the question of difference was pressed further: differences and identities formed out of them were no longer conceived as relatively durable 'structures' as the famous binary oppositions of structuralist analysis might suggest. Instead a new sense of the mutability, contingency and continual flux of meaning around terms was increasingly matched to the fast-moving developments in culture, technology, economics and politics. The rather static understanding of meaningful structures that structuralism had developed, was exploded as a new sensitivity to difference and continual change emerged within cultural theory. The theoretical shifts in thinking about identity that structuralism and post-structuralism wrought definitely had a broadly political orientation. It amounted to an extraordinarily sustained liberal critique of conservatism as a political culture, with the latter's investment in rather more static and unified cultural understandings that could sustain a more assured hierarchy of value, a greater sense of autonomous development from a range of 'outsiders' and a firm sense of a boundary marking itself off from those apparently absolutely different others. The normative implication of the liberal critique of the conservative model was that difference and change should be embraced (was already with us in fact), while the normative underpinning of conservatism was that 'vertical' (i.e. hierarchical) unity, cultural homogeneity and historical continuity were to be prized above all else.

The linguistic turn blasted open two of the common traps which discussions of identity had typically fallen into previously: the notion that identity was more or less fixed in time, that continuities were far stronger and more significant than change; and the idea that identity was about unity and homogeneity, that who we thought we were (identity) must rest on similarity (of interests, of culture, etc.). Yet any identity, any drawing of a boundary that stakes out a claim for a distinctive and recognisable formation, not only depends on difference 'outside' it to define itself, it is always also made up of differentiated component parts internally. This is true of individuals, social groups, political cultures and national identity itself. 'Identity thinking' has had a tendency to play down these differentiated component parts, or at best recognise and celebrate them as part of the diversity of a broader unified identity 'beneath' the differences. Yet when we dig further into the component parts of an identity we often find that while they may be held together within the force field of a broader framework, there may be considerable tensions or even contradictions between the component parts and these tensions and contradictions are in turn historically mutable. This book will focus on the internally contradictory dynamics of the key political cultures that have fashioned Britishness. In particular I focus on how conservatism and liberalism, in a competitive partnership of alliances and tensions, have been central to the formation of Britishness. I also explore how their contradictory relationship with the British capitalism they otherwise support is also a key dynamic that has formed the national cultures.

If an appreciation of the temporal change and internal differentiation of identity has been hard won, then the question of grounding identity in the complex of powerful forces of a social and economic kind has been harder still. Here the linguistic turn has been less successful in helping us understand how and why identity forms and changes the way it does. Indeed, if liberalism has conducted a long cultural and theoretical 'war' against conservatism, it has also conducted one, in academia especially, against the discipline of political economy, the discipline which has most insistently raised those awkward questions about our social and economic model of capitalism. This 'war' against political economy as a discipline has its parallel outside academia in the mainstream institutions of politics, where a disinclination to 'burden' capital with any social responsibilities, has entrenched itself amongst the political class. The liberalism of the linguistic turn does not exactly reflect liberalism in the political institutions, not least because the latter, in the real world of politics, exists in complex alliances with conservatism, which academic liberalism, in theory can afford to appear to remain implacably opposed to (at the level of models of identity in particular). But there is a clear connection nonetheless between economic liberalism in the core political institutions and cultural liberalism in academic theory.

The political and methodological framework of this book does not accept that conservatism and liberalism exhaust the possibilities of discussing cultural politics, political cultures and their relationships. Even if conservatism and liberalism loom large as the most powerful philosophical and political actors at work in our historical moment (and historically) we need not accept their horizons as the methodological and political presuppositions by which to examine their movements and dynamics. For there is a vast terrain of social experiences which these political cultures struggle to properly accommodate or to even recognise. This 'political unconscious' provides the normative basis for speaking outside the conservative–liberal consensus. The aim of this book is to develop a model of national identity that can be adequate to the complexities of identity at the level of historical mutation, structured and internally differentiated composition *and* materially grounded in the play of social and economic forces. As we move to ground cultures and identities in their socio-economic contexts, so some of the assumed and easy pluralism of the linguistic turn begins to be reconceptualised within a framework that brings into view structured power relations, patterns of interest and reproductions of inequality.

The methodological and political framework that I deploy here, to meet the demands of complexity *and* power in the formation of Britishness, is an 'applied Gramscianism'. Antonio Gramsci's work continues to attract a lot of critical attention, much of it at the level of philosophical enquiry or in the field of international relations. Here though I seek to show how Gramsci's concepts, such as hegemony, historic bloc, civil society, molecular change, the national-popular, and so forth, can help us understand a specific social and historical formation, including those social experiences that lie outside the framework of the dominant conservative–liberal bloc. Gramsci's concepts must be brought to bear on the real historical content of Britishness and that in turn means revisiting a number of important debates and conflicting assessments of this national formation and different and even conflicting uses and understandings of Gramsci's concepts. In the 1970s and 1980s Gramsci was the theoretical inspiration for significant accounts of Britishness, especially by two political scientists, Tom Nairn and Perry Anderson, and the founding figure of cultural studies, Stuart Hall. With the benefit of hindsight we can draw critically on their work to think anew about Gramsci and Britishness. For example, I will show how Gramsci's concept of the historic bloc allows us to understand in new and powerful ways, how political cultures have reconfigured their dynamic relationships with each other over the long duration, in relation to broader socio-economic constraints and opportunities and how all that in turn has shaped British self-identities.

This is, I believe, a surprisingly rare undertaking, perhaps because it requires a multidisciplinary approach, which is difficult and risky. Here I combine critical political economy, political science and historiography, political communications, cultural studies, media studies and film studies. This interdisciplinary range is not accidental but broadly corresponds to the three terrains which Gramsci's analysis can help us cover: the social class-economic relations (critical political economy), the State (political science and historiography) and the cultural and communication practices of civil society (political communications, media studies, film studies and cultural studies). In terms of its argument, this book is structured in a rather non-linear way; it rotates through conservatism and liberalism in turn, exploring their relationships with economic liberalism and the dialogic relationship of competition and alliance between conservatism and liberalism for leadership of British capitalism. In the latter chapters the contradictions and discontents between conservatism, liberalism and economic liberalism intensify as we approach our own current turbulent moment. My hope is that the reader rotates through the arguments, the theoretical concepts and the historical narrative that is constructed from different angles, so as to build up a complex prismatic account of Britishness. Gramsci's methodological framework amounts to a revalidation of the important role of politics and culture in shaping historical outcomes. That is a vital and potentially empowering truth in an otherwise dispiriting age in which politics and popular participation have drifted apart. With that in mind, the final chapter of this book probes where we are now, how we got here and how we can go forward by reconnecting politics with popular participation. On the question of identity, Gramsci combined a sophisticated methodological framework with an urgent political project. A degree of philosophical sifting is required, he suggested, 'to work out consciously and critically one's own conception of the world … refusing to accept passively and supinely from outside the moulding of one's personality'.[1] The personality, he argued, was 'composite'; it is made up of many different ingredients that have been accumulated historically within the culture – itself a site of different and conflicting cultures – before one is even born.

> The starting-point of critical elaboration is the consciousness of what one really is, and is 'knowing thyself' as a product of the historical process to date which has deposited in you an infinity of traces, without an inventory. The first thing to do is to make such an inventory.[2]

What a resonant phrase that is! '[A]n infinity of traces, without an inventory'. It speaks to the need of any political, cultural and educational project to construct such an inventory. This book is a contribution to a critical inventory of Britishness.

1

Political cultures and national identities: a Gramscian framework

Introduction

British capital is not a singular unitary phenomenon. But in all its many differentiations it has been a decisive force in helping to shape British national identities. When we think of some of the main versions of British national identity we can correlate them easily enough to various fractions of British capital. Firstly, we have Britain's identity as a 'nation of shopkeepers' as Napoleon was said to have once described the country. He did not mean it as a compliment. The image rests in large part on the commercial capital, made up of merchants and retailers, which have formed part of the British capitalist class, including a large fraction of small business retail capital. In the eighteenth century, there was a veritable 'cult of trade' according to historian Linda Colley, where one in five families lived off trade and the distribution of goods, much of which depended on the product of slave labour in North America and the Caribbean and other land-holdings acquired overseas, such as India.[1] Between 1701 and 1750, the East India Company massively increased imports in the commodity that was to become quintessentially 'British': tea. It grew from 67,000 pounds of weight to nearly 3,000,000 (and smugglers brought in even more).[2] Growth in trade preceded, helped capitalise and then helped expand other forms of capital and therefore extend the material terrain for other versions of national identity. By the mid-nineteenth century, Britain was known as the 'industrial workshop of the world' and its industrial identity remained a significant if troubled and increasingly embattled part of its economy and identity right through to the 1980s, when under Thatcherism, de-industrialisation set in with a vengeance. But if industrial capital has played a defining part of Britain's identity, so too, and very contentiously, has the aristocratic and landowning class, around whom a powerful *mise en scène* of country life has been developed, widening to encompass sober bourgeois farmers and middle-class professionals brought up in the small villages in the south of England. Then again, another feature of British identity was the connection between the 'gentlemanly capitalists' of the landed oligarchy and the banking capital of the City of London, which grew in the late nineteenth century and which was an attractive alternative occupation for aristocratic families looking to sustain their wealth while avoiding the lower status occupation of industrial and commercial capital. The heyday of the City came to an end in many ways in 1914, at least for a time. After the First World War, the 1929 stock market crash, the 1930s Depression, the era of protectionism, then the Second World War and the subsequent international post-war financial architecture that reined in loose speculative capital, the power and the profile of the City was constrained somewhat. Yet its power started to grow again in the 1970s and it bounced back again in spectacular style from the 1980s, as the engine of Thatcherism, to leave an indelible mark on British national identity once more. To this we must add of course the history of empire – in which both the City and industry participated, and which has also shaped British identities in ways which are still being felt – for example in the need that British political and military elites have to be major players on the international stage of foreign affairs (with all that implies for sustaining barely affordable military spending – especially on nuclear weapons). The empire was emphatically a product of nineteenth-century British capitalism. It achieved its 'classic' imprint on British national identity towards the last quarter of the nineteenth century although it could draw on a much longer history of colonial entanglements and possession going back several centuries. The racism it helped to foster within some of the general population and the illusions of a 'civilising mission' it required are still very much with us today. The alliance between American neo-conservatives and British liberals – who unleashed their inner bomber – over the disaster that was the Iraq War in 2003, is only one example of how much the nightmare of an imperial past continues to weigh on the present.

But if the various fractions of British capital have provided the essential terrain on which different versions or facets of British national identity have developed, this has only happened because of the equally essential mediating work done by definite *political* cultures. These political cultures orchestrate those capital interests in particular ways and give them a definite sense of orientation, purpose, identity, and value system. Political cultures interpret the experiences of people shaped by their economic-class formations. In doing so, they work with images, values, and representations. The Italian Marxist Antonio Gramsci was one of the key thinkers on the Left to develop our understanding of the importance of parties and political cultures more broadly in shaping historical outcomes. He was unusually sensitive for a Marxist of his generation to the importance of language, which his studies in philology as a student in Turin had helped him to appreciate. As he put it:

> In reality, every political movement creates a language of its own, that is, it participates in the general development of a distinct language, introducing new terms, enriching existing terms with a new content, creating metaphors, using historical names to facilitate the comprehension and the assessment of particular contemporary political situations, etc., etc.[3]

This interest in language meant that Gramsci was aware of the importance of the relationship between politics and culture. In selecting, interpreting and amplifying certain experiences, certain ways of understanding, certain normative assumptions, political cultures marginalise and exclude others. Certain images of a class and its experiences become typical in the systems of representation at its disposal. In the course of political struggle, cultures will hope certain images become resonant more generally, 'symbolic' of the hopes and aspirations of broader strata of people than the ones who most immediately populate the landscape of the images and stories political cultures develop. As Michael Billig notes, 'Nationhood … involves a distinctive imagining of a particular sort of community rooted in a particular sort of place'.[4] Indeed, it may be that those people and places, their communities and their work, that receive the highest profiles in the representations of national political cultures are hardly typical of the broader sections of the population that are being invited to identify with them. This is because such people and places function as moral exemplars and have a rhetorical value in exhorting others to in some way or another adopt the exemplars as role models. To take rather contrasting examples from conflicting political cultures: both the image of rural England, which has been central to conservatism as a political culture and the image of the industrial manual (usually male) working class that was central to socialism and social democracy, figure people and places that were *never* statistically typical of what most people do or how most people lived in twentieth-century Britain. Even the image of the industrial working class, which was certainly far more representative of the lives of the majority than rural England, was behind the trend of ever-larger numbers being employed in the service sectors, even in the 1930s, when it first came to prominence.[5] But statistical representativeness, merely empirical facts, is not really the issue here. What matters is the rhetorical and exhortatory power of such images, their ability to crystallise moral feeling and forge identifications with political value systems. Tacitly, the image of southern rural England and a northern industrial working class, were constructed as moral–political critiques of each other. Gramsci calls such struggles, the struggle for hegemony or leadership in the moral–political field.

State and civil society

The State is that massive edifice for the administration of public affairs. It includes but is not identical with government, since the State spans a much wider range of institutions, personnel and activities (the civil service, the judiciary, the police, the army, the intelligence services, the monarchy) that outlast particular governmental regimes, especially formally democratic ones. Governments come and go but the State refers to a deeper continuity of the social order the State is essential to managing and protecting. The State, notes Stuart Hall:

> is itself a power – *the* central and supreme power – in the land. And it exercises the power by imposing its rule over us and commanding obedience ... Rule may take many forms – monarchy, democracy, dictatorship, etc. But wherever the State is sovereign – the *supreme* power – it involves the *subjection* of its subjects to the powers of the State.[6]

In formally democratic societies it is through governmental power that at least some State power can be captured, organised and constructed by 'the people'. Different political cultures – with their different constituencies and alliances – have quite different attitudes, conceptions and relationships to the State and this shapes their interaction with it and shaping of it. At certain times radical governments can substantially modify aspects of the State without necessarily changing the basic social order the State has served. The 1945 Labour government which brought to a climax several decades of developments in the formation of a social democratic political culture, marks one example of this. Margaret Thatcher's 1979, 1983 and 1987 governments, which fundamentally dismantled that social democratic settlement, marks another example of significant State modifications. In exceptional circumstances, the social order itself undergoes a fundamental transformation along with the State. We call these moments revolutions.

In the administration of public affairs, the State is widely held to be a means of arbitrating between the *different* social interests in society. For Hegel the modern State was supposed to be the representative of a 'general will', to be the embodiment of the life of the community, the whole of the nation. Yet Marx noted that the State rested on what he called in his early writings 'civil society', by which he meant the economic sphere of capitalist activity. For Marx 'the unsocial nature of this civil life, this private property, this commerce, this industry, this reciprocal plundering of different civil groups' had to cast extreme doubt on the ability of the State to embody the general will.[7] For the State was not separate from or above the individualism, egoism, selfishness, competition and the exploitation of labour-power which civil society (capitalist economic activity) generated. Rather, civil society (economic-class relationships in this conception) was the basis on which the State rested and depended (for example in the form of taxes and borrowing money) and it was the predominant and most powerful interests of the large property-holders which the State systematically tended to respond to most favourably. We can identify four axes of conflict which capitalist society poses and which the State historically has tried to manage.

1   Intra-class conflict. The 'warring' competitive nature of capitalist civil society meant that no coherent leadership in the long-term interests of capital as a whole could emerge from within civil society. This leadership had then to be delegated to a special social organ (the State) which could provide the legal and administrative support for expanding capital. In the 1700s for example, MPs would be lobbied by merchants for infrastructure projects on roads, bridges, ports, street lighting, as well as the legal frameworks required for capitalist exchange (e.g. standardising weights and measures, bankruptcy laws, and so forth).[8] All this required political power, political control and political leadership to be exercised on behalf of the dominant but

centrifugal class forces. Gramsci discusses this ability of a class to develop a political culture that can work on behalf of all its different sectoral interests as an essential component of its ability to secure its power and reproduction. As we shall see, in the case of Britain, the two key political cultures that have mediated this intra-class conflict over a long period of time have been conservatism and liberalism.

2 Inter-class conflict. If competition between capitals required the State to plan for the long-term interests of capital, then conflict between capital and labour required the State to respond to the demands of the class which capital exploits as its source of wealth. Two modalities of response were and remain available to it. One is coercion and force, using the repressive arms of the State apparatus (both legal and physical) to intervene in and regulate the relationship between the classes on the unequivocal behalf of capital. Famously, for the sociologist Max Weber, one of the defining features of the State is that it and it alone must have the ultimate authority on the legitimate use of violence domestically or abroad. The other modality is compromise, making some concessions on which basis a more or less active consent to the way things are can be won from the dominated classes. This latter mode requires complex political finessing, negotiation, persuasion and some small material benefits and opportunities to be distributed here and there to the general population. Gramsci will call this latter modality the formation of hegemony, the ability to set the agenda, to define the terms of the debate, to win groups outside and beyond the dominant classes to viewpoints that are congruent with the leading group's own interests, to make a particular cluster of interests appear universal or more universal than any other historically available option.

3 Nation-building. The modern State had to increasingly define itself as having a more or less clear territorial reach within which its authority to rule or sovereignty could be exercised without contest. The close link between territory and modern Statehood made the question of borders and boundaries powerfully resonant within modern culture and politics. States are defined by their territorial boundaries (where their writ ends) and territory is closely linked with national identities. The formation of national markets for capital accumulation according to laws established and policed by the State made the development of capitalism and modern Statehood a closely interconnected process. In the case of Britain, a single State established its authority over

multiple nations, including Ireland, until a campaign of military struggle led to the secession of the Irish Free State in 1922. Northern Ireland however, where most British capital and people from other British nations (especially Scotland) had relocated over time, remained part of the British State. The case of Ireland and Northern Ireland highlights the issue of how consciousness of national identity may be articulated to the supra-national identity that is Britishness or to political projects that demand either more autonomy or (much worse for any State) independence. In the contemporary moment this has been a particularly pressing issue in relation to Scotland (while in Northern Ireland it has been virtually ongoing since 1922). The preponderance of England within the multi-nation British State, the largest territory, by far the most populous and the most wealthy (although there are significant geographical divisions here between north and south) is a complicating feature in the supra-national identity that is Britishness. We may add that British capitalist civil society was from the beginning international in its activities and this too creates another very significant cleavage, i.e. between the national basis of State sovereignty and the international scope of capitalist activity.

Historically, the modern State, amid the pressures of establishing a unified political and economic national territory, has tended towards a conservative view that the culture that best accords with the State has a great deal of continuity and homogeneity over time and unity throughout social space (although again, as we shall see, this is complicated by the multi-national components that officially make up Britishness). This conservative ideal of temporal continuity and unity has been challenged by both Marxism and liberalism. For Marxists the imagined community of national identity, the sense of a 'deep, horizontal comradeship'[9] is fissured by class differences and antagonisms. For liberalism, especially in its meta-theoretical version that has powerfully defined cultural studies, the problem exists almost exclusively at the cultural level insofar as national identity is always more plural and diverse culturally than conservative notions allow for, with the international dimension of capitalism in particular appreciated for the way it breaks up insular national identities. As Marx himself noted as early as the 1840s, '[i]n place of the old local and national seclusion and self-sufficiency, we have intercourse in every direction, universal inter-dependence of nations.'[10]

4 Atomisation. If the drive for establishing a unified market pushes capitalism towards a preference for cultural standardisation, the atomising nature of economic competition, its implicit or explicit valuing of selfishness and competition, of an 'anything goes' mentality, drains the community of its reservoirs of moral feeling and sentiment on which some kind of ethical system can be espoused or lived. This dynamic is closely linked to the question of class divisions but because it refers to the way *capital* uses market relations to dissolve any and all forms of belonging (including but not limited to class belonging), it is worth specifying this process separately. Such economic forces weaken the bonds of trust which non-market relations are able to sustain better than relations that revolve around exchange (and profit). Commodification, the process by which everything can ultimately be opened up to becoming an 'exchange value' to be bought and sold on the market, such as education, health and culture, is inextricably connected to the capitalist tendency to universalise market forces in contemporary society. Our relationships become contract based, which itself speaks to the spread of an individualistic model of society held together by legal rights and the cash nexus but not shared resources, objectives and values. In this context, as Neil Davidson remarks, nationalism (which posits *community*) can provide a 'type of psychic compensation … unobtainable from the mere consumption of commodities.'[11] Yet there is also a potentially more positive gloss to this process insofar as the spread of market values can also help to disrupt and break up oppressive, static and hierarchical value systems, those 'motley feudal ties that bound man to his "natural superiors"' are 'pitilessly torn asunder'.[12] This side of atomisation, individualisation and commodification provides a material basis for liberalism and its investment in for example individual social mobility, meritocracy and the belief that the market is an educational experience that teaches self-reliance and individual autonomy and responsibility.

These four tensions or problems shape the political cultures of conservatism, liberalism (social and economic), socialism and social democracy, although in different and historically evolving ways. Conservatism, for example, invests heavily in the symbolic power of certain 'departments' of the State apparatus as a means of binding together a society otherwise characterised by cut-throat competition and a decided absence of neighbourliness. The monarchy, the Church, the military, these are some of the parts of the State apparatus that are supposed to represent the unity of the nation and a moral value system which civil society cannot itself generate. Conservatism favours those parts of the State that are primarily either coercive (the judiciary, the military, the police) or ritualistic and ideological (the Church, the monarchy, or in a previous era, the empire as a source of national pride). For social democracy by contrast, the State holds out the real possibility of actual and not merely symbolic compensation for the failures of civil society to produce 'civility'. This required the State to redistribute wealth and expand or build new institutions and services that saw the development of what we can call the social State, alongside the State's traditional coercive, juridical, political and ritualistic-ideological functions.

As capitalism develops extensively (in terms of reach) and intensively (in terms of intensity and complexity) so the State must manage on an ever-more grander scale both the competing affairs of the bourgeoisie among themselves and the costly business of meeting and containing the demands of those outside the core ruling forces (the power bloc). This is why Marx describes the State as:

> a mutual insurance pact of the bourgeois class both against its members taken individually and against the exploited class; this insurance becomes inevitably more and more costly and, in appearance, more and more independent vis-à-vis bourgeois society, for it is more and more difficult to bridle the exploited class.[13]

The development of the social State in the nineteenth century was the result of the fact that there could not be a merely coercive solution to the question of meeting the demands of the exploited classes. The tilt away from an over-reliance on brute suppression *as a long-term solution* does not mean that capitalism will not, in specific moments, require and enact the full-scale suspension of all democratic rights. It merely means that in a complex modern society, it is very difficult for this to be a sustained solution. As Gramsci puts it in relation to developments in France in the nineteenth century, but in terms that have a more general relevance:

> The 'normal' exercise of hegemony in what became the classic terrain of the parliamentary regime is characterized by a combination of force and consent variously balancing one another, without force exceeding consent

too much. Indeed one tries to make it appear that force is supported by
the consent of the majority, expressed by the so-called organs of public
opinion – newspapers and associations ...[14]

This tilt towards consent (which Gramsci explicitly says is balanced
by coercion, and coercion in turn is legitimised by the construction of
consent) underscores that the State acquires an independent life from
its *immediate* socio-economic base (capitalist class relations) as its
legal, administrative and political and cultural management of class
exploitation develops. This is what Marx means by 'appearance' – real
but also limited autonomy. The 1833 Factory Acts banned work for
children under nine and limited the working day for children between
nine and thirteen to nine hours a day. The bourgeois State even found
the resources for a whole four factory inspectors to be appointed to
enforce the law across the country! Marx shows how the factory bosses
campaigned against these infringements on their liberties by the capitalist
State and how in practice they found ways to break both the spirit and the
letter of the law.[15] And precisely this in turn produces further struggles
by the working class for effective legislation. So by the early part of the
twentieth century the entire domain of politics as the management of
intra-class struggles within the dominant class and inter-class struggles
between capital and labour had indeed become a complex art.

The development of the management of social conflict, of
compromise, concession, and persuasion poses methodological
problems for Marxism: the role of the political needed to be taken into
proper account in the development of the life of a nation. Already in
the 1890s Engels was critical of himself and Marx for having laid too
much stress on the principle of economic determination – because their
adversaries (the Hegelian philosophers and idealists) denied it. But this
bent the stick too far in the other direction to the detriment of the:

> various elements of the superstructure – political forms of the class
> struggle and its results, to wit: constitutions established by the victorious
> class after a successful battle, etc., juridical forms, and even the reflexes of
> all these actual struggles in the brains of the participants ... also exercise
> their influence upon the course of the historical struggles.[16]

Indeed it is just such developments within the 'superstructure' (those
institutions not immediately involved in economic production) that
are responsible for real differences within the historical development

of capitalism. Engels was highly critical of younger German scholars who called themselves 'historical materialists' but who used the general principles of Marxism developed by Marx and Engels to *not* study real historical conditions 'afresh' but instead reduce them to formulae.[17] Gramsci understood more than most that the political denotes the terrain of creative practice responsible for differential outcomes at the level of *national* formation.

Beyond economism

The terms 'civil society' and 'the State' work as an analytical distinction (for the purposes of study) of a whole social order, but also a methodological problem (what is the relationship between economics and politics?) and a political issue (wielding economics and politics together, despite the tensions between them, constitutes a practical goal in the struggle). For Gramsci, to take the analytic distinction between economics and politics as a real divide, or to fail to understand the methodological problem which thinking through the relationship between the economic and political sphere poses, or worse yet, to not understand that the subordinate classes must advance *beyond* the terrain of their own immediate economic interests and articulate a broader political agenda to address the problems of society, were all signs of 'economism'. This term may be said to refer to any philosophy or politics that assumes that a given set of economic relations or developments always produces a definite set of social and/or political outcomes. As a consequence, social and political struggles are seen as secondary to economic developments, because they are always already pre-determined by economic factors. Economism is therefore a form of economic determinism.

In contemporary cultural theory, economism has been a label readily applied to Marxism. Gramsci, very interestingly, has a much wider view of economism, identifying it with political abstentionism for example and syndicalism (the left-wing philosophy that conducts its battles on the terrain of the economic, inside the factory, classically, and which is suspicious of the role for political parties in such struggles). He also, very significantly, identifies liberal free-trade philosophy as an early form of economism, one that pre-dates Marxism and sometimes even influences it. Liberal free traders or economic liberalism believe that the State should not interfere with or attempt to regulate the doings of market actors. Gramsci notes that in practice however, 'even liberalism is a form of "regulation" of a State kind, introduced and maintained by means of legislation and coercion: it is an act of will conscious of its own ends and not the spontaneous, automatic expression of an economic fact.'[18] Economism of the liberal free-trade kind is characterised by a disavowal of the conscious mobilisation of interests needed to protect and develop private ownership of the means of production. In our contemporary era, liberal economism peppers contemporary political discourse. If, for example, commentators and political elites talk about economic growth as a good thing in and of itself, without referring to the iniquitous distribution of wealth, then that is a form of economism, since it brackets off social questions in favour of merely quantitative ones. When neo-liberals such as Margaret Thatcher asserted that free markets were equivalent to or guaranteed political democracy, that too was a form of economism. Leaving aside the historical record where capitalism has co-existed quite happily with the absence of political freedom (beginning with Britain's rule by a capitalist oligarchy for several centuries), the equation of the free market with political freedom empties politics of its most important substantive content: namely the participation of the people in developing the rules by which a community can live together. Such rules go well beyond 'the rule of law' but include crucially how wealth is produced and distributed and this fundamentally affects what kind of law is produced and whose interests it best serves.

If economism is very far from being an invention of Marxism or even the most important example of economism today, it is true to say that economism has attached itself to certain versions of Marxism. Gramsci in effect argues that economistic Marxism remains in the grip of liberalism and a certain form of superstition and fatalism. Gramsci's explanation of this retardation in Marxist philosophy, widespread in the years between Marx's death in 1883 and the 1917 Russian Revolution, was that the cultural level of the masses was generally very low – 'medieval' in the case of much of southern Italy, for example. That, combined with political setbacks and resistance from the dominant classes made a Marxist version of economism popular. This took the form of an argument that economic development was marching irresistibly towards socialism. It was a popular argument, for example, at the time that capitalism's consolidation into monopoly capitalism (ever-larger units of capital) would make the transition towards social ownership of private property easier when the time came. This evolutionary argument was attractive to intellectuals as it seemed an economic version of natural evolution, drawing on the prestige of natural science to make economic history explicable in terms of iron 'laws'. The same explanatory framework worked for the masses as nothing more than a modernised version of religious and superstitious beliefs with which they were already saturated thanks to the ideological work of Catholicism.

> When one does not have the initiative in the struggle and the struggle itself is ultimately identified with a series of defeats, mechanical determinism becomes a formidable power of resistance, of patient and obstinate perseverance. 'I am defeated for the moment but the nature of things is on my side over a long period,' etc. Real will is disguised as an act of faith, a sure rationality of history, a primitive and empirical form of impassioned finalism which appears as a substitute for the predestination, providence, etc., of the confessional religions.[19]

Sketching out an alternative understanding of the relationship between the economic and the political, Gramsci argues that the former simply creates a terrain more or less favourable to the 'dissemination of certain modes of thought, and certain ways of posing and resolving questions involving the entire subsequent development of national life.'[20] Nothing could be more foreign to Gramsci's line of thinking than that the economic – such as a crisis – determines mechanically, any particular outcome. Such a conception robs human agents of the necessity to forge political instruments – organisations and ideas – that must shape economic dynamics in particular directions. 'Laws' for Marxism are not, or ought not to be conceived in the natural science mode as, predictable linkages between causes and effects. Instead, social 'laws' are tendencies and counter tendencies, linked to antagonistic social groups that can, *within historical limits*, shape those tendencies in this or that direction. The political level is critical in terms of providing the ultimate legal, coercive and cultural conditions for a given set of arrangements to secure themselves. It is the moral and intellectual agenda that underpins the political guarantees of an era that must be challenged by the subordinate classes, and this means going beyond merely economic demands, or rather it means linking the economic to the moral–political.

Gramsci identifies various levels of political consciousness that might be active on the terrain of economic life. The most primitive type is restricted to a merely economic identity and identification with others of the same occupational or professional type. A tradesman 'feels *obliged* to stand by a tradesman, a manufacturer by another manufacturer' but there is not yet sufficient awareness of shared interests for the tradesman and manufacturer to recognise their mutual interests as different sections of a single capitalist class. Similarly a worker in one industry may identify with other workers in the same industry, but not see the shared interests between workers of that industry and those engaged in a strike for example in another industry. A more advanced stage of consciousness is reached when 'the solidarity of interests among all members of the social group' is forged, but still now only at the economic level. Group activity for the subordinate classes is limited to making adjustments to situations 'within the existing fundamental structures.' This is the stage of 'trade union consciousness'[21] at which most labour movements without revolutionary leadership stay stuck. Strikes for higher wages for example generally fall into this category of political consciousness.

A third moment, 'the most purely political phase' sees a group translating awareness of its own economic identity and interests into a broader political project and agenda. This 'marks the decisive passage from the structure to the sphere of the complex superstructures' argues Gramsci and involves an attempt to link economic interests to an entire moral-ethical, cultural and political *narrative* about the past, present and future direction of the nation-state. At this point a social group has achieved political maturity as it were, because it is in a position to pose 'all the questions around which the struggle rages ... on a "universal" plane, and thus creating the hegemony of a fundamental social group over a series of subordinate groups.' The concept of hegemony is one of the centrepieces of Gramsci's political science. It specifically denotes the blend of consent, compromise, persuasion, enticement, administrative fiat, legal power and if necessary coercive force, by which a social group achieves a moral and intellectual leadership over society as a whole. The 'development and expansion' of a particular class interest is translated into and presented as being 'the motor force of a universal expansion, of a development of all the "national" energies.' When a particular group with its particular economic interests can make itself stand for the interests of all the other classes and class fractions, then it has achieved a leading position in society. This means that enough of the other groups can identify with the dominant group's way of framing national identity and see themselves in, find a 'home' or place within, that representation.[22] But this ethical-cultural and ultimately political authority is not and cannot be merely a matter of representation. It has to have an economic component. The 'leading group makes some sacrifices of an ... [economic] kind.'[23] These 'sacrifices' are real and provide the material basis for winning support beyond the core power bloc. These 'sacrifices' of an economic kind may be initiated by the dominant classes themselves because they also help those classes or they may be sacrifices *forced* upon the dominant class by the other classes (e.g. concessions won by the working class through struggle). In the context of capitalism, all such socio-economic concessions are often time-limited, plagued by the gap between rhetorical invitation and practical experience, far more vulnerable to economic shocks and downturns and far more exposed to a range of social problems which the pursuit of the class interests of the dominant classes causes the rest of the population. So the:

> interests and strivings of the groups over which the hegemony will be exercised are taken account of, that a certain balance of compromises be formed...but it is also undoubted that these sacrifices and compromises cannot concern essentials, since if the hegemony is ethico-political, it must also be economic, it must have its foundation in the decisive function that the leading group exercises in the decisive sphere of economic activity.[24]

One of the key institutional organs that frames the questions and poses the solutions that confront the social protagonists and antagonists is the political party. The political party emerges from and in turn cements a definite 'collective will'. Gramsci defines 'collective will' as a 'working consciousness of historical necessity, as protagonist of a real and effective historical drama'.[25] Collective will then requires a degree of self-consciousness at an individual and collective level about one's role within a 'historical drama' and it is the role of parties to shape and refine that self-consciousness. However Gramsci was very aware that political cultures more generally, through media representations as well as in everyday life – the exercise of opinion-formers within peer groups for example – were also influential in forging degrees of consciousness about one's place within a historical situation or context. Gramsci for example cites the role of some newspapers as having leadership functions for a party, a sort of 'intellectual High Command'.[26] This certainly strikes a chord within the context of contemporary Britain where the right-wing press in particular have considerable power in setting agendas for political parties to follow.

Gramsci saw political cultures as having a directive and 'educative' role (even if that education was deeply one-sided, partial, and aligned to the needs of the business class). To the extent that there is at least some necessity to communicate within modern mass societies, there is philosophically, or immanently, an educative element built into them (an argument also made by Habermas). Practical activities, suffused with modern techniques and technologies means that learning is 'interwoven with life'.[27] In such circumstances, the role of the State which politics and policy making steers, is not to leave the development of society to a 'haphazard and sporadic germination' but to rationalise, accelerate, reward, solicit and encourage the 'right' kind of behaviours, attitudes, knowledge and actions conducive to the economic development and class interests of the dominant groups, which do not necessarily see eye-to-eye in all respects (intra-class struggles) and which must also learn to not rely exclusively on force in relation to the exploited classes (hegemony in inter-class struggles).[28] Thus for Gramsci, politics matters in terms of effecting outcomes. But it also matters normatively as a means, because it is the basis of democratic consensus governance which can only be substantively expanded and genuinely realised with the passage to socialism. Gramsci's recognition of the moral–political dimension of the State went beyond the traditional Marxist view of the State as *only* a coercive force at the disposal of the ruling class to crush their working class opponents using the police, the army and the law. It is not that this modality of class power in the State disappears. Gramsci spent the last years of his life in prison under a fascist regime, so he would hardly argue that force had disappeared as an option for the capitalist State. But in the context of modern mass society, force has to be blended with some degrees of popular consent – which may range across the spectrum from active support to resigned defeat. The State itself is an active promoter of such consent but it also works in conjunction with a whole range of organisations that extended the State into society at large. Here Gramsci adopted and reworked the concept of civil society, whose development in the west Gramsci contrasted with the situation that had confronted the Bolsheviks in Russia in 1917:

> In the East, the State was everything, civil society was primordial and gelatinous; in the West, there was a proper relation between State and civil society, and when the State trembled a sturdy structure of civil society was at once revealed. The State was only an outer ditch, behind which there stood a powerful system of fortresses and earthworks.[29]

In the west, political cultures embedded in the State also radiated out into what Gramsci called the '"private" fabric of the State', or civil society.[30] Describing civil society as the 'private' fabric of the State suggested both a connection and a distinction between the two. For Gramsci, civil society refers to all those institutions outside the State proper, which, while they are influenced by the State (through the law for example and politics) are 'private' institutions in a variety of senses. They may be 'private' in the economic sense that Marx used the term, referring to private capital, private ownership of property, the market for labour-power, and the competitive individualism characteristic of capitalism. But Gramsci seems to now reclassify this sphere as the economic structure of society and instead fills the term civil society with a new content that includes a range of institutions that are private more in the social sense (the family) or entered into through personal choice and preferences (religion) or used, consumed or engaged with as consumers or citizens (the media, social clubs, hobbies, education) or, from the point of view of the institutions themselves, organised by their own distinct set of concerns, not directly subordinated by the State. Gramsci writes of hegemony forming at least in part through a kind of decentralised process of individual or 'molecular' initiatives working broadly within the direction of the predominant social relationships.[31] Although it is a rather 'baggy' concept covering a wide range of organisations, they can broadly be differentiated from the more coercive or administrative arms of the State directly (the law, the police, the courts, the army, the civil service) and while civil society organisations may also be active economic agents (such as the media) they also have a social impact more in the realm of ideas, ideals and the shaping of public debate and opinion. Civil society in this definition works to organise 'the "spontaneous" consent given by the great masses of the population to the general direction imposed on social life by the dominant fundamental group'.[32] Essentially, Gramsci's conception of civil society absorbs much of what Marx and Engels called the superstructure (minus the State) into it. Arguably this tripartite conception encourages thought to approach society as a spectrum of interlinked practices that are analytically distinct but in practice complexly interwoven. In this it may avoid the dangers of the classic dualistic base–superstructure model, which, in the hands of at least some, relegated the superstructure to a rather secondary role, after the sphere of economics and production, as we saw Engels complain. At the same time, for Gramsci civil society is not as liberalism conceives it:

an autonomous sphere having no relation to class interests but merely the exercise of individual freedom or professional expertise in the sphere of politics, the media, education, religion and so forth. Instead, civil society plays a crucial role in linking the economic structure to a broader set of cultural and normative agendas as well as the State, which provides the juridical protection or backstop which economic and civil society organisations need, as well as financial assistance. Private schools in Britain for example, so crucial in reproducing social stratification in the State and economic sphere generation after generation, have charity status in Britain and therefore benefit from tax breaks. Gramsci's conception of the relationship between the State and civil society provides the theoretical framework for thinking of the way 'politics' in the narrow sense of the term and 'culture' in the broadest sense of the term (as an everyday set of practices and value systems) are conjoined into political cultures. As for political parties, they straddle both State and civil society. As mass party organisations depending on voluntary membership, political parties extend into and are part of civil society. But where they participate in the legislative and executive branches of governing, they are also part of the organs of the State. So we see that Gramsci's conception leads us to think the social order through the prism of a dynamic tripartite structure that consists of the State, civil society and economic structure. It is important, I think, to hold onto this tripartite structure in contrast to some versions of Gramscian analysis that focus instead only on the State and Gramsci's reconstructed version of civil society, excluding how both relate to the question of economic-class interests, the 'decisive sphere' as he put it.[33]

Political cultures and cultural politics

Political cultures are certainly hybrid formations. British conservatism for example typically combines at least four distinct strands: Christian conservatism; a strong nationalistic conservatism that can at its more extreme edges bleed into fascism; a Burkean view of the sanctity of 'traditional' British institutions whose great merit is their slow evolution; and fourthly, an economic liberalism that defines liberty as the freedom to dispose of private property as the individual wishes.[34] Political cultures require organisations to sustain themselves and extend their influence. Party-type organisations are the most important here from an instrumental point of view – that is in terms of exercising power that most immediately guarantees the economic – class interests that political cultures represent (or proclaim that they represent). Parties that are integrated into the upper echelons of the State apparatus at legislative and executive level are clearly the most important over the long term. But just as political cultures are internally hybrid formations, political parties are themselves typically made up of *different* political cultures, the difference between parties being found in the weight and configuration given to those political cultures within any given political organisation of the party-type. Thus when I write of conservatism or liberalism or any other political culture, the reader should not assume that I am referring to one specific political party unless I expressly do so or assume that a political party has only a single political cultural current flowing through it.

At the same time, this heterogeneity and complexity of cultures and parties is embedded at the State level in the necessary business of instrumental power play. The more power is linked directly to the 'decisive sphere of economic activity'[35] the more a certain closure on permissible heterogeneity comes into operation. One only has to think of how Tony Benn, the most radical left-wing minister in Harold Wilson's government in the mid-1970s, was undermined, contained and neutralised by his own civil service, the intelligence agencies, the right-wing press and his own party leader to see the closure of permissible heterogeneity at work.[36]

As we move from the State – the most important terrain of power for political cultures and parties – to civil society, political cultures bleed into cultural politics and a certain reconfiguration of the 'structure-heterogeneity' dynamic I am sketching here may take place in favour of heterogeneity. The motif of 'structure' has been most consistently developed in the Marxist tradition, while the motif of heterogeneity (or synonyms such as diversity and pluralism) has been most consistently developed in the liberal tradition. Part of the intense theoretical debate that has occurred around the meaning and legacy of Gramsci's work arises because it can be read as an attempt to critically synthesise these motifs of structure and heterogeneity. Different political cultures have attempted to lay claim to that critical synthesis and define it. Gramsci left a rich range of concepts that can help us think through the question of structure and heterogeneity although, given that his major work was written as a prisoner of the Italian fascists, he did not produce an overall ready-to-hand theoretical synthesis.

What he did leave, however, were exemplary applications of his methodology in action. In his remarks on the Catholic Church he suggested that beneath its apparent superficial unity 'in reality a multiplicity of distinct and often contradictory religions' were at work.[37] Class differences mean that there was a Catholicism of the peasants, of the petty bourgeoisie, the urban proletariat and the intellectuals. There was even a gender-inflected Catholicism of women according to Gramsci. At the same time, such a degree of attention to the heterogeneity of Catholicism must be coupled with a re-embedding reflex, where analysis reminds itself that we are still dealing with a definable conception of the world operating within a definite institution (the Church) which for all practical purposes can *act* in a coherent way (it is not paralysed by the fact of its heterogeneity) and which is in turn embedded into and has close contacts with the dominant class and other key institutions of the dominant class. If we can hold onto the two ends of the chain, the heterogeneous and the organised structure, then we are well placed to sustain an analysis that is both sophisticated and politically robust. However, holding onto the two ends of the chain, has proved difficult both because it is an intrinsically complex methodological operation and because social and political pressures work to push thought in other less politically robust directions (away from Marxism and towards a species of liberalism for example) or less complex directions (towards a version of Marxism but one not adapted to the complexity and diversity of modern society). This extraordinary passage from Gramsci on the methodological complexity of thinking about the birth of a political party gives a sense of how he tried to hold onto the two ends of the chain:

> It requires an extremely minute, molecular process of exhaustive analysis in every detail, the documentation for which is made up of an endless quantity of books, pamphlets, review and newspaper articles, conversations and oral debates repeated countless times, and which in their gigantic aggregation represent this long labour which gives birth to a collective will with a certain degree of homogeneity – with the degree necessary and sufficient to achieve an action which is coordinated and simultaneous in the time and the geographical space in which the historical event takes place.[38]

As we move on a spectrum from political practice to culture more broadly and from culture more broadly to specific cultural products –

especially those that have an aesthetic dimension to them – Gramsci's idea of hegemony as an 'unstable equilibria', that is to say, as a deeply contested terrain, and social life as a dynamic between 'a certain degree of homogeneity' sufficient to accomplish given tasks, combined with difference at a molecular level, is even more in evidence. For as the Marxist linguist V.N. Voloshinov argued, the same linguistic community divided by class and other social interests refract the same language in different semantic directions (as we saw in Gramsci's example of Catholicism). Thus signs are 'multi-accentual', which means they are accented towards different meanings according to the struggle to define the world and make it intelligible from the perspective of the different class and other interests in play.[39] As Raymond Williams argued, no *dominant* culture 'in reality exhausts human practice, human energy, human intention'.[40] Certain media and cultural practices may be more open to articulate alternative conceptions than others. Music for example, because of its low capital requirements raises far fewer barriers to entry than something like film-making and so it is not surprising that it has always been fertile territory for alternative conceptions of life and identity for subaltern groups, from rap music, punk, and mod subcultures through to folk. Such alternative cultural politics may be ignored or seen as a moral threat to the dominant order depending on circumstances. They can also be articulated to a coherent alternative political conception, programme and practice. The Black civil rights movement in America had a clear soundtrack in Black popular music culture for example, while in the UK, Rock Against Racism, a successful anti-fascist organisation of the 1970s and 1980s, is another example of precisely this articulation between cultural politics and political cultures. These, however, are examples of cultural politics that are self-consciously articulated to political cultures. However, this articulation goes on continuously, across the spectrum, inevitably and perhaps often with little sense that this cultural activity always has a political hinterland.

The national-popular

Gramsci's concept of the 'national-popular' is a way of thinking about the relationship between political cultures, and the class struggles that have shaped them, and cultural politics; that is to say the political dimension of seemingly 'non-political' artefacts such as novels, magazines, radio, films, theatre and so forth. How – the concept of the national-popular asks – do such cultural practices mediate certain visions and versions of national identity and make them popular? Take for example Gramsci's analysis of the lack of an indigenous popular literature in Italy. He read this as a symptom of the gap between Italian intellectuals and the people: 'they [the intellectuals] have not and do not set themselves the problem of elaborating popular feelings after having relived them and made them their own', he argued.[41] The Italian public's preference for French popular literature in the form of classic stories serialised in the newspapers indicates that the Italian intellectuals do not play an educative role in relation to any deep contact with the workers and/or the peasants. By contrast French popular literature represents a 'modern humanism' which Italy's intellectual strata have failed to produce.[42] This cultural situation was intimately connected with the respective histories of the political cultures of France and Italy. The former successfully pursued a thorough-going revolution in the late eighteenth, and early nineteenth century, while the latter's struggle to unify Italy into an independent nation did not, Gramsci contended, sufficiently involve the popular masses in the same way that the Jacobins had during the French Revolution or even the popular enthusiasm for Napoleon across Europe in the early years of the nineteenth century.

Gramsci's discussion of how political cultures shape a popular culture and how both may be understood in relation to important historical battles and developments has been influential in thinking about the 'national-popular' in relation to Britain. The argument has been, similar to Gramsci's in relation to Italy, that Britain's popular culture has been marked by a gap between the intellectuals and the working classes and that its popular culture is dominated by the middle classes and the upper classes (especially the old landed aristocratic class) and tends to be elitist and hierarchical rather than democratic and plebeian in spirit. Along with this analysis of popular culture has gone an influential analysis of the broader failure of the British bourgeoisie to properly modernise the British State and society and release it from the inhibiting grip of reactionary class fractions such as the landed gentry and the City. We shall examine this critique, associated with political scientists in particular, Tom Nairn and Perry Anderson, in later chapters. For now we can merely note that there is some evidence to argue that Britain's national-popular culture shows signs of either a narrow social base for a strongly middlebrow British culture, which has not included the working classes, except in a very marginalised way; or a deep split between the tastes of the working classes and the other classes with little sign of dialogue between them.

Film is a good example of such deficiencies in the national-popular culture. Just as the Italians showed a taste for French popular literature over their own, so the British working classes have consistently shown a preference for the less class-bound popular culture of Hollywood films than the products of their own British cinema, which has been suffused with the cultural-moral value systems of the upper middle classes.[43] The close links between British cinema and the theatre – traditionally a bastion of upper-class elitism – has hardly helped. This is not to say that British cinema cannot produce popular stories (although their popularity often has a skew towards the middle classes in terms of audience and dramatic scenarios), but they are very often filtered through a decidedly upper-class optic.[44] Heritage culture focuses on the past as a place where only the middle and upper classes lived. For example, Harry Potter (the books and films) with their location in what is essentially a private boarding school, and James Bond, a hero still playing out British fantasies of imperial power, are all symptomatic of a national-popular culture that has little space for the working classes. Sherlock Holmes is equally resonant and fascinating in this regard: an upper-middle-class character whose intelligence alienates him from the arrogant and corrupt aristocracy, whom he nevertheless often serves; the bureaucratic agencies of the modern State (the bumbling Inspector Lestrade) who again he nevertheless helps in order to preserve law and order; bourgeois domesticity and normative heterosexuality (Dr Watson's fiancé and later his wife) which he must tolerate; and of course the working classes who swarm around London as a backdrop to his adventures and with whom he has very little contact. In this sense Sherlock Holmes is a somewhat tragic figure, unable to find authentic satisfaction in his relationships to the various social groups around him, a figure who in miniature represents the crisis of the social function of the intellectuals that Gramsci suggested was evident in Italy. It is perhaps this paralysis and social alienation that accounts for Holmes' addiction problems. But although Holmes represents a crisis of the independent intellectual, he does not represent a crisis of hegemony. Instead, on a spectrum of the national-popular from hierarchical through to democratic, the British national-popular is decidedly at the former end of the spectrum, with plebeian voices and agency very much marginalised and backgrounded. The success of Britain's elitist construction of the national-popular relies in part on its export value selling a version of Britishness to the rest of the world, especially the United States, which is popular abroad, rather than being particularly engaged with contemporary life in all its diversity within Britain.[45]

If such images correspond to a broadly conservative culture, we can also find, especially on television, a version of the 'national-popular' that seems to have been decisively shaped by the new economic liberalism or neo-liberalism that has reshaped the political economy, culture and politics of Britain since Margaret Thatcher's governments in the 1980s. The value system of economic liberalism has achieved a hegemonic presence across many 'factual' entertainment and apparently 'educational' genres of television. The need to compete, to sell yourself, to be individualistic but also to be a 'team player' without the 'team' being allowed to forge any traditional worker-solidarities, to be flexible and adaptable to any fast changing conditions imposed by those in authority, are some of the core values of neo-liberalism. Bearing in mind Gramsci's argument that the forging of hegemony requires a strong 'educative' dimension (even if that education is deeply ideological), it is interesting that the talent show quest format exhibits a strong emphasis on 'learning'. Participants in shows such as *Britain's Got Talent* and *Strictly Come Dancing* are provided training, mentoring and are encouraged to articulate to the camera how much they have developed on their 'journey'. This gives 'an ethical veneer to an otherwise bruising, stressful and sometimes humiliating process' as Joel Windle points out.[46] The profusion of entrepreneurs on British television has been another facet of the percolation of neo-liberal values in popular culture. While public trust in large-scale corporations remains low and hardly improved by various scandals, as well as the general perception that they are extremely predatory in relation to workers and consumers, the figure of the entrepreneur has emerged as the acceptable, and apparently popular face of capitalism.[47] From *Dragons' Den*, *The Apprentice* or numerous shows featuring celebrity chefs, television, among other media, has played a key role in making the apparently self-made men or women look appealing and a model to emulate and look up to. Business is thus associated with innovation, do-it-yourself success, opportunity, economic reward, a certain 'coolness' in relation to the digital and internet economy (e.g. Steve Jobs) or a certain carefully cultivated maverick image (e.g. Richard Branson or Alan Sugar). The maverick image of Alan Sugar in *The Apprentice* has allowed neo-liberalism to promote the bullying and unaccountable authority figure with 'charismatic' power over either democratic accountability or the norms of bureaucratic power.[48] Yet even *The Apprentice*, apparently an uncomplicated hymn to neo-liberalism, has an element of self-parody to it (Sugar himself and the frankly silly tasks the contestants are set), which speaks perhaps of an element of popular scepticism that these people really do constitute models of behaviour to emulate.[49] This may complicate how people are actually using and reading such a series, whatever its overt rationalisation of the neo-liberal ideal.

This televisual celebration of the entrepreneur is all a far cry from the actual fragility and historic weaknesses of British capitalism, the failure rate of small businesses, the reluctance of the banks to lend after the 2008 crash or the way the figure of the entrepreneur functions ideologically to conceal the hardships and precarity of self-employment for the vast majority of 'entrepreneurs'. Nevertheless, this promotion of economic liberalism clearly has the potential to appeal to wider layers of people than traditional conservatism. When added to conservative political culture, as it was by Margaret Thatcher, it brings an element of meritocracy to a culture that otherwise depends a great deal on deference and what sociologists call ascribed (by inheritance or birth) social position.

Conservatism and economic liberalism represent the two dominant political cultures within British identity in the present conjuncture. But we must add to them three more, which we can briefly identify now before a more extensive discussion in the next chapter. A significant third political culture is that of *social* liberalism. This played an important role in rehabilitating economic liberalism in the 1990s, after its popularity and durability as an electoral force started to falter. Social liberalism, especially as institutionalised by the Labour Party after the rise of cadres around Tony Blair's leadership, offered economic liberalism a more modern, progressive model of citizenship than the one associated with conservatism. In short, social liberalism sought a new alliance with economic liberalism. Within academic theory a parallel investment in multiculturalism and various new models of identity inspired by post-structuralist philosophies were developed. Measured against the traditional and dominant conservative models of national identity, these new liberal and multicultural models looked and felt radical and progressive as they challenged many of the myths and assumptions which conservative-based models of personal and national identity are based on. However, they shared a broad indifference to questions of economic power and structure that matched the new political alliance between social liberalism and economic liberalism. This blind spot when it comes to analysing capitalism has meant that liberalism has been ill-equipped to understand the ferocious return of right-wing conservatism, as a 'solution' to the insecurity and anxieties generated by the very economic liberalism which conservatism itself has implemented. Conservatism in short cannibalises its social liberal partner in the implementation of economic liberalism. Social liberalism for its part, an eager accomplice to extending economic liberalism, refuses to understand the link between that project and the growth of its opposite: illiberalism.

A fourth political culture, which is still a contemporary presence within the national-popular culture, is that of social democracy. Although embattled and largely abandoned by the political classes and parties in Westminster (although not necessarily by the Scottish MPs representing the Scottish National Party), social democracy remains an active and alive part of the political culture of the national scene. The contradictory combination of these political cultures is evident by the fact that the two most popular institutions that regularly top opinion polls when people are asked to identify what makes them proud to be British are: the monarchy or sometimes the armed forces (conservatism) and the National Health Service (social democracy).

Finally, a fifth political culture that has been historically important to the formation of national identity, even though never a majority current, is socialism. Its current real marginalisation, perhaps even virtual elimination, represents a considerable achievement from the point of view of its historic enemies: conservatism and economic liberalism. Social liberalism has had an oscillating role in relation to both social democracy and socialism, and indeed its gravitation towards them or away from them has been a key bellwether indicator of which social-economic alliances or what Gramsci called 'historic blocs' would dominate for a long duration. Thus conservatism and economic liberalism were dominant (in alliance with social liberalism) for much of the nineteenth century and again today from the 1980s (again in alliance with a contemporary social liberalism). Conversely, social democracy – and to a much lesser extent socialism – have been, if not 'dominant', at least accepted by conservatism in another historic bloc (that included social liberalism) that developed in the early part of the twentieth century, was cemented after 1945, and lasted up until the 1979 election of Margaret Thatcher. In this hegemonic bloc that included conservatism, social liberalism, social democracy and, at the outer edge, socialism, economic liberalism was effectively excluded, sacrificed and pushed to the margins of the political life of the 'national-popular' political cultures. The 1979 election of Margaret Thatcher effectively saw the beginning of the popular rehabilitation of economic liberalism (after a long period of germination and elaboration by neo-liberal intellectuals in the preceding two decades) and the reconfiguration of a new historic bloc, a new hegemony, in which economic liberalism is the leading force together with conservatism and social liberalism.

Gramsci was also aware of how the national-popular was shaped by territorial differences that fracture hegemonic formations. His sensitivity to these questions of a geopolitical and cultural nature was shaped by the late unification of Italy and the continuing and sharp division between the industrial north and the rural and peasant economy in the south of the country.[50] Such geopolitical considerations are also potential fracture lines for a multi-national State as is the case with Britain. First empire and then social democracy played important roles in binding the constituent parts of the multi-national State together.[51] But with the demise of both and the rise of a new historic bloc in which economic liberalism predominates, not only are there new stresses between England and the other nations that make up Britain, but there is also the return of the deep-seated fracture line within England between the north and the south, which have, for more than 170 years at least, been underpinned by different political economies.

England is the core national base for economic liberalism and the south of England its core economic regional base within England. This is where the middle class is at its most dense and most dominant in the key institutions of the State, the media and the arts and where the middle class is most strongly linked with private capital rather than the public sphere;[52] this is where the economy is most open to international capital and so receptive to the ideology of global competition which has been an important driver for economic liberalism in its presentation of itself as 'inevitable'. It is also the location of London, the heart of finance capital. For many commentators, economic liberalism is characterised by a shift within capitalism away from investment in productive activities towards short-term financial speculation on the world's stock exchanges. London is also the heart of the neo-liberal supporting national press and the heart of the political elite that has been almost wholly converted to neo-liberal orthodoxy. Of course this geographical dimension to economic liberalism does not mean that there are no sites of resistance to it within the south. Or that economic liberalism does not have any institutional, economic and social bases of support outside the south of England. There are blocs of ruling classes within each region and nation of Britain, of course, as well as poverty. We are talking rather about tendencies here rather than any simple clear-cut divide. Nevertheless, England and the south of England in particular constitute a dense and compact network of socio-economic and political interests that are particularly plugged into the global neo-liberal order. Since the 1980s, there has been a growing political and geographical polarisation with Conservative Party voters amassing in ever-greater numbers in the south east of England.[53] Such geopolitical weightings and skews add a further level of complication to the business of building and sustaining hegemony (since polarisation and building consent and legitimacy are to some extent in conflict) and a further level of complication and diversity in terms of the heterogeneity of meanings within and across political cultures.

2

The formation of political cultures

The major political cultures that have forged the 'national-popular' in Britain have been conservatism, economic liberalism, social liberalism, social democracy and socialism. National identity is thus a composite and contradictory formation. No one political culture has ever dominated the political terrain on its own; no one political culture has ever been able to univocally speak to and mobilise behind it enough of the population, or even the dominant social classes, to secure its rule through a combination of consent and coercion. Thus political cultures have had to work together in different configured alliances in order to manage the contradictions between civil society and the State discussed in the previous chapter: intra-class conflict between capitals, inter-class conflict between capital and labour, the atomisation of the social fabric generated by commodification and competition and how all this impacts on national identity. Of course this does not exhaust all the constituencies around which political struggle and cultural identities are formed. There are many other identities that intersect with these class formations and processes. The ones which we will engage with in due course in more detail as the book unfolds are based on ethnicity and geography.

From the nineteenth century to the contemporary moment we can identify three great 'historic blocs' that have shaped the national-popular in particular ways. The term historic bloc, as we have seen, is Gramsci's. It refers to the configuration of social-economic interests that are brought together into a set of class alliances within a given political–moral framework that sets the agenda and terms of debate, the moral and intellectual leadership (hegemony) of the country. Another useful way of thinking about a historical bloc is to see it as a particular dialectical organisation of 'base and superstructure'.[1] The first historic bloc that was in place for most of the nineteenth century was forged around conservatism, economic liberalism and nineteenth century social liberalism. This partnership in governance did not preclude significant tensions inside it, but it does presuppose substantive areas of consensus as to what constitutes the 'common sense' parameters of social, political and economic life. Towards the end of the nineteenth century this historic bloc began to undergo a decomposition. The rise of the workers movement from the mid-nineteenth century and the not unconnected deepening split *between* economic liberalism and nineteenth-century social-reform liberalism, opened up a long-protracted period of reconfiguration. A new historic bloc slowly formed inside the old one during the opening decades of the twentieth century. This new historic bloc saw a new kind of class compromise between the workers movement and the defenders of private property. The compromise between conservatism and the labour movement was mediated by the strata of intellectuals linked to social-reform-minded liberalism which had broken away from economic liberalism. The resulting second bloc that was properly institutionalised in 1945 following the electoral triumph of the Labour Party, is the period of social democracy – a product of the labour movement in which its socialist wing compromised on its more radical ambitions with the social reformers of liberalism. Conservatism accepted this new configuration as necessary and inevitable after two World Wars, the Depression, the rise of fascism and communism. Economic liberalism was banished to the outer margins of political life. It largely vanished from the 'common sense' of mainstream political thinking, since it was constitutively impossible to reconcile with social democracy.

This second historic bloc lasted for a fairly brief time. The conditions of its possibility required a post-war booming capitalism. When that boom started to falter in the 1960s and decline acclerated in the 1970s, the coalition that had built social democracy began to fragment. At this point there emerges what Gramsci calls an 'organic crisis', when 'incurable structural contradictions have revealed themselves (reached maturity)'.[2] An organic crisis sets the terrain in which one can then study a 'conjuncture', namely the specific people, groups, tendencies, movements, strategies and so forth that are in play in a given moment and which, within the constraints of the situation, try to 'demonstrate that the necessary and sufficient conditions already exist to make possible, and hence imperative, the accomplishment of certain historical tasks'.[3] Gramsci probably had in mind here not only the forces of the Left – but also the forces of the Right which can just as well pose themselves as the leaders of certain 'historical tasks'. In a classic example of Gramsci's argument that political change requires a long-protracted struggle to build up the popular support for a philosophy among the people, economic liberalism had bided its time, kept alive by a cadre of dedicated intellectuals that began once more to win the ear of influential people in politics and business as capitalism faltered. The 1979 election of Margaret Thatcher provided economic liberalism with the opportunity to achieve some (much debated) purchase within popular culture once more. It was combined with conservatism in the 1980s and was reconfigured again in the 1990s as a new social liberalism now joined forces with economic liberalism and, at the level of electoral politics at least, for a time displaced the most reactionary wing of conservatism's social agenda, associated with Thatcherism. As with the previous historic blocs, the consensus that made this third historic bloc possible was also characterised by contestation, both from within the bloc's leading forces (the tensions between conservatism, economic liberalism and social liberalism) and from without (residual struggles launched from a social-democratic political base) including what was the last (for now) major confrontation in Britain between an explicitly large-scale mobilisation of the working class against the dominant historic bloc, namely the miners' strike of 1984–5. The defeat of that strike, which Perry Anderson described as 'the longest epic of collective resistance in the annals of British labour'[4] still haunts the national-popular today even as the substantial reconstruction of the working class since the 1980s makes the particular features of that confrontation now look a very long way away indeed. In this chapter we need to sketch some of the internal structural features of the five political cultures to understand their specificity and how they work together and against each other in complex patterns of consensus and contestation. Subsequent chapters will unpack the political cultures and their contradictions in greater detail.

Conservatism

Conservative political culture has a deeply contradictory relationship to capitalism, which it is easy to overlook, given its fierce support and defence of this socio-economic system. At the same time, it is the most successful and oldest of all the political cultures within Britain and this suggests that it is very adept at managing the contradictions between conservatism and capitalism. Like liberalism in both its economic and social wings, it defends the private ownership of productive property as synonymous with civilisation and liberty itself. Anything that limits the rights of private property and possessive individualism is seen as equivalent to an attack on freedom and liberty (which are more important than democracy and equality).[5] To the argument that private property itself may violate the rights of the worker, the citizen, the consumer or our obligations to the natural habitat, conservatism turns a deaf ear. For conservatism, the worker exists only as an individual whose interests are synonymous with private property.[6] For does not the worker own 'property'? Here the conflation between radically different kinds of property – that which we use for its use value or personal consumption and that kind of property (productive forces) which capital uses to generate more capital – serves conservatism well. It blurs essentially very different kinds of 'property' since owning a washing machine and owning a factory that produces washing machines are not just differences of magnitudes but rather involve entirely different kinds of social relationships.

When conservatism imagines the individual, it imagines the private person, in their private space (e.g. their garden, or in the patriarchal-feudal phrase, 'the Englishman's home is his castle') with their private goods. The citizen by contrast, is a category that conservatism is thoroughly suspicious of. From the French Revolution onwards, it smacks of the individual who has a strong political identity and therefore someone who has an interest in politics and who sees themselves as having certain political rights. This is uncomfortable for conservatism because political participation can lead to demands to diminish the hierarchies that conservatism prefers to keep intact. Freedom and liberty for conservatism is best exercised by the individual in the sphere of civil society (i.e. in the non-Gramscian sense, of the market) not the State. But this commitment to economic freedom is coupled with a belief in the inevitability of inequality. From the position of a traditional conservative, this is manifest in the ascribed position of social differences around status and esteem. But the belief in the inevitability of inequality also opens up a potential alliance with economic liberalism which is also relaxed about the unequal outcomes of a market society. However, economic liberalism in theory at least is less prone to endorsing ascribed (already cemented) social status but instead has a meritocratic element that suggests, unequal starting positions notwithstanding, that 'anyone' can or should make it if they have talent, drive, etc., etc. This creates a potential tension with traditional conservatism as it did in the case of Margaret Thatcher's brand of conservatism.

The tension between conservatism, with its investment in already established social hierarchies and economic liberalism which may not necessarily respect those already established hierarchies, is a long-running one which can be related to the dynamic transformational character of capitalism. While accumulation sits happily enough with conservatism, the broader transformational processes unleashed by capitalism does pose a problem for conservatism's desire to *conserve*. It was Marx of course who noted in *The Communist Manifesto* that conservation is in many ways the last thing that the bourgeoisie have on their minds as they embark on an:

> uninterrupted disturbance of all social conditions, everlasting uncertainty and agitation ... All fixed, fast-frozen relations, with their train of ancient and venerable prejudices and opinions are swept away, all new-formed ones become antiquated before they can ossify. All that is solid melts in to air ...[7]

The idea that capitalism is only a revolutionising and modernising force is something we will need to qualify later on, but it is certainly a very powerful aspect of capitalism and one which causes interesting and significant tensions for conservatism's inclination to protect already established hierarchies of class and culture. In periods of rapid capitalist derived change and the sudden expansion of market principles, those accretions of social status that have accrued to particular groups within the social structure may be challenged by new entrants into positions of economic power. This tension between the economic logic of capitalism based on recurrent change and the social and cultural logic of status, honour and esteem, which tries to defend already established hierarchies, was pointed out by Max Weber. '[A]ll groups having an interest in the status order' he observed, 'react with special sharpness precisely against the pretensions of purely economic acquisition.'[8]

This tension between social status and the 'pretensions' of purely economic power (e.g. the 'newly moneyed') has been observed as an interesting cultural fissure within British capitalism and may be mapped over the intra-class tensions between older landed capital and newer industrial capital in the nineteenth century. It was also much in evidence during the early years of Margaret Thatcher's decade in power, because her economic project involved unsettling established hierarchies of esteem and taste by re-injecting conservatism with the newly emboldened economic liberalism. Since social status requires some temporal duration to build up while economic power can be achieved relatively quickly, the tension between status and economic power often maps over onto the tension between tradition and change. The everlasting uncertainty and agitation of capitalist change, the anxiety and fear it can generate, requires therefore a compensatory invocation of tradition. Along with social status acquired over time comes immense reserves of legitimacy which radical change often lacks, especially when it is being driven from the top down in what Gramsci called a 'passive revolution' (i.e. one in which the masses are not invited to play an active role, but rather be the objects of change dictated by the leading, dominant social classes).[9]

For example, over the long term, the high social status and ideological efficacy associated with the aristocratic and landed gentry offers conservatism a rich resource from which to counterbalance capitalist change with the comforts of continuity. The potential, accumulated power and attractiveness for a general population of certain motifs around continuity, evolution, stability, hierarchy, deference and 'community' associated with rural England is considerable.

The tension between dynamic and transformative economic activity on the one hand and a powerful investment in images of stasis and continuity on the other, maps onto another binary opposition within conservatism: that between dynamic individualism and an obsequious deference and conformity to certain favoured social institutions, particularly those associated with the State. This is an example of where the common starting point of conservatism and liberalism in the individualism of private property bifurcates in different directions. Liberalism, a true child of the Enlightenment, remains committed to the supremacy of the individual's freedom of thought and conscience, and is instinctively suspicious of the threat which the State's coercive apparatus poses to liberty and the State's ritualistic-ideological apparatus poses to rational and critical thought. By contrast, conservatism's roots in a reactionary strand of romanticism, means that it invests heavily in feeling and sentiment even at the expense of rational self-knowledge. The German philosopher Herder declared for example, that prejudice and ignorance were *good* because they helped build a sense of communal unity and tradition that makes people happy.[10] This is an authentic conservative position and utterly at odds with liberal Enlightenment thinkers of the same period such as Kant.[11] While Herder was hostile to centralised State institutions and preferred concrete and particular, if hierarchical, communities to govern themselves, British conservatism grew naturally out of the feudal Absolutist State as it gradually oversaw the transition towards a capitalist economy.[12] It thus tries to straddle and unite in a single vision the particular community (emblematically represented in a rural but capitalist England) with the powerful apparatus of the State as the embodiment of the nation. Conservatism develops a distinctive concept of *service* rooted in honour, duty and obligation that is both deeply anti-democratic and prone to ecstatic investment in the rituals and ceremonial 'spectacle' of the State.[13] It is an anti-democratic concept of service because it is based on a presumed hereditary right to service (in the nineteenth century, the great aristocratic families) and an elitist notion of who is fit and capable to serve. Despite the professionalisation of the staffing of the State apparatus during the twentieth century, 'breeding' remains for conservatism, one of the best indicators of the ability to make a contribution. The conservative concept of State service is also anti-democratic because it is most invested in those parts of the State that are least susceptible to popular pressure and accountability and indeed least set up to service popular needs (unlike the social State). The military, the monarchy, the judiciary, the Church (of England) are powerful institutional repositories of conservative sentiment, identity and authority, which links conservatism to many parts of civil society (in the Gramscian sense as the 'private' fabric of the State). A certain version of the Houses of Parliament is also important – not as a symbol of popular representation (hence the importance of the House of Lords) but as a symbol of wise statecraft by the governing elite. The Burkean tradition of conservatism sees its favoured institutions in quasi-mystical terms in which nature and God merge together to endorse the particular arrangements that have developed in Britain.[14]

One may think that conservatism's in-built tendency towards authoritarianism, its almost erotic attachment to authority and obedience, comes into contradiction with its defence of individual property rights and the individualism associated with the latter. However, the State after all exists to defend the property rights of the property holders. The laws that it enforces and the obedience which it demands allow precisely for that activity of unhindered egoism in the economic structure of society which, from this perspective, is the cherished right of every freeborn Englishman. From the perspective of the subaltern classes, as Gramsci called the dominated groups, it is perfectly possible to imagine the economic structure of society as a sphere of your own activity and responsibility in which looking out for yourself is the dominant motive force, while regarding this set up as presided over by institutions of social control that guarantee and protect this 'freedom' and whose leadership and laws must be uncritically accepted as necessary and inevitable. Indeed conservatism's ability to recruit significant sections of the working classes to this vision has been essential to the success of the Conservative Party. But it is clear that while logically conservatism as a political philosophy can combine the concepts of individualism and authoritarianism together and explain how they complement each other, it remains a fault line and a potential point of attack from opponents for whom the tendency of excessive individualism to transgress juridical arrangements as well as moral norms and values, is clear enough.[15] Certainly within cultural critique (e.g. the gangster film or in an American context a satire such as *American Psycho*) it is a popular trope that seeds a line of attack that could be elaborated by political opponents of the conservative-economic liberal alliance, if they had the wit to do it. For conservatism however, one of the main political management skills that it has to perform is precisely to channel anxieties generated by both inequality and individualism into conservative repositories of identity, especially the 'law and order' State. This task which the Conservative Party has historically shown itself to be consummately skilled in, usually requires the construction of feared 'Others', whether from within the country (criminals, immigrants or better still 'criminal-immigrants') or outside it, onto whom fears and anxieties generated by capitalist change, trends and inequalities can be displaced. The displacement operation, whereby the causal drivers of anxiety and fear are relocated onto quite different, usually relatively powerless people and groups, is little remarked upon within the mainstream media and political discourse, even though it is routinely practised and quite structural to conservative political culture in particular. Thus the tensions between economic liberalism and conservatism may work as *enabling contradictions* for the culture, deepening and enhancing its hegemony through cunning political orchestration.

The tension between stasis and transformation, the old and the new, individualism and obedience, cause and displaced effect, can also be related to another 'dualism' within conservatism: that between a certain empiricism and bluff common-sense attitude and a broader sense of philosophy, worldview, theory or even metaphysics of conservative value systems. On the one hand, conservatism is characterised by its everyday pragmatic doing, in which experiential understanding based on immediate sense-perception (empiricism) is valorised and along with this goes a dismissive attitude of anything remotely abstract such as 'theory' (and of course 'intellectuals').[16] Indeed, for conservatism, it is precisely its antipathy towards theory that proves to itself that it is not an ideology, but rather just 'common sense'. Not for nothing did Gramsci associate 'common sense' with thought that uncritically assimilated existing opinion and thus was most likely to be shot through with ideology. For conservatism, philosophy, 'is a gentle additional illumination of the performances of the agent, not a powerful and detached instrument of decoding human conduct and of gaining crucial new insights into the human condition'.[17]

Yet despite or perhaps because of its relegation of philosophy and suspicion of theory, conservatism does what Gramsci recommended philosophy needed to do: translate its principles into an effective idiom that grips the masses. In this sense, conservatism's grasp of the tactics of forging the 'national-popular' are unparalleled. Of course, for Gramsci, integrating philosophical principles into practice – what Marx and Gramsci called 'praxis' – was designed to produce *critically informed action* (or 'good sense' rather than common sense). Conservatism, however, forges a popular idiom without the critical, reflective element. This absence of critical reflective judgement (and therefore the downplaying of theory in favour of 'gentle ... illumination') is inextricably linked to conservatism's very weak sense of social structure as a result of its commitment to individual property rights and stirring gut feelings, à la Herder's happy but ignorant folk. For Perry Anderson, a profoundly conservative British intellectual culture has displayed a 'deep, instinctive aversion to the very category of the totality'.[18] Margaret Thatcher was not articulating anything new in conservatism when she declared in an interview in 1987 that 'There is no such thing [as society]! There are individual men and women and there are families'.[19] 'Society' was plainly too abstract a concept for a philosophy that is mired in the empirical workings of market transactions. Whereas liberalism must complement its defence of private property rights with abstract universal concepts such as citizenship, rights, equality and so forth, in order to offer a social vision, conservatism finds a counterbalance for its lack of a sense of *social* structure by investing in the 'smaller' social units of 'community' or 'family'.[20] The latter offers a social unit larger than the individual to combat complete atomisation, but small enough to operate below the level of 'class' as a category while yet at the same time it is coextensive with individual private property rights (the 'assets' of the family) and it is a unit of consumption for advertisers. In addition images of the family in discursive practices are able to tap the wellsprings of Herder-like sentiment and feeling quite readily because it is easier to be moved by thoughts of people who are intimately involved with each other than more abstract conceptions of solidarity between acquaintances and strangers.

The contradictions between stasis and change, individualism and authority, cause and displaced effect can all be seen at work in a concrete example.

When Margaret Thatcher fixed the Conservative Party in the direction of economic liberalism in the 1980s, she simultaneously evoked a version of 'Victorian values' to lend legitimacy to her radical and unsettling transformation of British society. The conjuring of Victoriana had naturally very little to do with real history and everything to do with a highly selective representation of the past that suited the Thatcherite project. It was wonderfully analysed by cultural historian Raphael Samuel in the early 1990s. By referring to the Victorian values of the nineteenth century, Thatcher could evoke a comforting sense of tradition and a consoling feeling of greatness while also bypassing the second historic bloc of social democracy, erasing it from a fantasy history even as she was busy trying to dismantle it in the present. 'Mrs Thatcher's traditionalism allowed her to act as an innovator … while yet sounding as though she were a voice from the past' wrote Samuel. She appeared 'simultaneously as a fierce iconoclast and a dedicated restorationist'.[21] In relation to the welfare state she was a destructive iconoclast, but this was coupled with the appeal to restoring an older lost glory. Her version of Victorian Britain is interesting for what and who it left out: the self-help working-class insurance schemes known as Friendly Societies showed a collective mutualism that was definitely not welcome in Thatcher's version of Victorian Britain. Nor was there much emphasis on the Victorian philanthropy or array of charitable organisations that mushroomed in this period. Beveridge, the leading intellectual figure in the founding of the welfare state, traced its origins back to the self-help organisations of the working class and the charitable organisations of Victorian philanthropy.[22] This was a lineage then that had to be eradicated from Thatcher's Victorian Britain. Nor was there any place in Thatcher's version of Victorian Britain for the new libraries, the great Victorian railway system, or even the patrician class that actually ran the Conservative Party in the nineteenth century and who sit at the apex of the social structures of rural England as conservatism imagines it. Thatcher's Victorian values even downplayed very traditional conservative motifs such as Church and monarchy[23] although not I think empire, as Samuel suggests.

The people and values which did constitute 'Victorian Britain' according to Thatcherism's representation of it were remarkably like her: lower-middle class, from a small family business background, hostile to the older social elites at the top of society and cultured elites or the professions, in the middle. The latter were as much the enemy as the working class. The Victorians for her were embodiments of discipline, respect, order, hard work, duty, and self-reliance. Here we have a good example of an economic philosophy being translated into an idiom that has a chance of resonating with the wider population, stirring people to support this moral order against their long-term interests in most respects. This cluster of values reconciled or tried to reconcile a strong individualism with a traditional authoritarian moral order internalised by the individual. That this traditional moral order was quite at odds with the exultant hedonism unleashed by economic liberalism in the 1980s is another contradiction or tension that exposed Thatcherite conservatism to a charge of hypocrisy that eventually had a corrosive effect on its support base in the 1990s.[24] Another component of the value system was 'living within your means' which was a coded attack on the public sector both at the level of public-sector debt and at the level of the individual somehow becoming dependent and irresponsible because they needed the State to help them meet their needs. Once again the deeply ideological rendition of Victorian Britain worked not as a history lesson, but as a way of fleshing out Thatcher's attack on the welfare state. If the Victorians could live without it and be 'great' why could not contemporary Britain? Having eliminated the working class Friendly Societies and the middle and upper class philanthropy from her vision of the past, the answer happily confirmed her view that the welfare state was a morally enervating institution rather than an attempt to mitigate the failures of market capitalism. The apparently more universal discourse of morality (the Victorian 'character') neatly side-stepped the obvious class affiliations, investments and interests at play in attempting to withdraw socialised goods of various sorts and exposing more and more people to the 'rigours' and 'vigour' of the market in ever more dimensions of their lives. All of this was well recognised by people at the time. In a 1983 phone-in on the BBC1 TV programme *Nationwide*, Thatcher was challenged by a caller, Janet Blair, about 'Victorian values' which to her conjured up great poverty. The programme presenter Sue Lawley commented during the exchange that:

> It has to be said, Mrs Thatcher, that a lot of people who wrote into us on this point – and there were quite a few – did feel that perhaps your summoning up the virtues of the Victorian times were perhaps an excuse for reducing the welfare state, which is what I think Mrs Blair is getting at.[25]

Thus the invocation of Victorian values was also an invitation to conduct a struggle of ideas and values on deeply contested territory that was far from necessarily advantageous for Thatcherism. 'Victorian Britain' was already encrusted with many negative associations concerning deep levels of poverty, inequality and social injustice.

The backward cultural identity that Thatcherism grafted onto economic liberalism exhausted itself in the 1990s as an electoral force. Nationalism, xenophobia, naked class war, a brash materialism, greed and individualism, 'family values' (also known as intolerance for anyone outside heterosexuality), all became deeply unattractive to wider and wider layers of people. The Conservative prime minister who followed Thatcher, John Major, attempted to soften some of the hard edges of Thatcherism but maintained both its economic project (disastrously privatising British Rail in a way that led to fatal crashes) and its backward looking traditionalism. This last manifested itself in an equally disastrous but comic 'Back To Basics' PR campaign that unravelled against a background of financial corruption and press reports revealing that the sexual morality of contemporary Conservative politicians (including, we later found out, John Major himself) was a good deal more adventurous than it was supposed to be.

It was the Left that in many ways and perhaps surprisingly won the 'culture wars' on race, sexuality and gender, even if they seemed to lose the economic arguments. But those themes were quickly appropriated by contemporary social liberalism and in doing so, were watered down (what Freeden calls 'decontested') and became more acceptable to mainstream institutions. Tony Blair's leadership of the Labour Party from 1994 represented a grafting of social liberalism onto economic liberalism, the victory in the culture wars lashed to a catastrophic surrender on the economic arguments. In the 2000s, the Conservative Party, at least in PR and marketing terms, adopted a more liberal face in order to compete with Tony Blair's election-winning 'New' Labour. Theresa May, the then Chairwoman of the Conservative Party, memorably told the Conservative Party annual conference in 2002 that they were widely known as the 'Nasty Party' for their hostility to groups outside the parameters of traditional conservative love-objects. However, shifting the party towards a more tolerant position on sexuality, race and Europe opened up a space for the disenfranchised populist nationalism associated with Thatcherism to be captured by UKIP. Nevertheless, whether inside the Conservative Party or UKIP, conservative nationalism and conservative-economic liberalism remains a fault line whose management takes up ever more energy ever since Thatcherism. Invoking national identity while at the same time privatising national assets such as British Petroleum, British Airports Authority, British Steel, British Gas, British Rail and more recently the Post Office, is clearly a quite contradictory project. No more could such entities be portrayed as representing the 'national interest' – now they represented their own private interests. To an extent, economic liberalism was hollowing out conservatism's own resources for forging the national-popular in its image. UK PLC is a distinctly different ideological project from 'Great Britain' and perhaps one which can draw on less powerful Herder-like sentiments to bond people to the hegemonic bloc. Yet that is precisely why traditional conservatism remains a potent and dangerous force in which irrational projects based on displacement may fester.

As the national terrain is penetrated more and more by multi-national companies buying up great chunks of the economy, the ideological contradiction between conservative nationalism and conservative economics becomes quite glaring. However, the most disabling contradiction for British conservatism was between its own increasingly hollowed out version of the cultural-political national identity that should 'cap' its economic-liberalist political economy and an alternative cultural-political project for neo-liberalism that developed on mainland Europe around the European Union project. This project was a powerful one geared around a convergence between social liberalism and economic liberalism, hence New Labour's strong identification with Europe in

the 1990s and 2000s. The European Union's project of greater political
and monetary union acted as a lightning conductor for a core part of
the Conservative Party because it threatened to offer an alternative site
of identity and identification that had nothing whatsoever to do with
the historic strengths of conservatism in the British State. Yet while
legitimate questions about State sovereignty from an undemocratic EU
loomed large within the conservative optic, threats to State sovereignty
and popular democracy posed by international capital were predictably
invisible to this political culture. The cultural correlate to subordinating
workers, consumers and citizens to international capital is to let the
cultural industries sell conservative England to the world as heritage
culture and tourist playground.

Liberalism: social and economic

One of the benefits of integrating a discussion of neo-liberalism into
Gramsci's concept of a historic bloc and then differentiating that bloc
into three distinct political cultures (conservatism, economic liberalism
and social liberalism) is that it meets the objection that the concept of
neo-liberalism assumes too homogeneous a phenomenon. The concept
of the historic bloc allows us to address for example the national
specificity of neo-liberalism in Britain in terms of the other political
cultures it must work with to secure its hegemony. We have seen that
the relations between conservatism and economic liberalism are not,
however, smoothly harmonious. Neither is there a seamless integration
between economic liberalism and social liberalism, nor again, between
social liberalism and conservatism. To some extent conservatism and
social liberalism vie as the most effective partner for economic liberalism
which in practice uses both to secure its hegemony. We must beware,
however, that social liberalism's critique of conservatism often disavows
its own role within the first and third historic blocs as managers of the
system.

   In thinking about liberalism, we must distinguish between economic
liberalism and social liberalism and understand their historically
changing relationship. Social liberalism began life as virtually the
political culture of economic liberalism in the late eighteenth century.
The two *were* identical. A busy commercial society premised on the
initiative and autonomy of people engaged in market exchange
laid the natural material conditions for a language of freedom and

Enlightenment progress. With the development of manufacturing, the combination of the application of scientific principles to the technology of production further linked the market and capital accumulation to progressive change. Richard Arkwright and his partners and commercial backers developed the water-powered cotton spinning mills that massively enhanced productivity around the same time that Adam Smith was writing *The Wealth of Nations* (1776). Although Adam Smith is today recruited as the philosopher of contemporary economic liberalism, especially by the Conservative Party, this rests on abstracting from a complex book with many different perspectives on the new business society a single phrase about the 'invisible hand' of the market producing beneficial outcomes for society as a whole through the pursuit of self-interest. This then supports contemporary economic liberalism's belief in the market as a self-correcting engine of growth, always returning to the equilibrium of supply meeting demand. The role of the State in such a conception is to facilitate the operation of the free market rather than get in its way and avoid appropriating to itself a conception of the social good.

But the adoption of Smith's political economy by contemporary economic liberalism also requires suppressing not only his many comments on the potentially harmful effects about the free market, but also the fact that he operated with an early model of the labour theory of value, namely one that acknowledged that the wealth of nations originated in the labour of those who work. Adam Smith's focus on the productivity of labour being enhanced by specialisation and machinery meant that liberalism retained a philosophical opening to labour as value-producing and therefore to its moral claims for 'fair' recompense once it became an organised political force. Yet this also meant recognising the limits of free-market capitalism in meeting those moral–political claims, something contemporary economic liberalism need not do since for it, it is the subjective desires of the consumer or capital itself (e.g. the 'genius' of the entrepreneur) that accounts for profit. This *neo-classical* economics that became dominant towards the end of the nineteenth century as a response to Marx, is the true philosophical point of origin of contemporary neo-liberalism.[26] But of course Adam Smith is a far greater ideological prize as the 'father' of neo-liberalism than its true progenitors. Appropriating Smith to economic liberalism smoothes over the real history of liberalism and the painful parting of the ways between economic liberalism and social liberalism in the nineteenth century.

Nineteenth-century liberalism had to learn that its hopes for progressive reform were not identical with the free market. Two key pieces of legislation marked the high tide of the free-market liberals. The Poor Law Act of 1834 stopped state aid to the very poor and instead funnelled them into the oppressive workhouses. Here liberalism was in alliance with conservatism, its partner in the historical bloc of the period. The Repeal of the Corn Laws in 1846 meanwhile marked a victory for economic liberalism *against* conservatism's social base in landed interests (intra-class conflict) which had had taxes slapped on imported grain to protect their own profits (but which raised prices for domestic food consumption and thus put pressure on industrialists to pay higher wages to their workers). At the same time as extending market forces, liberals in the early and mid-nineteenth century, agitated for social change, among other things, electoral reform (The Reform Acts in 1832 and 1867), prison reform, educational reform and public sanitation. Their class base was the industrialists and the growing numbers of the intelligentsia: press men, educationalists, scientists, engineers – the emerging professional middle class. This class base for liberalism as a political culture was to be short lived, however. In the last quarter of the nineteenth century, industrial capital, growing larger, but still small by US and German standards, and the provincial middle class, began to fear a reform agenda and drifted away from Gladstonian Liberalism towards the Conservative Party.[27] This was entirely rational from their perspective, since a reform agenda that was becoming increasingly 'economic' could only hurt their short-term interests (albeit moderately). Liberalism's social base narrowed to sections of an expanded and heterogeneous professional class, and the labour movement whose heartlands were in the north, prior to the displacement of the Liberal party by the Labour Party after the First World War.

The identity between laissez-faire economics and social liberalism in the nineteenth century was broken at first by attempted State regulation and then subsequently direct State involvement in the effective provision of essential services (such as gas and water) that the free market was systematically failing to deliver.[28] John Gray makes a distinction between a market society embedded in social life, where law and customs modifies its workings and a market society where the market is uncoupled from having social obligations.[29] He suggests that England had been the former kind of society *before* the mid-nineteenth century and only latterly and briefly a laboratory for a laissez-faire experiment which he pins wholly on those formally describing themselves as liberals. Here Gray wants to dissociate conservatism from nineteenth-century liberalism and 1980s Thatcherism, with its apparently novel marrying of conservatism and economic liberalism. Yet the whole trend of English society from the sixteenth century was precisely to develop market relations against the body politic. Conservatism's alliance with economic liberalism is a long and tacit one and economic liberalism was not the sole preserve of liberalism in the nineteenth century. Where Gray is right is that the free market was curtailed by the rising demands for change and increasing electoral enfranchisements of the population (the organised working class) during the last quarter of the nineteenth century.[30] This fundamentally pushed a good section of liberalism towards social reform in the genuine sense of the term and towards a politics of dialogue with the socialist and labour movements. It is this lesson, that economic liberalism and progressive social reform are *not* identical with each other that social liberalism has had to unlearn as it once more converges with economic liberalism in the current context. This means that today the 'reforms' it undertakes essentially unravel the reforms that it helped put in place across much of the twentieth century. This self-contradiction makes contemporary liberalism a particularly sorry philosophy.

If the economic development of capitalism towards big monopoly capital resistant to reform was one contradiction for social liberalism, another was the tendency of capitalism to develop economies that seem to be very different from the typical dynamics of industrial capital, which involve productivity gains through technological innovation. By contrast, empire, banking capital, landlordism, speculation and so forth all indicated that large chunks of the political economy of British capitalism depended on 'unequal exchange', hyper-exploitation, parasitic revenue streams such as rent and casino-style betting on the future as well as the use of debt and interest as a form of economic profitability or extortion. All of this has proved painful for a philosophy otherwise deeply supportive of capitalism. A normative distinction thus emerges between 'good' capitalism and 'bad' capitalism, and one may even detect this within Marx's critique. It is certainly evident in subsequent Left debates as well as radical liberal critiques of 'bad' capitalism that could be associated with, say, empire and its interlinkages with banking capital.[31] But what this normative distinction has tended to underplay is the extent to which 'good' and 'bad' capitalism are necessarily, structurally interrelated. Still, liberal critiques of capitalism's 'reactionary' developments are important signs of intra-class conflicts and significantly expand the repertoire of critique available for critical thought (Lenin, for example, famously drew on Hobson's liberal critique of imperialism).

Despite expanding the repertoire of discourses, the normative distinction between 'good' and 'bad' capitalism that emerges from intra-class tensions indicates the limits within which liberal thought must move, namely that there *must* be a 'good' capitalism to champion against the rentier capitalism which liberalism associates with conservatism. That investment sets the parameters for the oscillations of liberalism. Responses by subaltern classes and groups to social inequality at home and imperial power abroad have constantly pushed liberalism back and forth, but frequently towards the coercive State and therefore towards an overlap with the conservative political culture which has dominated the coercive State. The identity between civilisation and capitalism which liberalism ultimately insists on means that when imperialism generates the 'barbaric' other, the threat to the international political and economic order, to civilised values (which includes of course the regrettable but necessary deployment of high-tech killing machines against the low tech 'barbarism' of the enemy),[32] liberalism swings uncritically behind conservatism. The conversion of liberal media commentators to support for the Iraq War in 2003, or the crude attacks on Islam displayed by, among others, *Observer* columnist Nick Cohen, one-time author of a sharp critique of Blairism,[33] is indicative of liberalism's oscillations on this score.

The disavowal of the link between economics and politics is also evident in the domestic scene as social liberalism uncoupled itself from social democracy and re-aligned itself with economic liberalism. In terms of the social and economic cleavages that have deepened within Britain since the 1980s, a liberal middle class political culture that is particularly invested in a European identity has subtly codified its differences from the working classes (especially outside metropolitan London) as the cultural correlate to the demise of social democracy. As Michael Kenny argues: 'There is an increasingly marked inclination among sections of the middle class to disavow any association with nationalism, and to establish a distance from the working classes by tarring the latter with the brush of atavistic and regressive forms of chauvinism'.[34]

Islamic fundamentalists abroad and working-class reactionaries at home are both liberalism's 'Other' – that popular term within cultural theory that indicates how a group or people become a repository for all the fears and sometimes the fantasies of those with the power to define and classify them. In doing so, the 'other' is ripped out of their historical context and is thus essentialised in their supposed characteristics. The role of the dominant group in asserting social, economic and discursive power over the group that is 'othered' is typically denied. In particular liberalism disavows the connection between defensive forms of cultural identity that invest in traditional conservative inspired identity formations such as 'nationalism' and the pursuit of economic liberalism. When the latter generates insecurity and anxiety it can (if there is a political culture willing to interpret this condition in a particular way) lead to the antipathy towards the very multiculturalism and 'openness' liberalism says it wants to encourage. The role which liberalism plays in generating illiberalism is one of the key contradictions of social liberalism once it merges again with economic liberalism. In the contest between the two different cultural projects which conservatism and social liberalism have in their alliance with economic liberalism, there can be only one winner. The discontent generated by economic liberalism at the bottom end of the social scale will always be more easily channelled into a conservative political culture than liberalism, since the former is rooted in a sense of belonging and tangible community that offers some (albeit in material terms, very little) compensation to insecurity, inequality and powerlessness. For the working classes experiencing the hollowing out of their communities following de-industrialisation, the liberal values of a cosmopolitan internationalism very explicitly embrace the forces of globalisation that are responsible for their predicament. With conservatism, this is much less clear, to the evident advantage of conservatism. While losing out to conservatism in terms of the reactionary political dynamic which economic liberalism generates, social liberalism is pushed back towards the very coercive State which in other matters it regards with suspicion, since it poses a threat to individual liberty. The complex dynamic of attraction and repulsion between social liberalism and conservatism, includes the former often helping the latter realise when it is time to introduce reforms in order to safeguard the longer-term future of the system. These intra-class tensions aside, conservatism and liberalism overlap in their political cultures to a considerable degree. There was nothing especially surprising about the coalition government between the Liberal Democrats and the Conservative Party between 2010 and 2015. Similarly, it is hardly surprising that the consensus politics of the current historic bloc means that the Labour Party has a very porous border, and is home to economic liberalism, social liberalism and conservative political cultures. The only political culture that is not welcome in the Parliamentary Labour Party, which instantly merits the return of border controls, passports and the thought police, is social democracy.[35]

Social democracy

Liberalism's finest hour, which lasted several decades, was to provide the political and intellectual mediation between the socialist workers movement and the capitalist social order that produced a fourth political culture: social democracy, a new 'historic bloc' as Gramsci would say, a new set of terms for an alliance or compact between the classes. The development of social democracy from the liberal side can be traced back to the works of Joseph Chamberlain in Birmingham and the policies of local municipal reform in gas, water and sewage that he pursued or inspired. Several decades in the making, it was only after two World Wars, the Depression and the rise of fascism and communism that social democracy was widely institutionalised in Britain after 1945. If it was a compromise formation from the perspective of the socialist movement, social democracy nevertheless represented real concessions to working people. John Gray defines social democracy as involving:

- The pursuit of greater equality of income and wealth through redistributive tax and welfare policies;
- The promotion of full employment through economic growth;
- A 'cradle-to-grave' welfare state defended as the social embodiment of citizen rights;
- Support for a strong labour movement as the principle protector of workers' interests.[36]

Today not only has liberalism turned its back on this social-democratic programme but so too did the Labour Party under the leadership of Tony Blair and Gordon Brown. Yet although no mainstream political party, at least in England, can be said to represent a social-democratic political culture, the culture itself survives in the sentiments and desires of wide layers of social groups for whom an unleashed capitalism is not a happy prospect. As a political culture, social democracy is currently what Raymond Williams would have called a *residual* culture. By this Williams means values and experiences that were formed in the past (possibly but not necessarily the pre-capitalist past) but which are still *active* elements in the cultural process and active to a substantial extent outside the dominant culture: 'Thus certain experiences, meanings and values which cannot be expressed or substantially verified in terms of the dominant culture, are nevertheless lived and practised on the basis of the residue – cultural as well as social – of some previous social and cultural institution or formation'.[37]

Williams distinguishes between the actively residual and the 'archaic'; the latter referring to historic elements that have been wholly incorporated as part of the dominant order, such as the aristocracy and the monarchy in contemporary Britain. Other residual elements, such as religion or ruralism are more ambiguous, having been in many ways significantly incorporated within conservatism and made archaic, but still in some respects and manifestations 'actively' resisting the dominant historic bloc.

But the residual posture of social democracy means that John Gray was not quite right to say that social democracy is 'a political project without a historical agent'.[38] What it has lacked is political party representation and leadership at that level, but it certainly has historical agency, as the vibrant independence campaign in Scotland testifies to. The growing popularity of independence within Scotland cannot be understood without reference to the political desire to reconstruct a social-democratic project in that country (we may leave aside the question as to whether the SNP, which has articulated the independence question with social democracy, really can deliver on that aspiration). Gramsci, as we saw in the previous chapter, writes of the 'vertical' axis on which hegemony is organised; that is to say the way political and class interests intersect with geo-political concerns. The elimination of social democracy from the political consensus has exacerbated a material-cultural fracture line between the 'North' and the 'South'. The north here includes Scotland, the north of England, and Wales. In the modern period, the north and the south (England from the Midlands down) have been underpinned by quite distinct political economies: between the tendential skews towards heavy-industrial capital located in the north and more 'rentier' forms of capital in the south, based on finance and property, with 'lighter' and more advanced industrial capital also a feature in the Midlands and south. One can see here how the intra-class tensions between conservatism and liberalism, between a 'bad' and 'good' capitalism from a liberal/Left perspective may map onto this geo-political split. In times of depression (such as during the 1930s and the 1980s) there has been a significant differential impact, with the north faring worse than the south. Under social democracy, this fault line was mitigated and conversely, with the decline of social democracy, regional polarisation has developed once more. On current trends the same bloc of dominant class forces, landed capital, finance capital and industrial capital, that was responsible for the enlargement of England into the British union by force, and then the enlargement of Britain again through imperial annexations, are the self-same class forces now contracting back to the 'core' of England in a way that threatens to not only undo Britain, but retrench even further to the England of the south-east. Former *Sun* editor Kelvin MacKenzie's call in the City paper *AM* for a new political party of the south,[39] suggests that the concentration of capital in the south/London may substitute the former empire as a route to profits with a local-global network that has a diminished need for the current British State (which some on the Right are now seeing as an invention of the Left!) or even an English nation (for some on the extreme Right 'the North' can go and join the Celts for all they care). MacKenzie is an ideological outrider for one possible future. Across the full range of liberal-conservative opinion today investments in Britishness and Englishness and their various meanings are certainly complex and contested, and reach well beyond the populist nationalism – to say nothing of the nascent separatism of MacKenzie – associated with one strand of conservatism. As Michael Kenny puts it: 'the panoply of sentiments associated with Englishness is more diverse and mutually disputatious than has generally been assumed. They encompass a relatively confident sense of national self-understanding rooted in familiar traditions of liberal and conservative discourse as well as harder-edged forms of populist resentment'.[40]

Nevertheless, such different shades of opinion across the conservative-liberal spectrum share a common reluctance to interrogate changing national identities in relation to economic liberalism, the crises of capitalism, the decline of social democracy or admit that socialism has been a constitutive feature of Englishness as well as Britishness.

The growing gap between the consensus politics among the political elites and the rest of the population who either consciously support social democracy or respond to its de-legitimisation in more displaced, disguised (and more right-wing) ways, is of course an international phenomenon, as is the spread of economic liberalism. Carl Boggs has, for instance, analysed how the public sphere and political participation and debate in America has withered as society has become increasingly commodified in the context of globalisation, a corporate media dominating and shaping the parameters of debate, and the diminishing obligations placed on corporate interests and power in general. The growth of what Boggs calls 'anti-politics' is evident in the general withdrawal from engagement in the public sphere, and the spread of feelings of powerlessness and paranoia. Even the Left's 'generalized hostility to state power'[41] can be seen as a form of anti-politics that is corrosive when politics could be a realm of self-realisation, collective empowerment, solidarity and action for the public good. As Boggs puts it: 'Viewed in … historical context, politics can be understood as the realm in which people seek to broaden their forms of identity, their sense of belonging, their capacity to influence the course of events, their ability to make a difference'.[42]

Peter Mair meanwhile finds similar trends across Europe, with western democracies being hollowed out as popular participation in politics and political parties is replaced by technocratic governance that de-politicises policymaking. He traces growing elite hostility to meaningful democracy and its replacement with 'constitutional democracy' which stresses legally codified rights in line with liberal values (freedom of assembly, equality before the law, elections, etc.) but little commitment to popular inclusion in the political process.[43] Instead the majority are largely seen as passive consumers that need to be managed and sold a political product (economic liberalism). A minority are encouraged to think of themselves as *citizens* – informed, knowledgeable, able to make political judgements. Here political participation and the knowledge tools required for it are increasingly stratified by educational provision and markets that commodify news and information for some and infotainment for the rest. While these widening gulfs between the political class and the broader political cultures have produced new social movements and left-wing populism across Europe, the biggest beneficiaries of an anti-political class stance until recently in England have been the right-wing populists UKIP and beyond them, far right street organisations such as the English Defence League.

If social liberalism and conservatism have a contradictory relationship with the economic liberalism they otherwise support, the relationship between economic liberalism and social democracy is quite simply a struggle to the death. Economic liberalism and social democracy must negate one another. The rise of one corresponds with the decline of the other, historically and logically. Social democracy represents the extension of democracy beyond merely the freedom and liberty to barter and trade, to dispose of one's private property as one pleases. In a capitalist society where various fractions of the capitalist class acquire vast accumulations of private property, the consequences of controlling that property and doing with it what they please, are increasingly profound and detrimental to the majority of the population who depend on that property for their livelihoods. As Engels put it in 1845:

> The bourgeoisie has gained a monopoly of all means of existence in the broadest sense of the word. What the proletarian needs, he can obtain only from this bourgeoisie, which is protected in its monopoly by the power of the State. The proletarian is, therefore, in law and in fact, the slave of the bourgeoisie, which can decree his life or death.[44]

Social democracy recognised this, recognised in a modified form the claims of labour, and extended the concept of democracy into the sphere of politics (which gradually become empowered to redistribute a modest amount of wealth from the minority to the majority) and across a wide social infrastructure that had to be constructed (housing, health, education, culture, etc.) so as to provide the real basis for some sort of participation in society. Social democracy's contradiction was that it was premised on the idea that a reformed capitalism could afford social democracy. But if we look at Gray's four-point definition of social democracy, it is not at all clear that capitalism can afford it, since equality and labour participation in policymaking cuts into profits. Greater equality through redistribution and welfare policies are essentially *political* goals, but the will to utilise political powers for these goals is shaped by the economic possibility of achieving full employment. On that, in turn, rests the possibility of constructing a welfare state and guaranteeing the labour movement a legitimate and empowered role in the construction of economic policy. But full employment was in all likelihood a brief and irretrievable moment within the unique circumstances of the post-Second World War period. In Britain, unemployment ran at about 2 per cent of the working population for much of the 1960s and into the mid-1970s. By 1979 it had risen to 5 per cent and by 1983 by more than 11 per cent.[45]

Gradually, unemployment was naturalised in the media. Tony Benn made the nice point that while days lost due to strikes constituted news, days lost due to unemployment were never reported. 'Each day that passes with four million unemployed' he wrote, 'means the loss of four million days' production. A billion days of production lost a year.'[46] High unemployment meant that the income of the poorest fifth of the population fell between 1979 and 1989 while the income of the richest fifth rose by over a third.[47] Successive Conservative governments 'solved' the embarrassing problem of unemployment by changing how the figures were counted. Will Hutton noted more than thirty changes to the definition of unemployment by the Department of Employment by the mid-1990s.[48] A more recent study by academics at Sheffield Hallam University found that the real rate of unemployment was around a million more than the coalition government of 2010–2015 admitted to,[49] meaning that unemployment has in reality stayed at about the level that it reached in the dark days of Thatcherism. At the same time, more and more workers in work are working in low-wage, low-skill and insecure jobs that have to be supplemented by more benefits, in effect a subsidy to the employers. One of the political effects of high unemployment of course is that it can break the power of organised labour to fight back against low-pay, poor working conditions and redundancies.

The growing reluctance of capital to invest its surpluses in production (unless it is worked by cheap labour outside the west) suggests that Fredric Jameson is right to argue that the central lesson to take from Marx's *Capital* is that it is not so much about work as the structural linkage between capitalism and unemployment.[50] Even if one does *not* agree with Marx's theory of the rate of profit, his labour theory of value, his theory of exploitation, alienation from species-being, or the working class as the agent of change, there is still one aspect of his critique that looms menacingly on the horizon. Marx's theory of the technologically driven displacement of human labour from the production process (automation, artificial intelligence and robotisation) still produces a devastating endgame for capitalism (and possibly us) around the mid-twenty-first century.[51]

Socialism

Socialism shaped social democracy from the Left and its main class base was the working class, although from Engels and Marx's time onwards, there has always been a fraction of radical middle-class intellectuals who broke with liberalism and aligned themselves to the working class against capitalism. Writing in 1845 from his base in Manchester, while working at his father's cotton factory, Engels produced, at the age of 25, one of the great classics of socialist literature, *The Condition of the Working Class in England*. Here he set out how early industrialisation shaped the life conditions of the first modern proletariat in the world, in terms of work, health, housing, city environment, diet, sanitation, education, family life and relations with the law and the factory bosses. In his chapter on the labour movement he analysed how working-class politics shifted away from individualistic responses to harsh inequality, such as crime, to the formation of trade unions. This was greatly facilitated when in 1824 working people received the right to free assembly – a right which before had been denied to them and which had made workers' associations necessarily secret. Through the trade unions the workers tried to defend their wages and conditions and withdrew their labour where necessary. An earlier tradition of vandalism and the destruction of factory machines or materials carried on alongside the new methods of organisation. Engels records armed conflict between workers and private security guards at Pauling and Henfry, a Manchester brick firm, in May 1843.[52] Such skirmishes though, whether violent or relatively peaceful, occupy the terrain of the economic-corporative as Gramsci defined it, the terrain of the immediate economic self-interests of a class fraction or even entire class. But for a class to achieve hegemony, it must move onto the terrain of political leadership and pose an all-encompassing agenda that knits together the economic, the social, the cultural, the ethical and enough of the other classes necessary to secure a power base. The dilemma and contradiction which this poses to socialism is that this requires engaging with the already existing institutions and practices of the society which socialism would like to fundamentally change. As E.P. Thompson put it:

> … each new advance within the framework of capitalism simultaneously involved the working class far more deeply in the *status quo*. As they improved their position by organization … so they became more reluctant to engage in quixotic outbreaks which might jeopardize gains accumulated at such cost. Each assertion of working-class influence within the bourgeois-democratic State machinery, simultaneously involved them as partners (even if antagonistic partners) in the running of the machine.[53]

The goal of socialism is to transform a society built around the private ownership of wealth to one where property is held in common and its uses democratically decided upon. Yet the institutions which exist and with which any large-scale political project has to engage, have developed within a society dominated by private elite power. These institutions have shown a remarkable capacity to absorb opposition and change its goals, especially by separating the leadership cadres of socialist movements from their base. Distinguishing between necessary tactical compromises and strategic co-option can be a complex and difficult judgement to make in such contexts.

After the demise of the working-class Chartist movement in the late 1840s, the labour movement delegated its intellectual leadership to the Liberal party. Eventually it reclaimed some independent political initiative with the formation of the Labour Party at the turn of the twentieth century. But the Labour Party and the labour movement more generally developed a particular culture that has been termed 'Labourism' which many critics saw as inimical to the goal of socialism. Labourism is the culture and politics of a movement trapped within the institutions it wanted – at least rhetorically – to change. It is the culture and politics of accepting the fundamentals of the British State, accepting the rules of the game, the inviolability of private property, the sanctity of institutions like the monarchy and the House of Lords, accepting the assumption that government equals power, that parliament equals power, accepting the fundamentals of unequal ownership of property and wealth, accepting that a mobilised working class is more akin to a mob and something to be feared rather than encouraged, accepting that winning elections is everything (and not what you do after you have won), accepting an imperialistic defence of 'British' interests abroad and accepting the traditional division of labour between the trade unions that focus on 'bread and butter' economic issues and the Labour Party which sees politics as the exclusive preserve of parliamentary representatives.[54] Theoretically, Labourism occupies the intellectual terrain no more radical than that staked out by the paternalism of the Fabian society. As a culture, Labourism is thoroughly economic-corporative, a movement in permanent deference to the existing order, it is the right wing of social democracy, the impetus of yesterday's socialist hopes congealed into the status quo. Its defensive intellectually meagre critical resources made its subordination to economic liberalism within the Labour Party, relatively easy.[55]

Yet beneath the sclerotic crust of Labourism's bureaucracy, pragmatism and passive acceptance of the status quo (with the 1945 administration the partial but significant exception), could there perhaps be a living working-class culture that was not identical to it – at least one that could potentially revivify the original socialist goals that required the agency of an independent working class more sceptical of the institutions of British society than Labourism generally was? In the 1960s and 1970s, as social democracy began to break down and expose the limits of Labourism, a number of cultural workers and intellectuals seemed determined to find out. But that first of all required reclaiming what constituted culture and who might have it. As Raymond Williams noted, there were powerful forms of elitism that suggested that ordinary people were too stupid and ignorant to have culture, which is supposed to be for the refined, the special and the few. For Williams, by contrast, culture refers to common meanings and value systems *and* it refers to the artistic expressions of those common meanings and value systems which allow for 'discovery and creative effort' and individual amendments of those common meanings.[56] Williams refused to read off from the 'observable badness' of mass commercial culture to the audiences themselves.[57] Coming from a working-class background himself, when he thought of his own family and friends, he found that mass culture did not hold up a simple mirror or index for moral condemnation of its audiences. '[T]he equation looks sensible', he noted, 'yet when you test it, in experience – and there's nowhere else you can test it – it's wrong.'[58] Audience studies of the mass media have since more than confirmed the essential rightness of Williams's argument, while cultural theory has explored the dialectic between mass culture and popular culture as one of continual and mutual appropriation and re-appropriation. It is interesting that while Williams came from Wales, where a strong working-class culture seemed self-evident to everyone as much as to him, he is quite concerned to write about the split between the dominant class associations of *English* culture and a working-class culture that presumably includes Wales and Scotland, but with the emphasis here, at least by implication, on the *English* working-class.

> There is an English bourgeois culture, with its powerful educational, literary and social institutions, in close contact with the actual centres of power. To say that most working people are excluded from these is self-evident, though the doors, under sustained pressure, are slowly opening.

But to go on to say that working people are excluded from English culture is nonsense; they have their own growing institutions, and much of the strictly bourgeois culture they would in any case not want.[59]

Williams's argument that culture is ordinary was timely because as he was writing these lines in the late 1950s, working-class actors, and scriptwriters were beginning to break through in theatre, television and film. New stories, new people, places, vernaculars, attitudes and values were getting a hearing in some of the biggest cultural institutions in a way that was unprecedented (especially for class-bound England). One of the key battlegrounds was television. Shaped by the social-democratic historic bloc, television was institutionalised as a public service medium, with the BBC as its cornerstone but stretching across to include the heavily regulated commercial channel ITV. Left to its own devices, social democracy filtered its cultural provision through a somewhat paternalistic middle-class intelligentsia. In the 1960s and 1970s, it was pushed by the Left to extend and democratise cultural participation and extend what counted as culture. That struggle was particularly important and fiercely fought out in television precisely because television, as a mass media, mattered. A number of actors, writers, directors and producers broke into the medium in the 1960s, having been beneficiaries of Rab Butler's 1944 Education Act that opened up grammar schools to a few bright working-class youngsters. But rather than be co-opted, by the time they acquired adulthood, a wider political context that was tilting towards radicalism encouraged them to articulate and represent the life they had emerged from. *The Wednesday Play* on BBC TV was designed by producers looking for new talent, new voices and perspectives on contemporary issues in the news at the time of airing. There was a strong working-class dimension to these programmes. Tony Garnett, one of the key producers of *The Wednesday Play* and collaborator with Ken Loach in this period, fought a battle to take the stories out of the BBC studios using the new 16 mm cameras.

The BBC film department at Ealing didn't want us to do this: they thought it was 'lowering standards'. Those 16 mm cameras were for news, not drama. Drama was posh. Anyway I fought the battle and we won. Indeed within two or three years no one wanted to work in a studio anymore.[60]

This nicely illustrates how aesthetics, culture and politics are all tied up. The move out of the studios, as happened in film a little earlier, opened up the possibility of engaging more authentically with the lives of ordinary people.

John McGrath, who worked in film and television but whose primary medium and first love was theatre, has written brilliantly about the complex ways an ordinary culture may provide the sources of inspiration for *artistic forms* that may express and comment on the culture. His book *A Good Night Out*, derived from a series of talks he did at Cambridge University at Raymond Williams's invitation. In one of the essays he reflects on a night out with the Manchester working class in Chorlton-cum-Hardy at a club in 1963. There is plenty of cheap booze at the bar and a variety of entertainments coordinated by the Master of Ceremonies, Ernie. A series of warm-up acts get things going: singers, dancers, comedians, a ventriloquist, Ernie himself telling gags and singing a song or two. Then things get serious with the bingo and by now 'the booze is flying over the bar in gallons'.[61] After that, Ernie brings on the evening's wrestling bouts which is then interrupted by a striptease show performed by 'Carmencita – in reality a raw young redhead from Stockport'[62] Then back to the wrestling before Ernie plays the night out on the Wurlitzer. Like the Soviet filmmaker Sergei Eisenstein who was fascinated by such popular forms as the circus and the fairground, or like the German Marxist Bertolt Brecht, who was equally interested in integrating popular forms into theatre, McGrath is looking for those popular elements that could break up and break out of the staid cultural forms of the bourgeoisie with their rigid distinctions between performers and audience and preference for linear well-told stories populated by 'rounded' characters. McGrath tried to reconnect with a tradition from the 1920s and 1930s, which had explored the potential convergence between the popular and the avant-garde. The carnivalesque quality of popular culture seemed to be a fantastic resource for overturning authority and hierarchy, for disrupting hushed respect with corporeal boisterousness and quick-witted banter, just as the avant-garde had tried to do ever since Marcel Duchamp submitted a urinal to a New York art exhibition in 1917. 'The characteristics of variety, music, satire, physical action, immense energy, and simplicity, or rather, non-elaborateness of presentation, are features that recur in almost all kinds of working class entertainment'.[63]

And they would also recur in McGrath's own theatre work as he tried to fuse popular forms with critical politics, never more successfully than in his now legendary tour of the Scottish highlands with the play *The Cheviot, the Stag and the Black, Black Oil*, which also had a television version produced by the BBC's Play For Today in 1974. In the mid-1970s social democracy was entering into its protracted crises and the extent to which an ordinary but combative culture would be tolerated within the main cultural institutions was beginning to reach its outer limits, as battles between cultural practitioners and senior management within the BBC showed. Democratisation of the institutions, what Raymond Williams once called 'the long revolution' was about to be decisively rolled back by the long counter-revolution of the new economic liberalism. There would not be many more examples of McGrath's Marxist populism on the BBC after *The Cheviot* or Ken Loach's Marxist interpretation of working-class history in the inter-war years as in *Days of Hope* a year later.

In one important cultural sector where the national-popular was constructed, a few organic intellectuals of the working class managed to make an impact. The term 'organic intellectuals' is Gramsci's and it seems to refer to that strata of intellectuals that are most closely connected to and familiar with the life of a class and most equipped to help develop its self-awareness and self-consciousness. Their role for Gramsci was, as John Schwarzmantel argues, to 'give the working class awareness of its ability to emerge from subalternity. This would involve extending its horizons above and beyond the economic-corporate level.'[64] Organic intellectuals of the working class may be intellectuals who have come from the working class (such as Tony Garnett, Ken Loach or Loach's long-term scriptwriter Jim Allen) or who have aligned themselves to the working class (such as John McGrath). Gramsci democratised the concept of the intellectual. Everyone, he suggested is a 'philosopher' insofar as they articulate conceptions of the world in their various forms of communication. Intellectual activity and capacity is part of our species-being (what it means to be human) and not the monopoly of elite specialists. Philosophy for Gramsci is the work of developing an independent and coherent conception of the world at both the individual and group level. The task of Marxism, for Gramsci, was to make everyone a philosopher, to develop that is, on a mass scale, the latent potentiality of critical thinking which everyone has, class stratification notwithstanding.

> Having shown that everyone is a philosopher, even if in his own way, unconsciously (because even in the smallest manifestation of any intellectual activity – 'language' – is contained a definite conception

of the world), we pass to the second stage, the stage of criticism and awareness. We pass to the question: is it preferable to 'think' without having critical awareness, in a disjointed and irregular way, in other words to 'participate' in a conception of the world 'imposed' mechanically by external environment, that is, by one of the many social groups in which everyone is automatically involved from the time he enters the conscious world … or is it preferable to work out one's own conception of the world consciously and critically, and so out of this work of one's own brain to choose one's sphere of activity, to participate actively in making the history of the world, and not simply to accept passively and without care the imprint of one's own personality from outside?[65]

Cultural workers involved in cultural and communicative production are therefore part of this process of disseminating philosophical ways of thinking in a popular idiom. Since culture is an important site where self-awareness and self-consciousness are forged, culture is an important site in the development of hegemony and counter-hegemony by organic intellectuals. In order to develop a moral and intellectual leadership, a class and its expressive and most articulate representatives, must be able to link the smallest details of ordinary life to the largest political questions of the day. In the case of counter-hegemonic organic intellectuals, they function to expand the communicative confidence, range, knowledge and combativeness of a class otherwise subordinated to traditional middle and upper middle-class agendas and perspectives that dominate education, politics and the media for example. As a political culture socialism is quite different in its relationship to the working classes in comparison to liberalism. The latter is unable to commit to trying to raise the cultural level of the working class as a self-aware class, but instead seeks to keep working people in a state of intellectual tutelage and passive recipient of concessions handed down by the dominant classes (and then taken away again).

3

Conservative culture and the economy

Introduction

The paradox of modern British conservatism – as with, to some extent, all conservatisms – is that this is a political culture dedicated to the reproduction of the most revolutionary and un-conservative mode of production in the history of human civilisation. It is a paradox that has perplexed many commentators. As a political culture, we can identify four key strands to conservatism. The first, economic liberalism, is in some contradiction with the other three. The ethical-religious strand of conservatism comes into conflict with the prioritisation of profit and accumulation that is essential to economic liberalism; the nationalist strand of conservatism comes into conflict with the international reach and scale of capital, while the investment in a 'deep-history' of institutions and customs whose origins appear to reach back into the mists of time comes into conflict with the perpetual revolutionary changes that capitalism brings about. Historically, the dominant *symbolic–cultural* order of conservatism has been made up of the ethico-religious, the nationalist and the evolutionary/deep-history strands. Together these three strands attempt to create a moral framework for an economic system that does not have one, a point of national identification for a mode of production whose expansionary logic cannot be contained within the nation-state and a slowing down of historical change for a revolutionary change-obsessed mode of production. It is a symbolic–cultural order that is in some contradiction with capitalism precisely so that it can work as a set of compensations to capitalism. The contradictions *and* the compensatory functions are inextricably connected. The symbolic–cultural order *has* to be in some tension with the economic order so that it can compensate for what is lacking in the latter. Noting that there are contradictions between the three strands that constitute the symbolic–cultural order and economic liberalism does not mean that the two cannot work effectively together. At the same time, the tensions become an active part of the history of this political culture. In certain circumstances the contradictions may intensify as the economic commitments begin to substantially negate the moral–political universe of the symbolic–cultural order. Yet by skilful political management (the art of displacement) conservatism can turn this negation to its own advantage, find other causes to blame and mobilise public anxieties around even more retrograde versions of conservatism. The contradictions become a 'virtuous' circle (for conservatism).

It is clear that the relationship between the symbolic–cultural order of a traditional conservatism and capitalism needs to be thought through as complex. The paradoxes of the relationship have confused commentators and persuaded many that conservatism as a political culture has not been fully signed up to economic liberalism or, in another variation, that it is a political culture that has retarded British capitalism by promoting archaic anti-modern attitudes. There has always been a strand of conservatism that has wanted a fuller cultural-political expression of conservatism's commitments to economic liberalism, and this strand overlapped with liberalism in its classic phase from the mid-eighteenth century roughly through to the mid-nineteenth century. After 1979, this wing of conservatism became dominant politically and culturally for the first time with the election of Margaret Thatcher as Prime Minister. Social liberalism and the Left have inflected the same complaint about a traditional conservatism in other directions. For the Left it has been argued that an aristocratic, landed gentry conservatism aborted British capitalism's proper growth path (industrialism and preparation for a transition to a socialist society) while liberalism in an overlapping but differentially inflected position, again suggested that a more progressive or rational capitalism grounded in a larger manufacturing industrial base has been historically stymied by traditional conservatism.

In an era when the British economy has returned, with a vengeance, to a basis in landlordism, property values, commercial trading activities, financial services and debt-led consumer-powered growth – all features which have been linked to specific sectors where conservatism as a culture has dominated, these debates about the historical past remain highly pertinent. In this chapter we will begin by looking at the arguments made by two political scientists, Tom Nairn and Perry Anderson across the 1960s, 1970s and 1980s that made the Left argument that linked the difficulties of British capitalism to the dominant political culture of conservatism. These arguments, known collectively as the 'Nairn/Anderson thesis' were contentious and contested accounts of the British social and cultural formation. Despite that, they are particularly germane here because they were influenced by the work of Antonio Gramsci. The attention they gave to the political–cultural specificity of national contexts was a welcome change in many ways from a strictly economistic account of the British historical experience and they made many powerful observations on the historical development of conservatism within the British political–cultural context. Yet their assumption that the symbolic–cultural order of conservatism was a significant drag factor on the development of British capitalism was problematic for several reasons. It gave cultural factors an efficacy over economic development when other economic and historical factors might explain the course of British capitalism's economic development more persuasively. As a result of according the cultural domain greater explanatory power in the economic field than perhaps it merits, the political–cultural domain itself was conceived in a rather non-contradictory manner, giving an overly unified, seamless and functionalist cast to Gramsci's concept of hegemony. This in turn meant downplaying the role of social liberalism within the dominant alliances that make up a historic bloc, in a partnership of alliance and competition. It also tended to assume virtually complete incorporation of the labour movement into a conservative hegemony. Gramsci's stress on contestation and change, on hegemony as an 'unstable equilibria' was marginalised as a result. It misconceived how the symbolic–cultural order of conservatism actually worked *for* British capitalism at the economic level despite appearances. Finally the analysis missed how a cultural fissure *within* the ruling bloc did eventually become efficacious on the political economy of Britain as part of a new configuration of class alliances.

In this chapter I give a brief summary of the Nairn/Anderson thesis before proceeding to offer a historically grounded account of how the dominant conservative symbolic–cultural order developed and worked (productively) in relation to capital accumulation. When British capitalism runs into problems towards the end of the nineteenth century, there are deeper historical and economic forces that can offer an explanatory account for that than the thesis of cultural backwardness. Yet the symbolic–cultural dimension remains an important part of the overall historical development of both society and economy, especially in relation to the competition between conservatism and social liberalism for leadership of the intra-class bloc that makes up the dominant nexus of class interests. In intra-class terms conservatism added to its base in the landed class, trade and finance, the growing support of industrial capital in the last part of the nineteenth century as it eclipsed the Liberal Party. As capitalist class societies become formally democratic, any dominant bloc's value system and some material benefits tend to be successfully extended in order to manage the inter-class tensions which are the inevitable consequence of a social order based on exploitation and crisis. This means integrating, both economically and through the various institutions of civil society, culturally, at least some layers of support from social groups outside the dominant classes or power bloc. Conservatism thus won support from the urban middle class, from the petty-bourgeoisie or small business constituency, from the upper layers of the skilled working class, as well as from layers of the relatively atomised working class deferentially attached to the service sectors of the south of England. The latter were without access to the more solidaristic traditions developed around northern industry and more saturated by the presence of the military (especially the navy) along Britain's coastal towns. This formidable hegemonic and electoral constituency or relatively durable set of alliances, which the conservative news agenda organs of the mass media help to solidify and amplify, had a distinctive political economy underpinning it. Yet despite this success, even conservatism had to contend with the persistence and competition of social liberalism from within the dominant historic bloc as well as the contradictions between its symbolic–cultural identity and economic liberalism. It also had to maintain an alert awareness of the organised presence of the workers movement or other threats from outside the dominant bloc, such as anti-colonial resistance or revolutionary movements abroad. In short, there was always contestation.

We finish this chapter by jumping forward to Thatcherism, which marks a moment when economic liberalism within conservatism achieves a level of symbolic–cultural expression and political leadership in its own right. Yet while this gives conservatism a renewed vigour with which to remake British society after 1979, it also intensifies the contradictions between the economic-liberal strand of conservatism and its other strands (the ethico-religious, the nationalist and the deep history strands). These contradictions were significant in my view and helped lead to the exhaustion of Thatcherism and its displacement by social liberalism. Later something like a Thatcherite coupling of traditional conservatism and economic liberalism returns around the future of Britain in Europe. This produces a deepening fissure *within* the historic bloc of conservatism and social liberalism for leadership of economic liberalism (see Chapter 6).

The Nairn/Anderson thesis

The core texts of the 'Nairn/Anderson thesis' are Tom Nairn's collection of essays from the 1970s, gathered together in *The Break-Up of Britain* and Perry Anderson's 1964 essay 'Origins of the Present Crisis' and his follow-up more than twenty years later in 1987 in the evocatively titled 'The Figures of Descent'. The analysis has been influential, in part because it drew on widespread sentiments across the political spectrum, though they gave those sentiments a new historical and theoretical armature. As I suggested already, there is an economic-liberal version of their critique. Martin Weiner's significantly titled book *English Culture and the Decline of the Industrial Spirit* is one such example that is also useful to refer to later on. The popularity of the Nairn/Anderson explanatory framework for the Left was considerable. For example, according to Stuart Hall, the British social formation, '… never ever properly entered the era of modern bourgeois civilisation. It never made that transfer to modernity. It never institutionalised in a proper sense, the civilisation and structures of advanced capitalism – what Gramsci called "Fordism"'.[1]

Here the failure to enter modernity was closely linked with the failure to modernise Britain's *industrial* base. Nairn's book provided a particularly excoriating critique of Britain's elites in this regard. Nairn argued that British capitalism suffered from a constantly weakening industrial base, a dominant financial sector orientated towards foreign investment rather than re-structuring and updating British industry, and a non-technocratic State and civil service unable to impose a revolution from above.[2] The structural barriers to modernity in Britain were laid firmly at the door of the political culture of conservatism, 'the controlling element in British capitalism',[3] Nairn argued. He associated this blockage in the necessary re-orientation of State and capital with England in particular, and looked forward to an English dominated British polity breaking up as the subaltern nations reasserted themselves against a 'patrician' State.[4] For Nairn, the economic problem was and remains conservatism's commitment to certain forms of capital associated with the City, itself seen as the modern incarnation of an aristocratic or at least landed elite. This meant that 'if they did not actually approve of the industrial degeneration, [they] had no urgent reasons for redressing it.'[5]

Surveying the contemporary scene in 1964, Perry Anderson identified a number of reasons for the 'profound yet cryptic' sense of crisis that was by then widespread across British society, 'with its stagnant industries, starved schools, run-down cities, demoralised rulers, parochial outlooks',[6] an assessment that looks oddly like it may have been written just yesterday. Like Nairn he thought the main reason lay in the origins of British capitalism in a landed class. England's revolution in the mid-seventeenth century (1642–1651), was '*the least pure bourgeois revolution of any major European country*' [original emphasis] because it was so early.[7] The English Civil War was primarily a 'clash between two segments of a landowning class.'[8] That the dominant class were landowners meant that a *landed elite* installed themselves at the head of Britain's development away from feudalism and this was to shape, it was argued, Britain in an ongoing way. 'The pioneer modern liberal-constitutional state', Nairn argued, 'never itself became modern: it retained the archaic stamp of its priority'.[9] One of the key consequences flowing from the dominance of the landed elite, it was argued, was the retarding of the British industrial revolution later on in the nineteenth and even the twentieth century. For Tom Nairn, a patrician elite remained in charge: an aristocratic and landowning class and ethos dominated Britain's political and economic institutions and civil society down through the ages. This ensured a policy agenda and culture that was anti-democratic, elitist and later anti-industrial. Nairn concludes that: 'As a road-making state into modern times, it inevitably retained much from the mediaeval territory it left behind: a cluster of deep-laid archaisms still central to English society and the British state'.[10]

Anderson agreed that the saturation of the British State by a commitment to an anti-modern conservatism meant that it lacked the technocratic skills to develop a coordinating apparatus that could overcome an amateur individualism associated with the aristocracy in defiance of bourgeois professionalism.[11] Anderson characterised the crisis of British society as an 'entropy' resulting in Britain's inability to modernise because it was trapped in an 'archaic society'.[12]

Mobilising Gramsci's concept of hegemony, Anderson argued that the hegemonic class 'is the primary determinant of consciousness, character and customs throughout the society'. The cultural power of the hegemonic class has a peculiarly archaic quality in the case of British society which is 'notoriously characterized by a seemingly "feudal" hierarchy of order and ranks, distinguished by a multiplicity of trivial insignia – accent, vocabulary, diet, dress, recreation.' He goes on to acknowledge that this does not correspond with 'the primary reality of a system divided into economically based classes' but it is 'the projective image of society naturally held and propagated by a landowning class' whose cultural power has lingered on well after industrialisation due to its 'continued political leadership'.[13] This both makes British society peculiarly class-obsessed, yet obsessed about a class imaginary that does *not* cognitively map onto the fundamental realities of class relations in the twentieth century and now twenty-first century Britain. The urban industrial bourgeoisie succumbed to the cultural power of the aristocracy and this in turn produced a powerful ruling bloc in which the clear class antagonisms that 'should' have developed between the bourgeoisie and the working class were overlaid and defused by quasi-feudal cultural maps of the social order.[14] While this ensured an ideologically robust social order it also, in this view, ensured economic decline by stagnating bourgeois dynamism.

This anti-modern cultural order was in turn buttressed by the British Empire, especially ideologically from the late nineteenth century. While earlier forms of plunder and annexation were crucial to the economic take-off of British capitalism in the seventeenth and eighteenth centuries, the rapid military expansion of the empire in the 1880s formed the ideological culture of empire which secreted itself deeply into British culture and society 'consecrating and fossilizing to this day … [the] interior space … and ideological horizons' of Britain.[15] Yet while the empire provided conservatism with a significant ideological boost, Anderson and Nairn play down the empire's economic role. This is because the more one acknowledges the economic role of empire the more the course that British capitalism took looks like it conforming to the rational capitalist idea of making the most of comparative advantage. Moreover, as we shall see, empire was as beneficial to industrial capital as it was to finance and commerce. Finally, Anderson notes that Britain's ruling class has enjoyed an almost unparalleled continuity of power compared to its European counterparts. Undefeated in two World Wars, un-invaded for centuries, its confirmed transition to capitalism (the English Civil War or revolution) receding back before the Enlightenment properly got under way, its social structures were 'untouched by external shocks or discontinuities'.[16] This is the least contentious aspect of the argument, since it is a historical fact that the British State has not suffered a rupture the like of which has been common on the European mainland. There is much in this outline of the British historical formation that one intuitively recognises and which provides a purchase on the British social formation. But to get a sense of how at every point there are complexities, nuances and interpretive choices that have to be made, we can turn to a passage from Gramsci that seems to outline in embryonic form, the Nairn/Anderson thesis.

> In England the development is very different from France. The new social grouping that grew up on the basis of modern industrialism shows a remarkable economic-corporate development but advances only gropingly in the intellectual-political field. There is a very extensive category of organic intellectuals – those, that is, who come into existence on the same industrial terrain as the economic group – but in the higher sphere we find that the old land-owning classes preserves its position of virtual monopoly. It loses its economic supremacy but maintains for a long time a politico-intellectual supremacy and is assimilated as 'traditional intellectuals' and as directive [*dirigente*] group by the new group in power. The old land-owning aristocracy is joined to the industrialists by a kind of suture which is precisely that which in other countries unites the traditional intellectuals with the new dominant classes.[17]

This is a complex, highly compressed passage that could be the basis for taking further research in the field in a variety of directions. We may note a number of points. There is the assumption, which Anderson later admitted was uncritically imported into his own analysis,[18] of a norm of bourgeois political development as represented by revolutionary France in the late eighteenth century, against which British development was judged negatively. We may also add here that there was in Anderson and Nairn's work an assumption concerning the normal *economic* development of capitalism, which prioritised industrial capital. This may have come from a reading of Marx's *Capital* itself, but the notion of an 'ideal growth path' has been (rightly in my view) questioned by others[19] while the notion of industrial capital being somehow normatively superior to other forms of capital, while not irrational, needs to be exercised with a certain caution lest it collapse into an uncritical liberalism. We will return to these points later.

Returning to Gramsci, there is some ambiguity concerning the intellectual-cultural achievements generated by the industrial bourgeoisie in this passage. While their economic progress is not matched by progress in the 'higher' sphere of political power, Gramsci does nonetheless suggest that there 'is a very extensive category of organic intellectuals ... who come into existence on the same industrial terrain as the economic group'. Organic intellectuals are by definition intellectuals who actually transcend the merely economic-corporative limits of industrial capital itself, and so while they may not achieve *political* power, scientists, engineers, economists and English novelists, nonetheless had a very significant broader impact on bourgeois culture in the nineteenth century. This was very much underplayed by Nairn and Anderson, for whom everything was ensnared in archaic quasi-feudal customs. In his famous riposte to the Nairn/Anderson thesis, E.P. Thompson asked how such a culture could have produced a Bacon, a Newton or a Darwin? This is important because although conservatism was certainly not a negligible part of the culture and retains down to this day huge levels of esteem and status, it has always had to share its hegemonic position with a liberal culture and it itself, insofar as conservatism couples itself with an active capitalist economy, helps produce the *conditions* for that liberal culture even if it chooses to 'fit' a different cultural capstone to the self-same economic relations that liberalism espouses.

The second half of Gramsci's passage concentrates on the 'old landowning classes' and anticipates aspects of the Nairn/Anderson thesis, namely the capturing of political power by that older class (Gramsci does not imply that this is to the detriment of a 'healthy' capitalism, however). The aristocracy become akin to intellectuals, providing political–moral leadership, but also 'traditional' intellectuals because of their roots in a prior mode of production (feudalism). For Gramsci traditional intellectuals are assimilated into the needs of the rising class of a new mode of production (that is capitalism). Usually Gramsci means by 'traditional intellectuals' priests, scholars, artists and so forth, those who are distant from economic activity directly, but here he re-defines the aristocratic elites in these terms vis-à-vis their political relationship to the industrial bourgeoisie. This risks downplaying the extent to which the aristocracy were in fact, as E.P. Thompson insisted, *agrarian capitalists* themselves. Landowners and farmers were 'a very powerful and authentic capitalist nexus'[20] and a 'superbly successful and self-confident capitalist class'.[21] They did not lose their 'economic supremacy' as Gramsci suggests, until the last part of the nineteenth century. Gramsci argues that the two classes are joined by a kind of 'suture', but the exact nature of the stitching remains undisclosed. The aristocracy are at once 'assimilated' and 'directive', which suggests a certain ambiguity. In fact within the Marxist literature, there remains a deep uncertainty around the terms of the relationship between the aristocratic/political/governing class and the industrial bourgeoisie. As Anderson noted in the later 'Figures' essay, Marx and Engels began by thinking that the aristocracy had been 'delegated' power by the industrial bourgeoisie, which makes the former, the representatives of the latter. But as time went on they were less sure that this was the actual relation or the balance of power between the two wings of the capitalist class.[22] They became increasingly disillusioned with the failure of the British industrial classes to seize the political policy making agenda and make it unequivocally their own. Yet perhaps this indicates the persistence in *their* thinking of an ideal growth path that favours the 'classic' model of capital accumulation mapped out in *Capital*, whereby competition drives technological innovation which in turn drives higher productivity. Normative investments in industrial capital, which is the driving force of this development model, can be found in both liberalism and Marxism. But the model forgets that accumulating profits need not require and perhaps never completely rests on the 'classic' or 'ideal-typical' dynamic to be found in industry. *At the end of the day it is profits rather than developing an industrial base that motivates capitalism.* Anderson himself notes this in a reference to the geographical splits between the different sectors of the capitalist class, but there is a reluctance to draw the necessary conclusions for his own historical analysis and its theoretical underpinnings:

> the bourgeoisie of London was commercial and financial in character, clustered around brewing, stock-jobbing, merchanting, warehousing, retailing and shipping, as opposed to the manufacturing and mining that dominated the North. It was probably more numerous than that of all the provincial cities put together, and was certainly wealthier per capita … By contrast, Northern industrialists were typically smaller figures. Making history and making money were by and large two different things: most of the concerns which helped to reshape British society yielded a good deal less profit for their entrepreneurs than others which tended to reproduce it … Even within the manufacturing sector itself, it was not

pioneering industries – textiles, railways, chemical – that generated the major dynasties, but those closer to pre-industrial activities: above all, food, drink and tobacco.[23]

My reformulated Gramscian critique of the British formation situates conservatism as an important but component part of a hybrid historic bloc, which it shared with economic liberalism and from the late eighteenth-century social liberalism. Contradictions between conservatism and economic liberalism could be destabilising while competition as well as partnership between conservatism and social liberalism also complicated the field of hegemony. Social liberalism's critique of conservatism is often built on a disavowal of its own role within the historic bloc as a necessary partner in an economic–political–cultural alliance that welds together the intra-class forces of the dominant interests. Yet it can at least seed some critique and intellectual resources for the emergence of more radical critiques. At the same time, if these more radical critiques do not sufficiently think through the limits of their influences, it can be problematic in terms of their political projects. The whole discourse around a 'blocked' entry into modernity is an example of an unfortunate uncritically absorbed inheritance from liberalism into Marxism. The idea of a blocked entry to modernity downplays the contradictions immanent within the mode of production in favour of the tensions between the old and the new.[24] It suggests, as Meiksins Wood argues in her assessment of the Nairn/Anderson thesis, that problems derive from 'the incompleteness of capitalist development' instead of 'the inherent weaknesses of capitalism itself.'[25] As we shall see, conservatism was not a check on agricultural capital in any case, but rather gave it powerful ideological resources while at the same time giving economic liberalism all the autonomy it desired. The 'old' was functional for the 'new'. If there were contradictions, it impacted more on the symbolic–cultural order than the economic order, although from there it could feed into further political outcomes. A defence of industry as a signifier of modernity says as much about normative investments in industrial capital that are questionable as it does of conservatism's priorities. There was a cultural fissure between conservatism and liberalism on the question of industry and it was efficacious but not in the way that the usual critique of conservatism has suggested (as a fetter on modernity and on industrialism). Instead this fissure on the question of industrialism helped generate new political possibilities for reform via a class alliance between the labour movement and sections of the professional middle class who became detached from the old historic bloc as industrial capital itself moved, in the late nineteenth century, into the conservative camp. Here culture and political culture (social democracy) did eventually have an impact on the capitalist economy in the form of a new set of redistributive policies and social obligations on capital, at least for a short period. That, however, is the story we will pick up in more detail in Chapter 5, but it should at least be flagged up here as we flesh out the history and nature of conservatism's cultural domination and its relationship to a differentiated economic base.

Conservatism's symbolic–cultural order

In his critique of the Nairn/Anderson thesis, E.P. Thompson noted: 'Despite disclaimers, neither Anderson nor Nairn appear to be able to accept, *au fond*, the notion of an agrarian class, whether rentiers or entrepreneurs, as a true bourgeoisie'.[26]

For Thompson, the conservative aristocratic culture that was grafted onto a dynamic commercial farming economy represented not an archaic check on capitalism, 'not some adjustment of interests between a tenacious feudal superstructure and an embryonic capitalist base, but an arrangement exquisitely adjusted to the equilibrium of social forces at that time'.[27] What was this 'exquisitely adjusted' arrangement and between whom? It was primarily between the old landowners who could trace their family line back to the aristocracy, the smaller landowning gentry whose numbers developed over several centuries and the expanding merchant class whose trading tentacles had an international reach. The nature of the arrangement was a fusion between the high-status cultural style of the aristocracy, which had its roots in the pre-capitalist feudal formation, but which was re-functioned for a new epoch or mode of production, and the economic imperatives of capitalist accumulation shared by landowners large and small and the merchant class.

The aristocracy were the thousand or so families that owned large landholdings and titles (Earls and Dukes). David Canadine divides them up between those who owned between 10,000–30,000 acres (the middling sized aristocracy, around 750 families) and the top elites (250 or so families) who owned more than 30,000 acres. The gentry were the small landowners, sometimes described as the 'untitled aristocracy' who like the aristocracy, worked their own land and rented out their land to tenant farmers who in turn employed a landless proletariat to produce commodities sold on the market. The gentry numbered around 6,000 families.[28] In all, around 7,000 families owned four-fifths of the land in Britain[29] and it is on *this* extraordinary concentration of material wealth that the symbolic and cultural potency of rural England and sometimes rural Britannia, rests. At the centre of this landscape, at least viewed from the hegemonic perspective, is the country house, what Raymond Williams, in his masterful book *The Country and the City*, describes as the 'visible centres of the new social system'.[30] As feudalism mutated into capitalism so the castle and the fortified manor becomes the country house as power becomes more directly and centrally founded on economics first rather than military prowess as in the feudal era.

Thomas Gainsborough's 1748 painting of Mr and Mrs Andrews, commissioned to celebrate Robert Andrews' recent marriage to Frances Mary Carter, offers a visual document of the gentry class and their relationship to the land. A combination of portraiture and landscape painting, Mr and Mrs Andrews situates the couple on an elevated hill overlooking and showing off the estate that stretches back in naturalistic perspective to the horizon.[31] In the distance behind the trees, two churches are visible, one at Sudbury and one at Long Melton (on the Suffolk and Essex border) providing both an Anglican blessing to the wealth laid out before us and perhaps the implication that the Andrews' authority stretches into the local parish institutions. Mr and Mrs Andrews are placed on the left of the frame before an iconic oak tree (a Burkean symbol of Englishness, historical/natural continuity and indeed the landed class themselves) while on the right sheaves of wheat lie stacked ready for transport to market. Of course, all trace of the workers and work that went into producing this happy outcome is eliminated, since the occlusion of labour, the source of wealth, is deeply embedded into both conservative political culture and capitalist disavowal and fetishism (the bracketing off of social context). The isomorphic connections between conservatism and capitalism are deep and deeply obscured. Rural exploitation has been 'dissolved into a landscape.'[32]

In the background of the picture, we see the sheep grazing the land in an enclosed field, linking the farm to the important wool trade. Along with the missing agricultural proletariat, Mr Andrews himself is depicted very much as the gentleman of leisure, leaning casually on the rococo bench his wife is sitting on, with his hunting gun in the crook of his arm and his faithful hunting dog sniffing around at his feet. At one level this presentation of Mr Andrews is a nod to the culture of the aristocracy with its long-established interest in blood sports as an extension or substitute for its military conflicts. However, although Mr Andrews is in leisure mode and referencing an aristocratic pursuit, unlike the authentic aristocracy he was both a rentier and involved in the running of his own acres. The well-tended and planned farm in the painting shows that this is very much a carefully looked-after commercial concern. What E.P. Thompson called an authentically bourgeois 'acquisitive ethic' that had converted land into private property[33] saturates the picture. Even Mrs Andrews, whose dowry carefully extended Mr Andrews' land holdings, may be seen as part of the intensively commercialised possessions on display.[34] His proximity to the sheaves of wheat, to the sign of direct labour and a commodity ready for market, suggests that the aristocratic gesture towards hunting is made in deference to the social status of the aristocracy but *not* at the expense of him taking an interest in the value of his capital. This proximity to his own commodities works to counterbalance the pose of the leisured gentleman and suggests an aristocratic style could be re-functioned as a component or ornamental part of a thriving capitalist concern on the land.

It is important to stress this reconciliation because it is extraordinary how often the cultural style of the elite are read as in conflict with, rather than complementing, the economic imperatives of capitalism. Perry Anderson argues in relation to the merchant class, that they 'suffered a constant haemorrhage of its profits and pioneers towards the countryside, as successful traders abandoned their background, investing in estates and becoming members of the landed class.'[35] This haemorrhage is read as depleting the capitalist class of their acquisitive and dynamic ethic of capital accumulation just as handing out knighthoods to the business class is sometimes supposed to do. Yet neither now nor in the past was the adoption of a certain cultural style fatal to the accumulation of capital. In the 1700s the landowners made money in government securities and merchants and bankers invested in landed estates to secure status, since, as Weber noted, wealth and status can be relatively independent variables within capitalism. Paul Langford is surely correct to argue: 'Whether they considered themselves country gentlemen with a continuing investment in business, or business with a stake in the country, was very much a matter of personal taste and circumstance. Most, but by no means all the Hull merchants who bought land did so without forsaking their trade'.[36]

Raymond Williams, similarly, in his discussion of how the country and the city came to be arranged as cultural opposites, reminds us of the real material inter-linkages that persisted: 'We must not be tempted to forget the regular, necessary and functional links between the social and moral orders which were so easily and conventionally contrasted'.[37]

The rural/urban distinction, which mapped in turn onto the tradition/modern distinction, was an important means of *spatially distancing* the gentry culture from the economic-class dynamics of capitalism. It was coupled with a temporal distantiation through the use of cultural value systems that seemed to refer back to the aristocratic feudal era. Through this cultural reference point there was also a social distantiation which equated culture with a particular class or sector of the dominant classes while others were seen as being without culture. It is these distancing devices that have often been interpreted as a sign that the gentry and aristocratic class were 'paternalistic', anti-capitalist and hostile to the profit motive. Our understanding though of how this symbolic–cultural order worked *with* the new capitalist order is facilitated if we think in terms of its *external* relation to the economy. Distance means that the symbolic–cultural order is not part of or integrated into the economic-class dynamics, but far from this being a cultural drag factor on the development of capitalism in its free market period, it actually facilitates it by giving economic motives a wide room for manoeuvre, unencumbered by the restraints of culture and custom. What happens to the symbolic–cultural order runs parallel to what happens to the relationship between politics and the economic sphere.

Before capitalism, the extraction of surplus value by the dominant classes had been enmeshed with the customs, traditions and social and community values that flourished in seemingly endless variety from mediaeval England to the South American Aztecs. Capitalism was the first mode of production in which the economic extraction process becomes uncoupled from the wider life of the community and asserts its own autonomous logic which now becomes, unchecked by custom or tradition, accumulation for the sake of accumulation. As the economic sphere achieves this formal differentiation from the surrounding culture, so it begins to naturalise itself, de-politicise itself and appear as an objective set of laws that transcend norms. As Ellen Meiksins Wood puts it: 'In capitalism, there is a complete separation of private appropriation from public duties; and this means the development of a new sphere of power devoted completely to private rather than social purposes'.[38]

As private economic power separates from public duties, so public duties or the whole realm of the political, becomes *external* to private appropriation, which asserts in classical political economy its absolute property rights. Adam Smith's *The Wealth of Nations* represents the philosophical expression of what had already become a pressing and extensive historical reality, namely that the new economy of the market 'was disinfested of intrusive moral imperatives' as E.P. Thompson puts it.[39] Whereas custom and tradition had once provided labour with some hard-won rights, whether access to common land or some controls on the price of basic foodstuffs such as corn, the advocates of the new market insisted that a proper modern 'rational' economy should have no blockages according to moral arguments.

In the eighteenth century, prior to the emergence of socialism as an alternative *future* society different from capitalism, the plebeian culture was 'rebellious, but rebellious in defence of custom.'[40] This was a conservative resistance to the encroaching free market in the name of what E.P. Thompson called the 'moral economy'. This moral economy which was still sporadically and patchily institutionalised in old laws and customs, restrained the free market by, for example, restricting the extent to which farmers could sell large quantities of basic food stuffs to merchants who might then hoard and push up prices. Instead farmers were legally obliged to sell at least some of their produce in the open market direct to the poor.[41] Yet over the decades these political compulsions weakened as the rights of private property strengthened.

The moral economy of the poor made an appeal to the past that was rather different from the 'traditional' culture that the aristocracy and the gentry developed within the new mode of production. The moral economy of the poor maintained the *integration* of economy and morality and its legal-institutional base in politics. The culture of the dominant classes, however, made an appeal to the past that was diametrically opposite, one in which the economy separated itself from culture and culture disavowed its roots in the economic-class relations that gave rise to it. The externality of culture to the economy manifests itself as a distantiation from the economic with culture valued the more it is distanced from the economy. To achieve this, the old feudal values of the aristocracy were re-functioned for a new age. If Sir Thomas Smith could in 1583 define a gentleman as someone 'who can live idly and without manual labour',[42] this seems an odd cultural identity for an economy based on the massive expansion of labour power productivity two hundred years later and at face value it seems counter-intuitive that it would be congruent with such an economy. Yet it was, providing class distinction and authority to the rentiers while also underscoring the freedom of the economy *from* custom, culture and morality.

The aristocracy, as Veblen argued in his discussion of capitalist culture, were exempt or excluded from direct labour, which was regarded as the preserve of the 'low-born'. Instead, activities such as warfare, priestly offices, government and sports (especially hunting) absorb aristocratic energies.[43] This list corresponds closely to the preferred routes of social engagement typical of the English aristocracy after the transition to capitalism. The reference point to activities that were both high-esteem and extra-economic (and were high-esteem *because* they were separated from the economic) is deeply symptomatic of the symbolic–cultural order more generally. Anticipating Bourdieu's later work investigating different forms of 'cultural capital', Veblen argued that the aristocracy of 'taste' serves the purpose of class distinction by referencing its distance from economic necessity for aristocracy and gentry alike. 'Refined tastes, manners, and habits of life are a useful evidence of gentility, because good breeding requires time, application, and expense, and can therefore not be composed by those whose time and energy are taken up by work'.[44]

Gentility is a style of class identity that signals through a social distance from direct labour and 'vulgar' culture. Sir Thomas Smith's idle gentleman has become the basis of culture. Culture depends on that most important value concept: time. Those who *have* time against those who do not: those who can distribute time into activities other than labour or immediate need-satisfaction. In all sorts of ways this is a form of cultural distinction based on *leisure* as the honorific 'non-productive consumption of time … from a sense of the unworthiness of productive work'.[45] But if this symbolic–cultural order serves the old conservative purpose of class distinction it also serves the purpose of classical political economy since this world of work has a value dimension that is simply incompatible with normative values and what is to be valued culturally. Culture and economics sit side by side but are not seen to substantially inhabit each other.

The symbolic–cultural order was dualistically related to the autonomous economy, not in the sense that it was substantially opposed to it but in the sense that it accepted the absence of a normative dimension from market development and the repression of the material class context from the cultural life-world. It was a culture that was external to the economic dynamics on which it depended and which it in turn disavowed.[46] It offered for the elites the sense that their world was governed by moral sentiments embodied in 'gentle' breeding, even though normative codes governing life where it mattered most had increasingly *less* purchase than the previous, less dynamic, less innovatory feudal mode of production. While the old feudal class were socially distanced from the world of direct labour, they were embedded nonetheless into reciprocal arrangements by custom and tradition that established certain 'rules' of exploitation. Despite the temporal reference point back to the aristocracy, the new bourgeoisie had no such obligations and culture and custom had no such reach into the field of economics.

Surely though, it could be argued, the cultural disdain for production might logically become a drag factor on *industrial* development, given the need for an intense involvement in a dynamic, constantly changing environment which industry promoted? And if this is true at the level of the individual industrial operation, it might also be true at the level of the need for State policy coordination, which such a dynamic environment would seem to call for. Yet it is peculiar for Marxists to argue that the cultural distance from labour, work, production – which could be reconciled with the slower tempo of agricultural capitalism – then transferred poorly to the industrial age and in effect hampered its development. From a materialist perspective, the causality runs the other way. The aristocratic disdain for production *could be sustained* because the economy of England was never *primarily* of that industrial sort and because, as we shall see, historical circumstances were such that there was little capitalist economic incentive to radically change course.

Conservative superstructure and economic infrastructure

Examining the conservative contribution to the nineteenth-century historic bloc means examining conservatism's particular orchestration of economic base and cultural-political superstructure. So what was that economic base and how did it make sense for a particular conservative cultural identity to flourish in relation to it? The conservative cultural identity has been described as 'gentlemanly capitalism' by Cain and Hopkins. The term seeks to capture the paradox that: 'The peculiar character of the modern British aristocracy was initially shaped by merging its pre-capitalist heritage with incomes derived from commercial agriculture'.[47]

An old form is thus combined with a new economic content, one which must also change that form, *re-functioning* it so that it is compatible with the new imperative of capital accumulation, rather than against it. This is something which Cain and Hopkins are very clear about – not for them the image of conservatism as an archaic culture holding back the 'modernisation' of British society.

> The gentlemanly capitalist had a clear understanding of the market economy and knew how to benefit from it; at the same time, he kept his distance from the everyday and demeaning world of work. In an order dominated by gentlemanly norms, production was held in low repute. Working for money, as opposed to making it, was associated with dependence and cultural inferiority.[48]

The gentlemanly capitalist began life as an emblem of stability, of that immoveable property, land, that embodied the nation. In this it was contrasted as early as the eighteenth century with the growing power of stocks and shares in the City, whose internationalism and mobility began to be viewed with some trepidation.[49] Later however, things changed as landed wealth and the City find a common cultural ground. The gentlemanly capitalist becomes a cultural model signalling resistance to and distance from *industrial* capital (working for money) with the spatial distance between urban locations and the countryside (or boardroom) becoming increasingly significant. Culturally, conservatism becomes strongly associated with the interlinked revenue streams of landed wealth, commercial capital and, increasingly, banking capital: all united by certain 'rentier' characteristics such as unearned income on rent or interest, or 'unfair' exchange using slave or colonial labour. Gradually a cultural alliance develops between landed wealth, the City and mercantile imperialism *against* (at the cultural level) industry (reflecting the latter's subaltern position). The fissure between conservatism and liberalism on social and political matters begins to grow deeper in the mid-nineteenth century as a result. Both conservatism and industrial capital (liberalism) were committed to laissez-faire economic doctrine at this time (the one major exception being the dispute around the Corn Laws tariffs for imports) but one becomes increasingly linked to industry, science and technology and a belief in progress through Enlightenment rationality, while the other becomes increasingly defined by its relations to landed, mercantile and banking capital that stressed tradition, nature, continuity and leisure as opposed to energetic work and perpetual transformation. Later, as industrial capital saw conservatism as its defence against the rising claims of labour, the progressive aspects of liberalism continue to find a class base in at least sections of the professional and technocratic middle class as industrial capital drifts towards conservatism.

The culture of landed wealth rested on a particular set of revenue streams that did not require the kind of cultural value system that industrial capital fostered. The landed capitalists made their money in a variety of ways. They invested in slavery when it was legal and had agricultural interests abroad in tobacco, sugar, cotton and tea – in other words, in the various parts of the empire (mercantile imperialism). When slavery was abolished within the British Empire, slave owners were handsomely compensated, to the tune of the equivalent of tens of millions of pounds each. Research released in 2013 found that the then prime minister, David Cameron, had ancestors who were the beneficiaries of the public purse as had the then newly appointed chairman of the Arts Council for England, Peter Bazalgette[50] and the actor Benedict Cumberbatch.[51] The Slave Compensation Commission had ensured that 46,000 slave owners in the UK received an astonishing 40 per cent of total government expenditure in 1834 (one year after the abolition of slavery).[52] Such public payouts were in effect pump priming for further rounds of capital investment and accumulation, a sort of early Keynsianism for the rich which was played out again after the 2008 crash, with rather less effect, using 'quantitative easing' for the banks.

Landed wealth also invested money in urban real estate. For example, the current Duke of Westminster, one of the richest men in Britain, benefits from land purchases his family made in London's Mayfair and Belgravia districts back in the 1700s and 1800s. The landed class, both aristocracy and gentry, invested in transport systems that crossed their land (the circulation of goods, not their production) such as canals and later railways. The fictional minor aristocrat Clifford Chatterly owns mines in D.H. Lawrence's *Lady Chatterley's Lover* and this was true also of real-life upper class landowners. Mining was closer to production than transport systems, but again this involved the extraction of a natural raw material, an input into industrial production (or domestic consumption) rather than an output (as with manufacturing industry). The common denominator in these revenue streams is a certain distance from industrial production proper and this was typical, although, given the debate among historians about whether industrial or other forms of capital were dominant, it is worth saying that no insuperable barrier separated landed wealth and merchant capital from industrial capital.

The Bristol merchant Henry Bush, who was awarded £7,247 as compensation for the abolition of slavery (a sum worth around ten million in contemporary prices) also owned ships in the 1840s and was subsequently an investor in the Great Western Cotton Works factory that imported cotton – using Bush's ships presumably – from the slave plantations of the United States. The factory, opened in 1838, employed 900 people initially but later increased to between 1,500 and 2,000. Bush also invested in the Bristol and Gloucestershire Railway Extension in 1837, with 50 shares worth £2,500.[53] In one person then we find united agricultural capital (the plantations) commercial capital (circulating goods through shipping and rail) and industrial capital. The Great Western Cotton Works closed in 1925, but it was not a victim of an anti-industrial culture among Britain's elite gentlemanly capitalist class. Rather, the problem for the British cotton industry was the disruptions to access to world markets caused by the First World War and the rise of competitor nations such as Japan, who could start from a higher, more sophisticated level of industrial development than British cotton factories who had sunk their investments in older and now less-productive fixed capital.[54] This indeed was the more general problem of 'pioneer industrialisation' which British capital faced and which increased the likelihood of a long slow decline because later entrants could invest in more up to date technology.[55] Significantly, the Great Western Cotton Works venture was funded by the capital of the local Bristol bourgeoisie and not the City. One could argue that only the larger pools of capital the latter had at its disposal could have kept British industrial capital up to date technologically speaking vis-à-vis its competitors.[56] To that extent, a lack of interest in domestic industry in the City may have been a contributory factor, but as long as British capital as a whole had other avenues for making a profit, the cultural distantiation from industry among leading sectors of the British elites, was more a rationalisation of existing historical circumstances and, from the perspective of British capitalism, which had an empire to hand, a not irrational posture to adopt, as we shall see. Only a problematic political investment in industrial capital could imagine it as a progressive force blighted by a reactionary aristocratic bias built into an exceptionally and comprehensively archaic British class system.

Decline and the cultural dominant in British capitalism

Certainly the place of industry culturally has been at the least, ambivalent in the British context and was less embraced by the ruling political elites than the land, the countryside, the village and the pastoralist tradition more generally. For Martin Weiner, in *English Culture and the Decline of the Industrial Spirit*, it was the capitalist-agricultural elites who absorbed the industrial class into their cultural value system, one which robbed the industrial class of the Weberian 'spirit' of energetic accomplishment they required to be successful. For Weiner the values associated with industry (and Marx's core definition of capital accumulation) – efficiency, technological innovation, change and productivity – were neutralised by a dominant aristocratic-capitalist class more orientated towards stability, tradition and the non-productive pursuits of country living such as hunting, riding, shooting and so forth.[57] According to Weiner, The Great Exhibition of industrial innovation at Crystal Palace in 1851 was to be the high-water mark of industrial capital's cultural dominance. Thereafter it accommodated itself to a subordinate position within the already established nexus of landed property, banking and trade.[58] Weiner's story is a kind of reversal in the British case of Weber's argument that a rationalised culture of capitalism emerges to push it forward by promoting a cost–benefit calculative mentality in the allocation of resources.[59] Weiner argues that status, honour and esteem (the old aristocratic values) rather than working for money were more important and that the rural, pastoralist tradition within Britain was its key cultural force.

There are, however, more compelling reasons than a ruralist or 'aristocratic' anti-business bias to Britain's dominant classes as to why its industrial capital base was on one level losing the international battle of competitiveness. With rising competition from the United States and Germany in the last quarter of the nineteenth century, British capital as a whole was faced with a choice, and the decision it made was, from the perspective of the dominant class if not the liberal technocratic class, quite rational. One option would have been the German or United States solution: fusing banking capital and industrial capital into what Lenin and other Marxists called finance capital, leading to the growth of large industrial conglomerates dominating the national terrain and hungry to expand overseas as domestic markets are conquered and demand saturated.[60] This would have been the preference of Anderson, Nairn and Weiner, no doubt, and it would certainly have transformed British culture, providing the material ground for the kind of urban, industrial modernist culture that flourished in Germany but which, with some notable exceptions, struggled to put down roots in Britain.

The kind of integration between the City and industry that was producing finance capital in the USA and Germany was much less pronounced in the UK. 'Even by the 1880s the largest 100 industrial firms in Britain accounted for less than 10 per cent of total production – and this had only risen to around 15 per cent by 1909'.[61]

This is not to say that City-led mergers and the growth of large industrial organisations were entirely absent: the late nineteenth century and 1930s saw significant developments on that score, with the latter period even being encouraged by government policy as a response to the 1930s Depression and overseas competition.[62] Perhaps it is not a coincidence that this was the moment when some sort of modernism did emerge in Britain. But comparatively, which is all that matters according to the law of competition, British industry was struggling in terms of scale and productivity. By the turn of the twentieth century, Germany did have an enormous lead over Britain. Lenin compares the production of pig iron for example: 17.6 million tons (Germany) against 9 million tons (Britain).[63] The German shipping magnate Albert Ballin noted in 1910 that:

> the British can really no longer compete with us and were it not for the large funds they have invested, and for the sums of money which reach the small mother-country from the dominions, their saturated and conservative habits of life would soon make them a 'quantité négligeable' as far as their competition with us in the world markets is concerned.[64]

Rather than invest in industrial production at home, then, the British dominant classes in 'the small mother-country' could instead use the empire, the largest in the world, to offset German and American industrial productivity. 'Instead of organizational or technological renovation, British industry drew on the assets of empire, settling into an easy reliance on customary and (in the case of India) captive markets' notes Anderson.[65] This is right but on what normative basis are we entitled to conclude that British capitalism had failed in some historic mission, the gist of his narrative? The German solution (organisational renovation and technological investment) had the unfortunate consequence (for

German capital) of laying the foundations of the best-organised working class in Europe before the First World War and with a significant communist base established in it after 1917. By contrast British capital took the course of least disruption, the course that went with the grain of existing historical conditions for British capital, namely its 'immense accumulated historic advantages in the undeveloped world … the greatest commercial power, and … the greatest source of international loan capital'.[66] The empire, it must be stressed was beneficial to industrial capital as well as banking capital, providing both cheap labour and raw materials from the colonies and export markets for British industry's finished commodities. The importance (and success) of the empire in propping up Britain's industrial economic importance in the world can be seen in the statistics laid out in Table 3.1.

Table 3.1 Share of major British exports going to empire markets: 1870–1934.[67]

	1870	1900	1934
Textiles	26.6	39.9	44.2
Machinery	19	22.3	51.2
Locomotives	16	49.5	65.3

Cain and Hopkins argue that, after 1850, the predominance of landed wealth was gradually eclipsed by the wealth of the City, which in turn reasserted the primacy of London and the south-east against the industrial provinces that had briefly rivalled the capital for economic and social dynamism.[68] Yet that rivalry never got to anything like a level of parity. The truth is, as W.D. Rubinsten argues, that Britain was historically an economy primarily built around commerce and finance.[69] Its overseas possessions were absolutely central to this economic base. In the late nineteenth century, the City continued a pattern established earlier and poured overseas investments into Canada, Australia, New Zealand, the Cape Colony (South Africa) and some Latin American[70] countries as well as investments in railway extensions in other colonies such as India (the civilising mission!). It is hard though, for anyone reading Rosa Luxemburg's *The Accumulation of Capital* to conclude that this international orientation of British banking capital was to the detriment of British industrial capital. As she noted, British loans abroad to companies and young capitalist States, were followed by orders for British textiles, coal, iron, steel and other goods to those self-same countries. Britain's empire needed to have transport links and that meant plenty of bridges and railways supplied by British iron and steel companies.[71] Nor does the international orientation seem to mark British capital out as 'exceptional' in any qualitative sense, despite complaints from Anderson to that effect. As Luxemburg notes, '[e]nlarged reproduction, i.e. accumulation, is possible only if new districts with a non-capitalist civilization, extending over large areas, appear on the scene and augment the number of consumers.'[72] The issue though is less a question of under-consumption as Luxemburg suggests, than the over-accumulation of capital which needs to find profitable sites of further investment, since capital cannot 'stand still'. The problem is that continued investment in the domestic economy can only produce a decline in profits (for example by increasing the leverage of labour and therefore wages against capital by diminishing the 'reserve army of labour', i.e. unemployment).[73] If reason alone governed the direction of history as Hegel had hoped, then capitalism would have abolished itself some time ago, when it was discovered that its very surpluses were a threat to its own existence. Too much investment in the domestic/home nation must be avoided since the production of use-values is not the prime aim of the system, but the production and appropriation by the few of surplus value from the many. Hence capitalism always has to find something 'outside' of itself to counteract the fact that the barrier to capital is, as Marx noted, capital itself.[74] In the empire, British capital had an extensive 'outside' zone ready to hand. Harvey calls this need for capital to be 'geographically expansionary', a 'spatial fix' to the problems of over-accumulation.[75] In this early form of globalisation, linked to the political, military and territorial power of empire, capital generated according to Marx's core definition (surplus-labour extraction through productivity gains) found outlets, supplements and markets in what were strictly speaking non-capitalist social relations of 'tax and tribute'[76] as well as cheap labour.

If industrial capital sustained itself in the medium term thanks to the empire and the City's overseas orientation, this is not to say that the City was positively disposed culturally towards industry, it is just that the 'aristocratic' culture was a high-esteem rationalisation of a model of accumulation that could hardly be said to conflict with the interests of either wings of British capital even if one was the dominant partner. Although landed interests were subsequently displaced by the City as the dominant economic pole within the hegemonic complex, there remained a cultural affinity between the landed capitalists and the City. 'When agrarian property lost its weight,' notes Anderson, 'it was not industry but finance which became the hegemonic form of capital, in a City socially and culturally in many ways closer to the wealth of estates than of factories.'[77] Leaving aside the problematic normative investment in the 'good' capital of the factories, we can note that both landed and City wealth were drawn to accumulation strategies that did not require direct involvement in industrial production (land, agriculture, mines, property, commercial capital involved in the circulation of goods such as shipping and railways, loans to governments, insurance, speculation on the stock exchange, etc).[78] Even where investors invested in industry 'proper' as it were (and not mines, plantations, docks, etc.) they were investing in industry abroad, maintaining a spatial distance from industrial activity (and of course benefitting from cheap labour). The cultural model (temporal, spatial and social distanciation from industry) fitted perfectly with the particular historical conditions which British capitalism and the British Empire found itself in. A whole complex 'superstructure' of more traditional moral and cultural value systems could be supported by this less dynamic (but still, *contra* Weiner, *profitable*) political economy. The debate among historians as to whether British industrial capital was subordinated to commercial capital has often turned on whether circulation activities such as railways and shipping count as industrial or commercial.[79] The important thing from our perspective is that they do not involve the classic industrial *transformation* process that Marx associated with being central to capitalism, its dynamism and its technologically driven extraction of surplus value through quantum leaps in productivity. This kind of industrial capital Britain's ruling elites were moderately fearful of within the domestic economy as a breeding ground for social change, working-class organisation and sometimes fierce class conflict. They had after all, been through it once already and the mid-nineteenth century Chartists were a most unwelcome consequence. For the gentlemanly capitalist on land or in commerce or in banking, impersonal systems processing large quantities of workers and raw materials within a situation of dynamic change was a foreign and unpalatable moral and cultural universe. What is more, it was not necessary. Exploitation of labour was achieved within less dynamic socio-economic systems protected by imperial possessions where continuity and with it social authority and leadership over subordinates, based on interpersonal relations embedded in traditional hierarchies, was much preferred. Of course this meant that British capital would eventually face a 'reckoning', once the imperial protective shield was removed, but that could be safely deferred further down the historical line, perhaps in the hope that 'something will turn up.'[80] Capital is not noted for its long-term thinking, as its current blindness to the consequences for capital accumulation which environmental destruction portends, suggests.

As the rural basis of landed wealth in Britain was declining in economic importance, its symbolic and cultural importance grew. Lenin cites evidence that an increasing proportion of land in England was being taken out of *cultivation* for the use of sport (especially by the English ruling class in Scotland) in the last quarter of the nineteenth century. On horse racing and fox hunting alone, England was spending some £14 million annually, a real material infrastructure to underpin the symbolic importance of these cultural practices for the dominant classes. The number of people living off dividends from shares had climbed to one million while the percentage of the population employed in basic industries, while increasing in absolute terms between 1851 and 1901, had *decreased* relative to the population from 23 per cent to 15 per cent over the same period.[81] As the material base of industrial England declined in *relative* terms, the *economic* base of gentlemanly capitalism was transferred from agriculture (itself in decline) to commercial and banking capital.

In this context the expression within liberal-left discourses of certain normative preferences for certain forms of capital formation become tempting within a teleological view of historical progress. Comparing American society with European society (and Italy in particular) Gramsci concluded that the latter were held back in their economic development by the 'numerous classes with no essential function in the world of production, in other words classes which are purely parasitic.'[82] The economic life of Italian cities, Gramsci argues, turns on the non-productive trades that serve the needs of the landowners. Evoking an earthy peasant metaphor to illustrate this nexus between landowners and the rest of society, he notes: 'Where a horse shits a hundred sparrows feed'.[83] It is the demographic composition of 'old' Europe that to varying degrees sustains parasitic and unproductive layers of the population, and this in turn hinders the development of a dynamic Fordist style capitalism. Fordism thus incarnates the ideal-typical model of capitalist surplus value production through new technology. In America, the historical conditions existed:

to rationalise production and labour by a skilful combination of force (destruction of working-class trade unionism on a territorial basis) and persuasion (high wages, various social benefits, extremely subtle ideological and political propaganda) and thus succeed in making the whole life of the nation revolve around production. Hegemony here is born in the factory and requires for its exercise only a minute quantity of professional political and ideological intermediaries.[84]

Gramsci's analysis is hugely suggestive and acute, but it can be read within a normative framework that we need to be wary of and that needs to be stripped out of the analysis. The establishment and expansion of industrial capital is often seen within the Left as the 'normal' growth path for capitalism, the one which establishes the conditions for its own overthrow (the proletariat become the gravediggers of capitalism). Industrial capital seemed to Marx to embody the core characteristic of the capitalist system: competitive transformation of the techniques and technologies of production that raises productivity and lowers costs per unit of production. This critique is buttressed and overlaps with the radical liberal critique which links imperialism to a parasitic aristocratic-City nexus that retards industrial development. The liberal thinker John A. Hobson remarked in his classic critique, *Imperialism*:

> Great Britain is becoming a nation living upon tribute from abroad, and the classes who enjoy this tribute have an ever-increasing incentive to employ the public policy, the public purse and the public force to extend the field of their private investments, and to safeguard and improve their existing investments.[85]

What we must avoid though is any sense that British capitalism was peculiarly archaic or exceptional or irrational in pursuing this strategy. Hobson for example argued against imperialism's logic of exporting capital abroad: 'there is no necessary limit to the quantity of capital and labour which can be employed in producing goods for the home market if the productive power is disposed in industries which meet the rising demands of the consumer'.[86]

Yet as we have seen, there is no 'necessary' limit to such good proto-Keynesian sense except capital itself. The demands of the domestic consumer are linked to the demands of the collective labour force. In fact, the political economy of British capitalism found a way of very modestly increasing the purchasing power of British workers and increasing the internal market for such consumption goods as food, drink and tobacco where British capital had made substantial investments and profits, *without* increasing the *organisational* power of the British working class in an expanding *domestic industrial* sector. High overseas investment meant a high exchange rate for the currency and this in turn meant cheap imports, including raw materials that could be processed by the food and drink manufacturers based domestically.[87] Within the protective force field of empire (access to markets) manufacturing could survive this policy framework that would have otherwise made the cost of *exports* crippling in genuinely free market competition with capital from other nations. For the workers, exploitation at home was modestly offset by some small crumbs thrown their way via the highly mediated transfer of value from the exploitation of colonial markets and labour abroad. For capital *profits* trumped any supposed historic mission to transform the productive forces for universal progress and what some Marxists thought was its historic mission to abolish itself.

The political economy of British imperialism provided the basis for a reactionary political culture to extend into a wider cultural politics within the national-popular imaginary in the last years of the nineteenth century and up until the cataclysm of the First World War (1914–1918). In 1882, Engels, writing to Kautsky, bemoaned the alliance which the British bourgeoisie had managed to forge with the workers on colonial policy. 'There is no workers' party here, you see, there are only Conservatives and Liberal-Radicals, and the workers gaily share the feast of England's monopoly of the world market and the colonies.'[88] Hobson complained of the interconnections and interdependencies between the national press and the financial interests linked to imperialism as a means of shaping public 'beliefs and sentiments'.[89] In this period both a English national culture and British national identity was self-consciously forged around empire, patriotism and the monarchy while rural England provided the symbolic culture of civil society underpinning an economy increasingly orientated towards the City and reaping the rewards of Britain's international monopoly. Popular cultural forms and the emergent mass media were strong promoters of the empire.[90] Anderson is withering about the nature of this renewed imperial nationalism with monarchy as its core State institution: 'The "manifest" function of the monarchy was (by assertion) to unify the nation; its "latent" function was (by example) to stratify it. The two were equally important. Probably at no period in peacetime history was English society so suffused with chauvinism and so glutted with rank'.[91]

This development was the product of the interaction between political cultures dominating the State (especially conservatism) and what Gramsci called the decentralised, molecular activities of myriad institutions within civil society. An example of the latter can be found in the preservation movement that developed in the late nineteenth century. It sought to protect places of 'natural beauty' and historic interest (especially the symbolically important country house) from the ravages of someone wanting to make a quick buck (economic liberalism). The formation of the National Trust, Patrick Wright has observed, had to overcome conservative objections to this infringement on private property rights, which it did by largely 'generalising bourgeois into "national" culture', and making the 'public interest' equivalent with the celebration of private property now preserved as aristocratic heritage spectacle.[92] The National Trust in turn required State backing to constitute itself as a legal entity that could buy and preserve land. This is a perfect example of a State–civil society hegemonic operation and partnership, in which civil society functioned as the educative private fabric of the State (educative to both the State and the public).

The national identity that emerged from this State–civil society process was, however, not exclusively dominated by 'aristocratic' conservatism, *contra* Anderson and Nairn's overly functionalist use of Gramsci's concept of hegemony. Instead a more composite fusion of conservatism *and* liberalism shaped the national-popular; the latter for example making headway in the professionalisation of State administration, education and as we shall see in Chapter 5, around 'industrialism'. For within 30 years of Lenin's statistics on the relative decline of the manual working class in Britain, a new image of the national-popular would emerge to rival the gentlemanly capitalism of rural England from a position that developed out of the cultural fissure between conservatism and liberalism but went beyond it, pulling a good chunk of liberal middle-class opinion with it. Its imagined Britain was 'the North', the basic industries and the manual working class. What is clear is that while imaginings of national identity require some material base, the economics of the situation, the quantitative dimension of people or contribution to GDP, are alone not enough for a contribution to the national imaginary. Instead it requires the formation of a political culture to translate certain features of economic-class existence into a cluster of images that coalesce into a popular identity for 'the nation'. It requires in short political–cultural leadership to turn 'objective potentialities' into real historical forces.

Contesting rural England

Rural England as the cultural dominant is really southern rural England, as Alan Howkins notes.[93] Its key counties are Kent, Sussex, Surrey, Hampshire, Berkshire, Wiltshire, Dorset and bits of Somerset. It can range as far north as Shropshire or the fictional town of Borchester in the long-running hymn to the farming community and country life that is the BBC radio soap opera *The Archers*. Any further north and rural England begins to bump into the great city-states of Liverpool, Manchester, Sheffield and Leeds, while the now multicultural cities such as Birmingham and Leicester a little further south also have to be carefully bracketed off from any conceptions of village and country life venturing that far north.[94] Howkins argues that in earlier periods the English landscape was associated with more northern and rugged landscapes such as the Lake District (Wordsworth, Coleridge) or Yorkshire (the Brontë sisters). But rural England moved south in the last quarter of the nineteenth century in order to be strongly and spatially differentiated from the industrial north, with its unpleasant urban squalor, social class tensions and radical transformations in ways of living. Relocating the heart of England in the south also put it in greater physical and imagined proximity to the political, economic, media and social power nexus of the conservative establishment, including the City.

In *Criticism and Ideology*, Terry Eagleton argued that the English literature of the late nineteenth and early twentieth century was fundamentally structured around the tension between bourgeois liberalism and rural conservatism. Literary works by George Eliot, Charles Dickens, Thomas Hardy, D.H. Lawrence and so on struggled to reconcile the tensions between these political cultures but each political culture is also marked by internal ambivalences, revealing the pressure of the other tradition's 'critique' as it were. Bourgeois liberalism risked atomising social relations with its aggressive and spiritually empty pursuit of the cash nexus, yet the image of rural England, while it offered a counter-image to that in the form of community and tradition, threatened also to suffocate individual energies into a fixed and static framework. While liberal rationalism brought with it great scientific and technological advances that could combat what Marx called 'rural idiocy' (and progressive forces entering organic rural communities are often celebrated in the novels of this period), liberalism was also associated with an abstract rationalism and calculating spirit remote from the life of the senses, the emotions and feelings. Again, paradoxically, while the organic rural community can be, in one accentuation, crushingly conformist and intolerant of individual desire and initiative, because it also embodies natural vitality and fertility (think of those sheaves of wheat in Gainsborough's painting) it can also be the source to renew and regenerate it.[95] The dynamics and ambivalences that Eagleton explores in relation to literature between the 1850s and the 1930s, can still be seen at work decades later in a film such as *Local Hero* (1983) where now liberal capitalism in all its ambivalences is represented by America and rural England in all its ambivalences, is represented by a Scottish village.[96]

This discussion of rural England and liberal capitalism as it is framed within political cultures and popular culture can be tabulated below (see Figure 3.1), with the oppositions between and within the two traditions marking out the parameters within which both political cultures and cultural artefacts move.

We must remember that because this tabulation maps the spectrum of intra-class divisions between conservatism and liberalism, this is also a somewhat limited and indeed ideological framing of the issues, although cultural artefacts can explore these tensions in rich and endlessly mutating ways that speak of utopian desires that may transcend them. One significant absence though from the oppositions tabulated, because it is an 'absent cause' within the literature itself, is precisely that larger international political economy of empire discussed above. It is significant that when he wanted to illustrate his concept of cognitive mapping and the difficulties which art has in articulating representations (or figuration) that can be authentic to their real conditions of existence within a *global* system, Fredric Jameson chose English literature and its circumference by an invisible empire as his example. It is worth quoting Jameson at length:

> The problems of figuration that concern us will only become visible in the next stage, the passage from market to monopoly capital, or what Lenin called the 'stage of imperialism'; and they may be conveyed by way of a growing contradiction between lived experience and structure, or between a phenomenological description of the life of an individual

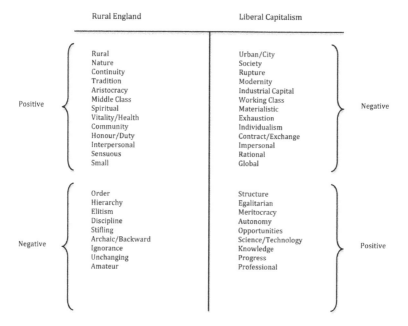

3.1 The structural tensions between rural conservatism and liberalism in English literature.

and a more properly structural model of the conditions of existence of that experience. Too rapidly we can say that, while in older societies and perhaps even in the early stages of market capital, the immediate and limited experience of individuals is still able to encompass and coincide with the true economic and social form that governs that experience, in the next moment the two levels drift ever further apart and really begin to constitute themselves into that opposition the classical dialectic describes as ... essence and appearance, structure and lived experience. At this point the phenomenological experience of the individual subject – traditionally, the supreme raw materials of the work of art – becomes limited to a tiny corner of the social world, a fixed-camera view of a certain section of London or the countryside or whatever. But the truth of that experience no longer coincides with the place in which it takes place. The truth of that limited daily experience of London lies, rather, in India or Jamaica or Hong Kong; it is bound up with the whole colonial system of the British Empire that determines the very quality of the individual's immediate lived experience and are often not even conceptualizable for most people.[97]

There is a paradigmatically strong dichotomy within the English national-popular between its focus on the land, the locality, the small, the homely, the domestic, the self-fashioning of the English identity as modest, unadventurous, unassuming, quiet and deferential on the one hand, and how all this is connected to the most astonishing ambition, aggression and spirit of adventure that had spread itself out across the world as empire. Remarking on this cultural dualism of Britishness, Nairn comments: 'Hierarchy and deference became the inner face of its outward adventure.'[98] The contradiction is nicely captured by artist David Mabb who discovered that the nineteenth-century socialist designer William Morris's floral prints were used, of all places, to furnish the officer-class quarters on British nuclear submarines from the 1960s to the 1990s. Here the signs of England as small, pastoral and homely encased in a symbol of imperial world power status, brings together in a single image one of the key tensions that structure British national identity. Mabb re-appropriated Morris's designs and brought them into a more fitting relationship with the signs and slogans of the anti-nuclear protest movement.

As the twentieth century wore on, the more the image of rural England would become interrogated and beset by a wider range of social forces. The suppressed violence of the middle class on which the serene tranquillity of its rural social order is based, becomes a popular trope (Cavalcanti's *Went the Day Well?* (1942) or John Wyndham's *The Midwich Cuckoos* (1957)). The penetration of the rural idyll by the State's imperialist military-industrial complex can now be interrogated (Greenham Common Women's Peace Camp in the 1980s, the film work of Derek Jarman or Patrick Keiller's *Robinson in Space* (1997)). The excluded or dominated others in Gainsborough's ur-image of rural England, the working class, women, the Black and Asian colonial labour that pump primed rural nature's conversion into capital, begin to fight their way into the picture (the mass working-class rambling movement of the 1930s trying to get access to the countryside against aristocratic landlord rights,[99] Ingrid Pollard's 'Pastoral Interlude' photography that explored the black presence/non-presence in the English countryside in the 1980s[100] and a broad 'post-colonial' awareness that re-reads the literary heritage, such as the 1999 film remake of Jane Austen's book, *Mansfield Park*, which in no uncertain terms brings the remote economic and sexual exploitation of colonial people back into the rural English frame). The contradiction between economic liberalism and the image of rural England flares up again in the resistance to corporate and State penetration of the countryside, such as the anti-road building campaigns in the 1990s, the anti-genetic modification campaigns in the 2000s, and anti-fracking campaigns in the present moment.

Conservatism and economic liberalism

Thatcherism was in many ways a return to prioritising the capital bases of pre-social-democratic Britain. Domestic manufacturers looking to export finished goods were hit by high interest rates and a high pound which exacerbated competition from the Newly Industrialising Countries in the Far East.[101] With the protection of empire now gone, the return to a policy of making overseas investment more lucrative through a highly valued pound was devastating to domestic industry. The government, however, was determined not to subsidise 'failing' industries as the price worth paying for crushing working-class organisation (especially strong in the nationalised sectors). Between 1979 and 1992, some 2.8 million jobs were lost in the manufacturing sector, or around 40 per cent of the sector total.[102] However, because manufacturing was in fact divided into different economic interests (such as between small national and large international conglomerates) there was no 'natural' manufacturing interest that could speak with one voice and object to its contraction during the 1980s (and beyond). As Colin Leys put it:

> The problem of why manufacturing capital has not resisted the Thatcherite economic project cannot usefully be posed as one of failure to defend a pre-existing common interest, but must be understood in terms of the conditions absent so far in Britain, which can lead to the construction of such an interest; in other words, we are led back to the issue of hegemony …[103]

There was no pre-given manufacturing interest distinct from the rest of British capitalism ready to 'express' itself, but instead the expression of any interest required a *political* construction, as Gramsci argued. Yet certain material class interests as well as prior histories made the construction of some political interests more likely than others. Faced with the choice of an alliance between an organised working class, which in the 1970s was becoming, from the point of view of the industrialists, 'dangerously' politicised, or an alliance as a junior partner to international and finance capital, manufacturing predictably chose the latter. Here we have reached the outer limits – set by the interests and imperatives of capital – of what alliances it is possible for politics to construct.

In the 1980s the traditional economic orientations of 'gentlemanly capitalism' once again represented the leading trends within a new globalising capitalism, but one that would have significant implications for the *culture* of traditional conservatism. Symbolic of this was the rise of the City in the 1980s, culminating in the Big Bang of 1987[104] and the international orientation of capital, both going out of the domestic economy and the invitation to foreign capital to come into the country as the trade unions were tamed and made compliant by big set-piece defeats and a battery of legal constrictions. A property boom underwrote increasing levels of personal consumer debt against second and third mortgages, while easy 'plastic' credit testified to the deep instinctive reflexes of conservatism's economic compass. Will Hutton notes how deeply the conservative gentlemanly hegemony continued to dominate in the south-east – loyally returning massed ranks of Conservative MPs in the Home Counties even during the 1992 election that saw the unexpected triumph of John Major's Conservative Party, 'in the middle of the longest post-war recession'.[105] The social world of the gentlemanly elites continues to be high profile and high status, evident in the great sporting events of the English summer season (Ascot, Wimbledon, Henley, Derby Day, Lords).[106] This is the cultural face of political power that stretches deep into the interior of the State, with the Treasury and the Bank of England 'both lobbyists for the financial over the producer interest, benefitting the southern rentier – now often in the form of the great financial institutions – rather than the northern manufacturer.'[107] For Hutton, gentlemanly capitalism was associated with short-term thinking and the demand for quick profits, rather than building the institutions necessary for long-term investment, especially in R & D, training and education. This sort of social-liberal critique would eventually be decisive in displacing the *culture* of economic liberalism in its early Thatcherite incarnation, but not economic liberalism itself. However, Thatcherism had two faces – a traditional conservative one linking back to conservatism's historic political–cultural resources and a new political–cultural identity that appropriated and updated the political–cultural identity associated with classical or economic liberalism, circa the end of the eighteenth and early nineteenth century.

While the economic base of pre-social-democratic conservatism was revived under Thatcherism and the high status of traditional conservatism affirmed, conservatism's renewal of vows with economic liberalism also required a new cultural identity based more directly on expressing the virtues of the economic in direct contradiction with the cultural style of spatial, temporal and social distantiation from the economic characteristic of an earlier gentlemanly capitalism. With this style of social authority it had been through disavowal and/or a clear separation between the moral worlds of culture and economics that left the economy to function 'freely' without intervention or undue interference. It was compatible with economic liberalism on the basis of a dualist structure between all the traditional motifs of conservatism's moral–political order and the economy. This structure, based on dualism and disavowal, could not on its own succeed in re-establishing the hegemony of economic liberalism because between its decline in the early part of the twentieth century and its re-emergence, the social-democratic State and the welfare state had embedded itself deeply into British society. Thatcherism therefore needed to recruit a much wider support base and conduct a long and energetic cultural and ideological war against the social-democratic and welfare state to erode attachments to that residual hegemonic bloc. The traditional cultural style of conservatism was simply not up to what was needed (from a capitalist point of view), namely to blow apart the vulnerable but still embedded social-democratic settlement, with its implicit institutional memory and critique of the former hegemony built around a leisured class's hands off approach to the market.

The traditional conservative culture of gentlemanly capitalism did not provide the cutting tools required in the context of the post-war crisis of British capitalism. It was too elitist, too wedded to ascribed positions of social wealth, too culturally disposed to tradition and continuity and too invested in the requirement that due deference be paid to particular high-status social strata. The cultural authority of its leadership cadres actually depended in part on the idea that because they were already wealthy, they could be trusted with the administration of the State since unlike other classes and groups, they were too rich to be corruptible, i.e. interested in making more money.[108] We have seen that this was a self mythology that cannot be taken seriously, yet the shift into a new style of leadership in which making money would now become *openly* the generalised ethical value of the highest order, is still significant. We should remember too that Margaret Thatcher was only the second Conservative Prime Minister not to come from an aristocratic or landowning family (Ted Heath was the first in 1970).[109]

It was impossible for the older gentlemanly capitalism's distantiation or disavowal of its own economic-class power and rapacious interests to serve economic liberalism in the context it found itself in the 1980s. Instead economic liberalism had to be unleashed at a cultural level as well as restored at the level of capital formation and interests. In short economic liberalism had to shift from being merely an economic project to becoming a normative political culture in its own right rather than one that left culture and norms to a traditional conservative political culture.[110] To be sure there are still some potential points of convergence between traditional conservatism and economic liberalism: the aristocratic emphasis on service could be connected with the way the service economy bulks large in the national-popular from the 1980s onwards,[111] while the aristocratic value placed on leisure, will also find a strong echo in the new consumer society. Nevertheless, we can see tensions between traditional conservatism and economic liberalism under Thatcherism in the 1980s.

In 1989, the newspaper magnate Rupert Murdoch, who had recently moved into British broadcasting with the launch of Sky, gave the annual MacTaggart lecture at the Edinburgh International Television Festival. Murdoch used it to make his case for diminishing public service television which he associated exclusively with the 'British Establishment, with its dislike of money-making and its notion that public service is the preserve of paternalists'.[112] Conservatism's own accommodation to social democracy had to be ruthlessly unpicked which was another reason why Thatcherism could not rely solely on traditional conservative resources to advance its political and economic project. Murdoch, formed in a different national context from British capital (he was Australian) was a powerful apostle of the new market society that Thatcherism sought to bring into being. He argued that consumer choice was equivalent to democracy, conveniently eliding the role of powerful market actors such as himself in shaping that consumer choice or indeed the difference between consumer choice and political freedom. Evoking a traditional mythology of the press as the Fourth Estate, Murdoch compared the future of television with the liberation of the printed word from State control several hundred years ago. Harnessing digital technology to the free market, he claimed that enforced spectrum scarcity in broadcasting had underpinned public service broadcasting of yesteryear. Now with the end of spectrum scarcity, market forces plus technological developments would blow apart restrictions on choice and usher in a cornucopia of cultural riches.[113] In fact it was a political settlement (rather than just technology) that had established public service broadcasting in the UK, just as the balance of political forces ensured that the market reigned supreme in broadcasting in America during the early decades of radio and then television. Murdoch's place at the podium in Edinburgh that year expounding on the virtues of a market-led television system similarly represented a shifting political terrain in which the will and desire to keep market competition relatively constrained was certainly not a priority of the Thatcher governments. Murdoch thus redefined public service as 'a service which the public wants at a price it can afford'.[114] On this definition, soft porn channels, channels featuring a host of religious charlatans looking for donations, endless recycling of television's archive and today endless advertisements on sports channels encouraging a major problem with out-of-control gambling, constitutes, according to Murdoch, 'public service'. Only the market, which in Murdoch's classic economic-liberal vision is a relatively level playing field of exchanges between buyers and sellers, is democratic. A explicitly political conception of citizenship, of the need to be able to engage in debate, dialogue and representation across the genres of entertainment and news, smacks of elitism for Murdoch, of somebody else, 'the British Establishment', choosing what is 'good' for people. Of course, this establishment paradigm was *one* model of public service broadcasting and there is a powerful liberal narrative that posits the spread of the market as a democratising force against elites and elite tastes and the State.[115] To the extent that this was/is true, Murdoch's argument that British television was dominated by nostalgia and heritage (traditional conservatism) certainly hit a mark (although his own paper *The Sun* was not known for its anti-heritage republican sentiments). Yet what he could not contemplate, was the long history of struggle that had gone on to democratise this establishment model of public service broadcasting, a struggle that had woven its way into the establishment model, contested it and extended a different model of public service broadcasting that was certainly not elitist, but nor was it one that could thrive within the market-led model that Murdoch espoused.

If in Murdoch we see a member of the economic elite using the traditional social elite as a foil against which to cast himself as a revolutionary outsider, we can also see that the kind of individualistic consumer culture that Murdoch wanted to disseminate had at least some popular base and take-up. Central to the national-popular imagined by 1980s conservatism was the county of Essex, which added to the predominantly middle-class profile of southern conservative counties, an explicitly working-class county which represented the new hegemonic alliance Thatcherism seemed to have constructed with certain strata of the working class that identified with her project of individualistic aspiration and material wealth. Situated just north-east of London, Essex men and women were well placed to ride the meritocratic ideology of economic liberalism and enter the expanding economy of the City as bankers or traders or prosper by attaching themselves to the property boom as estate agents, home renovators or other forms of self-employment servicing the well-off. The political right were fascinated by this new working class embrace of economic liberalism but were also deeply ambivalent about it. Essex Man and Woman, as Biressi and Nunn have shown, both delighted traditional conservatives for their support of the Thatcherite project and appalled them because their conspicuous flaunting of new wealth and opportunity, their hedonistic immersion into the consumer culture, their social mobility and explicit articulation of values that it was best to be discreet about, as well as their lack of deference, struck an older middle-class cultural formation as vulgar, tasteless, disruptive of established class hierarchies and certainly not very 'gentlemanly'.[116] The bodies, clothes, jewellery, language and desires of these working class 'Thatcherites' were a site of attraction and repulsion for the middle class. Yet without harnessing such individualistic cultural energies, Thatcherism would have been a good deal less emboldened as a political project than it was.

At the same time there was a major problem with this mark one model of economic liberalism. It was extremely vulnerable to political and cultural critique on the grounds that this model of identity was based on sheer greed, an aggressive individualism (often blurring into the illegal), ignorant indifference to the public good and a moral indifference to those 'losers' unlucky enough to be left behind by the Thatcherite economic transformation of the British economy. Moreover, it was a relatively crude ideology that denied the role of the State in paradoxically extending economic liberalism across the wider terrain of institutional and social life. Education, training and the lack of long-term planning around research and development – the traditional and valid complaint from liberalism and Keynesian economists – were once again becoming important deficits as the ideological discourse of the knowledge economy took off in the 1990s.

We have seen how a high-status dominant image of conservatism constructed around the civil society of rural England developed out of a landed elite of aristocrats, gentry and merchants. Culturally, this elite forged a self-image that drew on and re-functioned pre-capitalist cultural raw materials, which constructed legitimation around a spatial, social and temporal distantiation from the economic realm that was the basis of their material power. The symbolic–cultural style of the English ruling class on its conservative wing drew on a matrix made up of nature, small-scale community, tradition, Church, nation and empire. It was so successful at concealing its economic roots that many opponents of conservatism across the liberal and left spectrum had come to the conclusion that conservatism was actually a block on the development of capitalism or hostile to making money. A cultural alliance with landed, mercantile, commercial and banking capital certainly fostered an attitudinal distaste for a specific sector, industry, but this did not prevent a real economic alliance between the different formations of capital which were interdependent with each other within an imperial political economy. The critique of this arrangement from the liberals and the Left was often compromised by investments in industrial capital that were both problematically normative (industrial capital is more progressive than other forms of capital) teleological (the growth path of capitalist modernity goes through industrial development) strategically flawed (ultimately industrial capital preferred an alliance with banking capital rather than social-democratic reform) and historically inaccurate (industry was never anything more than a component part of a British economy always predominantly weighted towards commerce, finance and inward trade). The complex relationship between different forms of capital in which industrial capital became a willing and benefitting subaltern part of the City's hegemony, both in the past and now, constitutes the political economic framework within which conservatism has dominated the national-popular, although never as exclusively as is often claimed.

Conservatism remains deeply attached to the image of rural England and gentlemanly capitalism, especially in relation to leisure-time pursuits; but it has had to relegate this cultural model very largely to nostalgia, fantasy, marketing and consumption, although the coercive departments of the State as well as a distinctive conservative nationalism remain very important practical resources. At the same time, since the 1980s and the return of economic liberalism, a different model of cultural leadership has also had to be developed for economic liberalism. This identity for economic liberalism could not be based on the older model of social, spatial or temporal distantiation from the economic, as it was developed directly *out of* economic imperatives and discourses. In its first wave under Thatcherism it took the form of a crude individualism and looked both vulnerable to a moral critique of greed and a social-liberal critique of a lack of rational planning and governance required to push the market into new areas of social and institutional life. Nevertheless it had great cultural energy, recruited a reasonable base among the skilled working class[117] and was able to articulate an ideology of meritocracy that cut against both conservatism's old elites and social-democratic corporatism. Once social liberalism had uncoupled itself from the social-democratic settlement and re-converged with economic liberalism, it was ideally placed to offer economic liberalism a more sophisticated identity for its operations. Economic liberalism shifted away from its alliance with conservatism because liberalism could protect it against the argument that it was simply powered by individual greed; it could also provide the necessary ideological justification for reshaping the social State according to the image of economic rationality. This reshaping could work its magic without much resistance. Economic liberalism no longer needed conservatism to use *brute* State power to tilt the balance of class forces in its favour. Thatcherism had achieved its goal in that regard and it had eventually suffered the exhaustion of its political capital as a result.[118] In addition, the cultural identity of Thatcherism came into contradiction with economic liberalism on the question of national identity. An economic model based on turbulent change and international flows of capital and commodities and powerful supra-national institutions sits uneasily with the traditional conservative sources of ideological power. British conservatism's belief that it can ally itself with economic liberalism in its contemporary phase of globalisation and not have its traditional values, emblems, structures and identities profoundly challenged by the changes economic liberalism brings about, is a root cause of conservative discontents.

4

Conservative culture and the State

We have seen that conservatism's relationship with economic liberalism has developed into two modalities. Historical precedence goes to what I have termed the dualist model between culture and economics based on distantiation from the process and source of profit making, which gave conservatism a distinctive style of social and political leadership that disavowed the origins of wealth in slavery, agricultural capitalism, parasitic and 'rentier' capitalism and financial dealings within a context of the imperial domination of markets. In this model, the ritualistic-ideological departments of the State and the conservative-dominated terrain of civil society develop a moral universe that is logically antithetical to the amoral profit motive and yet it can coexist with it through a kind of disavowal, dualism and compensatory value system in which culture and morality do not interfere with the market but establish their own bases outside it. More recently this modality of dualism and disavowal has had to coexist with a new cultural style developed in the 1980s which generates its legitimation strategies directly out of economic values rather than apparently non-economic values. Economic liberalism in this phase now attempts to remodel the superstructure in its own image, bringing it into contradiction with many of the ritualistic-ideological resources of traditional conservatism. Insofar as both modalities support economic liberalism, they are compatible in terms of their objectives; insofar as these modalities of support offer different and potentially incompatible types of support for economic liberalism, they come into conflict with one another.

We can identify at least six contradictions between traditional conservatism and the unleashed capitalism of economic liberalism, contradictions which the State tries to manage.

1   Conservatism's greatest wellsprings of ideological power remain, for historical reasons, grounded in *national* resources, contexts and points of reference. Capitalism by contrast is international and has none of the emotional bonds of loyalty to the nation which stirs conservative nationalism. This has been especially true of British capital, which, historically and today, has preferred to invest substantial amounts of its assets abroad. The FTSE 100 companies listed on the London Stock Exchange whose highs are excitedly quoted by the national media as if they are indicators of a healthy *domestic* economy, generate as much as 77 per cent per cent of their earnings overseas.[1] The disjuncture between the national framework of so much reportage and the international networks of capitalist activity has the effect of occluding various dimensions of the social totality. That is beneficial to conservatism in terms of public reception of its policymaking, but it also produces for the culture more generally a somewhat bewildered incomprehension as to why cherished conservative institutions, practices or values are under threat.

2   Conservatism's older moral–cultural orientation defends a cluster of values that are perceived to be important for shoring up respect for authority and hierarchy. The most long-standing battlegrounds on this score have been around the family, sexuality and representations of the body, where conservatism has been strongly shaped by its close affiliations with religion. The apparent atemporality of scripture powerfully reinforces and naturalises the continuities of conservative authority. Capitalism, by contrast, has little time or respect for such norms. The body and sexuality are highly lucrative as commodities and the more capitalist imperatives have been unleashed (by conservative policy-makers) in the sphere of media and communications for example, the more long-standing conservative moral norms have been eroded. Rupert Murdoch was a strong supporter of Margaret Thatcher's Conservative Party in the 1980s but he also put topless female models on page three of *The Sun.* One can barely imagine what the 1970s defender of 'moral standards' Mary Whitehouse would have made of Channel Four's *Naked Attraction,* but it was the commercialisation of the channel's public service remit via the Conservative Party's 1990 Broadcasting Act that laid the basis for such offences against conservative moral principles.[2]

3   Conservatism is a form of national identity that seeks to unify the nation and dissolve substantive socio-economic inequalities and

antagonisms in cultural reference points of shared belonging, whether of State institutions or the small rural community kind. Yet economic liberalism, or capitalism unleashed, inevitably leads to deepening class stratifications which also have strong geographical dimensions that in the present context are threatening the integrity of the British State. One can see conservatism negotiating the tensions between 'community' and profit in the 1986 television advert that promoted the privatisation of British Gas: the famous 'Tell Sid' campaign. The television advert is set significantly in that most symbolically resonant of traditional conservative locations, the English village, and moves from the local pub, to the street outside, where the postman takes the message of the chance to buy shares in the soon to be privatised utility to an old lady at the bus stop. All the characters ask their interlocutors to 'tell Sid' if they see him. The sense of the message being spread outwards is coupled with signs that wealth is also apparently spreading downwards. We start in the pub with the local Tory gent in bow-tie talking to a middle-class friend in a sweater with a more regional accent before moving on to the postman and the pensioner. Yet while the scenario is about telling people how easy it is to buy shares, the characters are all, rather oddly, *whispering* to each other, as if they are letting their friends and acquaintances in on a secret from which only the select few will benefit. This whispering is symptomatic of the reality of what was happening: a service to the community at large was becoming a private asset that would be handsomely beneficial to a few shareholders (through hikes in prices) and CEOs (in salaries). Here was a radical and large-scale transformation from public to private interests disguised by the small-scale traditionalism pictured in the advert, but given away by that odd sense that only those 'in the know', and with the means and the philosophy will cash in on this form of theft. National unity and community turn out to be fissured by the chance to make a quick buck.

4 Traditional conservatism leans not only towards disavowing the realities of socio-economic difference and the resultant antagonisms, but it also leans towards a national identity forged around cultural homogeneity. This requires both refusing or questioning the legitimacy of cultural difference as part of the national identity and (in contrast to the question of socio-economic difference, where antagonism is disavowed) insisting that *cultural difference itself*

leads to antagonism and conflict that undermines national unity. Again, economic liberalism drives in a contrary direction. Capitalist markets are cosmopolitan; they break down national exclusiveness and mix cultures through trade and migration. Social liberalism is at this level compatible with economic liberalism and this becomes a significant fissure within the Conservative Party once Tony Blair's socially liberal and economic-liberal New Labour achieves electoral hegemony. On the other hand, deepening class stratification does generate the fear and resentment that conservatism can mobilise against cultural difference through displacement strategies.

5 Conservatism downplays a sense of patterns and unities at the level of the social order (or synchronically) only to insist on patterns and unities on the temporal (or diachronic) plane.[3] It thus discovers 'structure' in history and in its particular interpretation of history as static tradition. This is combined at any particular point in time with a pragmatic adjustment to the engine of turbulence that is the capitalist economy while constantly folding change into a nostalgic and backward-looking attachment to the deep past. In his rebuke to the French Revolution, the conservative philosopher Edmund Burke wrote that in contrast to sudden breaks, historical change in England adopted a different principle: 'in what we improve we are never wholly new; in what we retain we are never wholly obsolete.'[4] In the balance between the new and the old the latter certainly prevails, giving a significant role for nostalgia. Within conservatism, the past is often a more glorious or comforting place and in the case of Britain this has given home-grown conservatism a distinctly post-colonial sense of loss, decline and melancholy.[5] Capitalism's temporality, by contrast, is radically orientated towards the now and the short-term future, always on the lookout for where some money can be made or some market can be opened up. Tradition and economic liberalism cannot always be seamlessly reconciled. Economic liberalism tears up established social relations, while the broader cultural consequences of capitalist modernity – the development of technology and science for example – may also pose great challenges to conservatism's investment in the pre-democratic era or its affinity with various taboos (especially around the body and sexuality).

6 Conservative investment in value accumulated over a long arc of time logically links it to that form of social status, wealth or power which sociologists call 'ascribed', that is inherited by dint of birth,

family or some other form of social network. By contrast, capitalism's present-tense and short-term future temporality makes it a potential challenge to long-held ascribed-status positions. Capitalism opens up opportunities for achievements that are seen as based on the skills and qualities of the individual (achieved status, in sociological terms) rather than advantages they have inherited. This was a significant tension within Thatcherism as a political philosophy. It drew on some of the traditional conservative motifs of the past in its attempts to reconstruct a link between the 1980s and a pre-social democratic Britain (e.g. 'Victorian values') but at the same time, it had a strong meritocratic element that attempted to galvanise and draw into its ranks new social layers that the upper echelons of conservatism were distinctly ambivalent about.

The political culture of conservatism provides important resources that try and handle all these contradictions. These resources are to be found in the State, in the image of rural England, in the City, historically in the empire and in the media. These resources of the political culture have all been subject to extensive critique, starting at the liberal end of the spectrum and ranging into the Marxist Left, and these critiques (especially their liberal versions) have certainly percolated into a good deal of the popular culture. We should avoid the idea of a conservative ownership of national identity. At the same time, these conservative resources also remain robust and effective, not least because they have enormously powerful and durable bases from which to sustain the political culture. Conservative discontent with some of the outcomes of economic liberalism which it itself has pursued, produces a culture of displacement, where effects cannot be traced back to causal generative forces, since if they were, conservatism would have to confront its ally and master, economic liberalism. Historically these displacement effects have pursued four main directions, or objects of conservative fear and loathing. They are:

1   Displacements onto class others. The working class as 'the enemy within' has a long history in conservative political culture. Margaret Thatcher famously invoked the phrase 'the enemy within' during the miners' strike of 1984–5 but it is a phrase and a sentiment that goes back to the Peterloo massacre of working-class radicals in Manchester in 1819.[6] In the conservative mythology of the 1970s,

the trade unions and striking workers were holding the country to ransom, making Britain 'ungovernable' and ruining her future. Both contemporaneously and subsequently, the strikes of December 1978 and early 1979 were framed by the British press as an apocalyptic 'winter of discontent' that helped seal a decade-long campaign from the New Right that 'something' (i.e. the social democratic, welfare state) had to change, and that Margaret Thatcher was the leader to deliver that painful but necessary medicine.[7] More recently, conservatism within both the Conservative Party and New Labour, has displaced the consequences of *their* economic policies onto a new political and discursive construction of the working class as conservative and *White*, resentful, angry and in a 'populist' mood thanks to cultural changes which, insofar as they have some 'economic' agency, are framed as the consequence of 'metropolitan elites' (i.e. social liberals). As an account of the social and economic forces responsible for the deterioration in the material and cultural condition of the working classes, this is no more adequate than the mythology of the 'winter of discontent'. It does, however, serve the purpose of framing and interpreting evident problems within the terms most conducive to not addressing those problems at any root and branch level. Here the working class are no longer 'the enemy' but a political force to be mobilised from above (Gramsci's 'passive revolution') as the explanation for the pursuit of certain policies that inevitably make the underlying problems (e.g. the lack of material security) worse.

2 Displacements onto national others. National enemies, especially those which Britain has been at war with, have, before, during and after such conflicts, been an extremely powerful and useful means by which conservatism has secured its hegemonic sway across sections of the population. France in the 1700s, Russia in the mid-to-late nineteenth century, Germany in the first four decades of the twentieth century, the Soviet Union during the Cold War (revived again for a time in the 1980s), Argentina during the Falklands War (1982), and today 'radical' (an interesting word choice) Islam. The conjuring of such opponents, especially nation-state opponents, is linked to British conservatism's need to continue to strut the world stage as a leading power. In 2013 there was a diplomatic spat between Russia and Britain at a G20 summit in Saint Petersburg. The then Prime Minister David Cameron had just been defeated in the House

of Commons in a vote as to whether to join the US in military action against the Syrian President Bashir al-Assad. It was reported in the British media that either the Russian president, Vladimir Putin or his spokesperson (or both) had described Britain as a small or little island nobody paid any attention to.[8] Here the choice of words is calculated to wound: the island status of Britain is selected to underscore both the sense of isolation (to whom no one listens) and the historic shrinkage of territory and power once its various imperial extensions overseas were lost, one by one.

3 Displacements onto ethnic others. If the working class are the enemy within and national others are the enemy without, then ethnic others are the 'problem' who *were* outside the borders and boundaries of the nation (and here the island image and identity of Britain plays another crucial role) but who are *now* inside (they have crossed the water, the protective barrier: they have metaphorically surmounted the symbolically loaded white cliffs of Dover) – a position which conservatism has historically seen as a threat to the 'purity' of national identity. Conservatism is characterised by a strong *impermeable boundary* concept of national identity, which makes symbolic entry and acceptance of immigrant populations difficult. This impermeable boundary concept of national identity is logically linked to the static orientation of conservatism: 'its typically binary system of representation constantly marks and attempts to fix and naturalize the difference between belongingness and otherness' writes Stuart Hall.[9] Liberal theories of national identity have noted that national identity is not, however, coterminous with the territory over which the State exerts sovereign power. The 'internalist' assumptions of conservatism, as Schlesinger terms them,[10] fail to acknowledge that the nation and the State have complex entanglements with economics, people, culture and communication systems that are global. Nor is this a new phenomenon, at least for Britain, which once had an empire that straddled the world. There is then a fundamental contradiction within the conservative national imaginary between its cultural understanding of national identity, as isomorphic with the territory of the British State and its economic commitments, which are aligned with the global imperatives of capitalism. This liberal critique is important, however; remembering that liberalism has been a dominant player in all the historic blocs of the last two hundred plus years that have shaped British national identities, we

may guess that there are problems to be explored with this liberal critique (namely how it has uncoupled itself from critical political economy).

4 Displacement onto social-liberal culture. Although social liberalism, as part of the dominant hegemonic bloc, is not attacked legally, politically or physically in the same way the preceding conservative hate-objects can be, intra-class tensions can still be significant and social liberalism may find itself being blamed for its distance from the people (its universalism or internationalism or 'intellectualism'). There may be a basis here for a legitimate critique of liberalism on the question of distance, and Gramsci were certainly critical of Italian liberalism on this score, but the terms of conservatism's critique are, needless to say, problematic. Another conservative framing of liberalism's failures concerns its collusion with those who would weaken the moral–political fibre of the conservative nation (social liberalism's tolerance on a wide range of social issues, e.g. sexuality and sexual mores, gender roles, race and so forth). Needless to say, there is no legitimate basis here for this latter complaint.

The political management of these displacement strategies is a crucially important task, which the political parties that conservatism intersects with (most notably, but not exclusively, the Conservative Party) must organise. Here the media and especially the conservative press have been enormously effective in shaping the daily political news agenda. This means that these displacement mechanisms shape the public conversation on the available policy options. The elements of capitalist interest, contradiction and irrationality to be found within and between conservatism and its paradoxical relationship to economic liberalism, has come to have extensive fertilisation across public opinion, in ways that help block the possibility for a more informed debate and better solutions to the problems Britain faces.

The conservative State and economic liberalism

The British State in the eighteenth, and for most of the nineteenth century, was economically liberal in a negative sense and conservative in a positive sense. It was negatively liberal in the sense that it followed the lead of civil society and the bourgeoisie both at home and abroad. The construction of the Great Western Railway in the 1830s is illustrative of this. The project was driven by local capital: that of Bristol merchants concerned to compete with Liverpool as a port of destination for goods from America by providing speedy access to London.[11] The role of parliament was to recognise the formation of private railway companies and give them the power to buy up the land on which the tracks would be built. Landed aristocracy would sometimes be on the company board of directors as their connections to the political elites were useful to smooth out any problems.[12] The coordinating role of the State is here *in the service* of initiatives that derive from economic interests and associated organs of civil society.

Abroad, the British State was happy to leave the startling conquest of India to a private corporation run from the City. The East India Company operated ruthlessly and with impunity in the eighteenth century not least because many MPs were shareholders. The State lent its military might to back up the company's own private army, before finally taking over direct control of the corporation's Indian empire in 1858 when the company's rapaciousness threatened British interests by triggering a mutiny in 1857.[13] Yet within popular culture and popular memory, this private acquisition of a country and a colony has been marginalised in favour of the post-1857 British Raj years. This is because it is very difficult to construct the activities of the East India Company as anything other than what it was: capital accumulation.[14] The conservative British State, however, brings with it a vaster cultural, historical, mythological, moral–political narrative in which the economic dimension can coexist (or preferably be back-grounded entirely) with other strands that have more esteem and status because of their apparent distantiation from the economic motive (e.g. the civilising mission, adventure and exoticism, glory, heroism, honour, cultural exchange, etc.).[15]

The State's relaxed attitude towards the autonomy of private capital both today and in the past, is and was combined with a punitive, oppressive and zealous use of the law and the courts to inflict punishment (in the past, capital punishment, transportation and imprisonment) on the criminal poor as well as trade union activity, in defence of private property. In the past:

> The Combination Act of 1721 made it illegal for the journeymen tailors to enter 'into combinations to advance their wages to unreasonable prices, and lesson their usual hours of work'. This is the earliest Act in British history designed to stop the formation of trade unions, and it was passed

at the behest of master tailors against some 15,000 journeymen tailors who had struck for better pay and shorter hours. Imprisonment and impressment forced them into submission.[16]

Conservatism's long-term engagement with economic liberalism has always had two primary aims in terms of hegemony. Firstly it aids various capitals in their fight against organised labour by increasing the power of capital and the market over labour and in other areas of civil society. Thus conservatism can never do without the law and order departments of the State to weaken the organised adversaries of capital and punish the individualised responses to inequality amongst the working-class population drawn towards infringing the rights of private property through crime. Secondly, having blocked the redistribution of wealth according to the norms of equality and solidarity which animate the labour movement, conservatism seeks to bind at least some layers of the wider population into the social order on an atomised *individual basis* according to material advancement via market opportunities. A classic example of this was the 'right to buy' council housing that was given to local authority tenants by the first Thatcher government. The policy transferred public housing stock into private ownership, which a booming housing market turned into a valuable asset.[17] It was no doubt hoped that such a material redistribution of wealth (from public to private) would also transform attitudes, cultures and politics. Naturally, both the aim of breaking down collective solidarity and offering material inducements of an individualist kind require a cultural battle and struggle and offer cultural-political rewards to the victor.

The welfare state that was institutionalised after 1945 represented an ideal of universality, which is to say that all citizens had certain social, economic and cultural rights that the State was mandated to deliver and resource. Housing, employment, education and health were some of the key areas that the welfare state sought to address. This universalism was not and could not be fully realised since it cohabitated with a capitalist class-divided society and the welfare state was grafted onto a capitalist State. Nevertheless it represented a real modification of the capitalist State and a modest redistribution of wealth. Welfare capitalism was a contradiction for both the welfare state and the capitalist State, one that could only be managed and stabilised within the same State for a few decades by compromising on the full unfolding of their different principles. The problem for capitalism is that the welfare state was premised on achieving near enough full employment. Yet a low level of unemployment and the other economic, social and cultural protections (the 'social wage') afforded by the welfare state provided the bases from which the working class could make more and more demands and claims on capitalism leading to a 'squeeze' on profits.[18] This was the real crisis of the 1970s: the economic pressure and growing political combativeness of the British working classes in a context of intensifying capitalist competition internationally.

It was this contradiction that Thatcherism aimed to resolve on the terms of the 'New Right' by reconstructing the British State and eroding its social democratic, welfare principles and practices. In his 1979 article in *Marxism Today*, the house journal of the Communist Party of Great Britain, Stuart Hall, Britain's pre-eminent Gramscian scholar, tried to analyse the specific political features of the rightward trend in British politics in the late 1970s. Taking his cue from Gramsci, Hall argued that a 'conjuncture', the precise synthesis of economic, political and cultural lines of force in a specific moment is defined by the political efforts of the contending classes and groups to organise the terrain on terms that are favourable to them. In a deep crisis – one that was 'organic', i.e. went to the fundamentals of the socio-economic system's contradictions – the political strategies in play cannot be merely defensive, argued Hall, but must be *formative*. This meant that political cultures must try and reconstruct an alliance of classes (Gramsci's 'historical bloc') and drive forward a new programme, construct a new 'common sense', a new way of seeing and interpreting the world that makes sense of the crisis and offers what appears to be some solutions to it. To do this the struggle over definitions must go beyond the economic and encompass as wide a range of social experiences as possible. For an organic crisis is not only one that goes to the heart of the socio-economic structure, but one that fuses with that crisis a whole range of cultural-moral-political problems. In the economic-political-cultural struggle, new orchestrations of social forces are likely to emerge with distinct strategies, languages, appeals, programmes and policies, marking a break with what went before, and inaugurating a new period of rule, or historic bloc. In that battle it was the political right that was winning, not the Left, according to Hall. Thatcherism represented the remaking of the British State and its 'compact' with the people, one that would lead in time to the dismantling of social democracy and the welfare state.

The outlines of this reconstruction was summarised by Andrew Gamble as 'strong state-free market', which marks a return (as I indicated above) to what had been essentially the norm for the British State prior to the social democratic interlude.[19] Another formulation of the same idea that was popular with the Left, was Stuart Hall's classification of Thatcherism as 'authoritarian populism'. The term authoritarian populism has its origins in the whole 'law and order' agenda which Hall and his colleagues had analysed in a pioneering book-length project called *Policing the Crisis* in the late 1970s.[20] In the first phase of the new law and order agenda, crime was linked to a supposed moral permissiveness unleashed by the 'Swinging Sixties'. This was then later 'connotatively linked with the more politicized threats, to compose a picture of a social order on the brink of moral collapse.'[21] With politicians, police and the press orchestrating moral panics around crime, moral deviancy and political threats to social order, sections of public opinion could be stampeded onto the terrain that most advantaged conservatism and an ascendant Thatcherism. In its simple dichotomies between good and evil, between the civilised and the uncivilised, between anarchy and order, decency and moral degeneracy, law-abidingness and lawlessness, the law and order debate was dominated by the New Right before they even achieved governmental power and laid the essential groundwork for persuading wide layers of people of the necessity and virtues of an authoritarian politics that could safeguard the 'silent majority' of society against its assailants (criminals, blacks, immigrants, subcultures, trades unionists, strikers, protesters, leftists, feminists, a whole series of equivalences and conflations or what Hall called 'magical connections and short-circuits').[22] The 'populism' part of the term at this stage referred to the orchestrated demands of 'the people' for 'strong measures' which 'served to win for the authoritarian closure the gloss of populist consent.'[23]

After the first election of Thatcher in 1979 and with the subsequent consolidation of Thatcherism (it was Hall who gave Thatcher's politics the 'honour' of an 'ism' in recognition of her hegemonic ambitions) the definition and terms of reference for authoritarian populism became more ambiguous, especially in relation to the 'populism' component of the term. While authoritarianism continued in Thatcherism's use of State power to advance its policy programme, 'the people' were constructed less as clamouring for rescue from the forces of disorder (since that would imply a failure of governance on the part of Conservative governments), than as *market actors.* Hall himself was not entirely clear about the logic of this shift within the concept of populism as Thatcherism moved from opposition in the 1970s into governmental power in the 1980s with a privatisation and 'free market' policy agenda.[24] But he did see the term 'populism' as having an economic content as it were, one that could be made to refer to Thatcherism's project to redeem and revalidate the free market as a model of freedom, choice, initiative and dynamism. The value of inflecting the concept of populism in an economic direction after 1979 is that it would bring into view the contradictory combination of traditional conservative themes (the authoritarian component of Thatcherism that stresses law and obedience and also traditional ritualistic-ideological complexes such as the family and nation) with a virulent brand of economic liberalism (that stresses a privatised freedom). Freeden cautions against thinking that Thatcherism constituted a radical new turn for conservatism. It occupies he argues 'fundamentally the same semantic field as its predecessors'.[25] Hall would not necessarily disagree with that:

> Some of the ideological elements currently being recast by Thatcherism are precisely the ones that coalesced into *modern* conservatism [in the late nineteenth century] – nation before class, the organic unity of the English people, the coincidence between the 'English genius' and traditionalism, the paternal duties the privileged owe to the lower orders, society as an orderly hierarchy of 'power', constitutionalism and so on.[26]

The context, though, was new and there was, as Hall argues, a process of recasting going on within the ideological universe of conservatism to reflect this. As we have seen, conservatism always assumed that private property should have as much autonomy as possible but its real symbolic–cultural investments were grounded elsewhere, not on the terrain of the economic. When the Liberal Party went into decline in the late nineteenth century, those who did not want to follow liberalism on the new emerging ground of the social State, joined conservatism, 'finding within it at least a fundamental commitment to the free-enterprise system, the ethic of possessive individualism and rugged competition'.[27] Before this current within conservatism could become dominant, however, there was a wider if gradual epochal shift away from laissez-faire that left economic liberalism marginalised. It returns of course with Thatcherism and now becomes dominant, while still drawing on 'the traditional emphases of organic Toryism'[28] even as it partially displaces the prevailing assumptions of post-Second World War conservatism and its compromise with 'one nation' politics.

What was new with Thatcherism's promotion of the market was that it was very explicitly designed to *oppose* the welfare state. Thatcherism cast the welfare state, the core institutions of social democracy, as a 'powerful, bureaucratic imposition.'[29] This recasting of the welfare state had some ground in reality, Hall argued, precisely because of the contradictions of social democracy for the Labour Party. The party formally committed to advancing the interests of the working class becomes *in government*, the party that must displace the burden of the economic crisis in the 1970s away from capital and onto the workers. The means for doing that was and remains making the welfare state institutions more 'disciplinary' and less generous. The subtle sleight of hand of the Thatcherite project was to offer the 'market' – whose failures the welfare state had been constructed to offset – as an alternative means of providing goods and services in key areas. Thus for Thatcherism the capitalist crisis is resolved by *more* capitalism. Sometimes, in relation to the privatisations of public assets such as British Gas or British Telecom, this was framed as 'popular capitalism', the contradictory idea that everyone could participate and benefit from buying shares. More typically, 'capitalism' was repackaged in the more universal and less class specific terms of 'the market', in which after all, everyone operated – even if on very unequal terms. Thatcherism's appeal to an individualistic, even hedonistic identity in which the free market could service our every desire (if only one can pay for it) continued to be combined with a strong new disciplinarianism of the State.

Thatcherism promoted the market against the bureaucratic welfare state, which was under pressure from the crisis of capitalism and promoted the coercive law and order State against a society that was cast as somehow not needing the moral-sapping 'nanny state' but the 'firm smack' of Conservative moral order. Thatcherism demonstrated the extent to which politics frames the debate and constructs a story of what went wrong and how to put it right. It did not just talk about the economic level of society, but also linked the economic to, or spoke across, a whole range of anxieties, desires and cultural–moral issues, on which it continually attempted to interpret events within its own framework.

One such issue was taxation policy. High taxation levels on wealthy individuals and on corporations in the post-Second World War era provided the funding base for redistributing wealth through various forms of socialised (public) services or nationalised industries (which kept prices on basic goods low). Thatcherism, however, helped redistribute wealth back to the wealthy by driving down taxation on rich individuals and corporations. Between 1980 and 2003, corporate tax rates dropped from 52 per cent to 30 per cent.[30] The top rate of income tax for the wealthy fell from 83 per cent in 1974 to 40 per cent in 1988.[31] This regressive economic redistribution was underpinned by a 'moral' case that attempted to make this look like something other than a wealth grab. This moral case talked instead of the individual taking responsibility for their lives and that, in order to do so, they needed to have only the bare minimum of income taken from them by the State in the form of income tax. By casting tax in these terms, the public sector (socialised services and nationalised industries) could be seen as morally enervating, fostering an unhealthy dependence on the State, draining away the individual's reserves of initiative, independence, their 'get up and go'. Lowering personal income tax would of course have an impact on public services, but the point is that this was desirable, since the public sector was, from this perspective, morally dubious as well as, it was argued, inefficient compared to the much-touted lean, consumer-sensitive private sector. Thatcherism could mobilise common-sense clichés that sound reasonable if they are not subjected to any real scrutiny (and the media ensured that they were not): people should stand on their own two feet; if people kept more of their money, then there would be more money to invest, to give to charity, to spend on what individuals wanted (and not what the bureaucratic State imposed); the best and the brightest would want to live and work in Britain, and so on and so forth. This case for lowering taxes (proportionally more for the rich) placed the *individual* and the pursuit of their own (self) interests as the moral centre of a new relationship between the State and the people. Since this new relationship meant a more unequal redistribution of wealth, it also meant a repudiation of the 'one nation' politics of the social democratic era. This in turn required accepting, tacitly for the most part, institutionalised inequality and what Jessop et al. called a 'two-nations' strategy, in which beneficiaries of the market-led growth strategy (especially associated with communications, finance and electrical engineering) pursued by Thatcherism would create enough of an electoral coalition to keep on winning power, while the other 'nation' (the losers), to be found in 'the North', the inner cities, the caring public sector, and the unemployed, were a problem to be managed and contained. As Bob Jessop and his co-authors noted, their 'existence is taken for granted rather than seen as a rebuke to society's conscience.'[32] With the British State beginning to be recomposed around economic liberalism once more, individuals are held to be ultimately responsible for their fortunes, thus those in need of State support come more and more to be seen as a drain on the resources of the individual, they are personal failures that 'we' cannot afford.[33] The failures of a capitalist political economy that has pushed people into a condition of vulnerability, are airbrushed from sight.

The aristocratic State

Although Thatcher herself was lukewarm towards the monarchy, this is not generally true of conservatives, even those who turned decisively towards economic liberalism in the 1980s. Along with the coercive power of the law and order State, conservatives generally appreciate the ideological-ritualistic contribution which the aristocracy and the monarchy offer. It was ever thus. From the late nineteenth century, there was a gradual separation between the symbolic power (still efficacious at the level of ideology) and economic power of the landed elites who had controlled the State since the English Civil War. Canadine provides, by implication, a devastating critique of the Nairn/Anderson/ Weiner thesis that British capitalism has been crippled by an archaic anti-business attitude (the right-wing complaint that Weiner seems to endorse) or anti-industrial capital attitude (the liberal/Left complaint). Quite simply the aristocracy, the target of their ire, went into decline as British agriculture began to encounter stiff competition from the USA. Both Houses of Parliament were dominated by the landowning elites up until the 1880s after which land values began to fall. At the same time the pressures of democratisation and the widening franchise in the 1880s at last began to impact on the composition of those in control of politics.[34] Yet because the 1880s saw the Liberal Party split over Home Rule for Ireland which guaranteed the ascendancy of the Conservative Party, Anderson sees this period as 'the final "feudalization" of the ideology and protocol of the dominant bloc'.[35] The persistence of the feudalism thesis strikes again, albeit qualified by the quotation marks. In reality, recruitment and selection for major parts of the State apparatus were opened up and partially democratised for the new middle class. As the State enlarged the scope and scale of its activities so it needed staff who were professionally trained:

In every profession, the old amateur, traditional, gentlemanly ethos was in retreat. The civil service was no longer an appropriate billet for literatti and dilettanti. The church was increasingly urban and professional in its structure and orientation. The law was becoming precarious and overcrowded. And in the aftermath of the Boer War, the army needed educated experts rather than ornamental horsemen.[36]

By the 1930s, Prime Minister Neville Chamberlain saw agriculture as a declining industry that needed to be rationalised with marginal and inefficient producers eliminated.[37] Where the landed elite did retain their dominance was of course in connection with the royal family and its offices and expanding bureaucracy. But as Canadine makes clear, this was a world in its own bubble, a world where aristocratic power had retrenched to a very small universe and where matters of State and economic development were shaped by powers and forces elsewhere, not least by Whitehall – a more powerful unelected check on radical change than the titular head of state. The aristocracy and the monarchy were recast for ornamental purposes, allowed to decorate institutional power complexes as directors of a company, mayor to a town, chancellor of a university, governor-general of a dominion, or later, patron to a charity.[38]

The cultural affinity between the aristocracy and the continued existence of the monarchy and certain aspects of capitalism helped ensure that it retained an ideological-symbolic role that should be neither discounted nor exaggerated. The success of a recent film like *The King's Speech* (Tom Hooper 2010) shows how tenacious the culture of hierarchy, deference and inherited social advantage remains, despite (or perhaps because of) the unleashing of economic liberalism and individualism over several decades. The film was released shortly after Britain had elected the most aristocratic prime minister since Alec Douglas-Home. David Cameron's family connections with the landed aristocratic elites makes him fifth cousin twice-removed from the Queen, according to Debrett's, the publisher which chronicles the elite and their social and cultural preferences. *The King's Speech* seemed to announce the new era quite perfectly.

The film was a major success in the UK, taking nearly $75 million at the box office and credited with getting an older (and more traditional middle-class) audience back into the theatres. It also demonstrated the economic value of the monarchy for international audiences. In America (the film was funded by the American producers Harvey and

Bob Weinstein) it took close to $139 million while box office returns also showed deep reserves of fascination for the monarchy in Commonwealth countries such as Australia and New Zealand and strong European interest in the British monarchy from France, Germany, Italy and Spain. The film is a good example of how one element of a political culture spreads itself into the 'national popular' as a dominant image through the cultural industries and how this internal dominance becomes even more consolidated as the image of national identity that outsiders buy into once it is projected internationally.

Weighed down with all the long-standing vices of British cinema (bloodless, sexless, devoid of drama, all talk and interiors, anti-plebian, mundane, anti-democratic and focusing on a social climber) this is a film absolutely desperate to convince us of the importance of the monarchy in assuming its ideological function in the age of war and the new mass media (specifically radio broadcast but also film). As a prince, Albert's inability to overcome his stutter in the 1920s and 30s means that public speaking is an excruciating failure of ideological efficacy, complete with many shots of his 'subjects' casting their eyes downward in that most British of emotions, *embarrassment* in a social situation. But with his ascension to the throne after his brother's abdication over his intentions to marry American divorcee Wallis Simpson, and with the Second World War looming, the gap between his personal performance – rooted in the appallingly rigid, fearful and loveless institution of the royal family – and the role of the monarchy as a point of identification for the whole of the nation, must be closed, or so it seems. This split between the person and the institution is always a potential fracture line in the smooth reproduction of the monarchy. When the person lets down the institution in some way (affairs, drunkenness, boorishness, corruption, etc.) there is always the possibility that thoughts might stray into wondering if there is a problem with the institution itself. But in the film at least, the king overcomes his impediment through a sterling selfless commitment to duty (the last thing he wants to be, it seems, is king).

This is a film about how the aristocratic elites adapt themselves to modernity: in this instance the cultural technology of the mass media that was so important in this period. But they do so only to keep the whole rotten hierarchical system intact, not to release the democratic energies and potentialities that slumbered within them. This capacity to adapt to modernity while retaining power is one of the key features of conservatism as a political culture. It was the central theme of the hit television series *Downton Abbey* during the years of the Conservative–Liberal coalition government (2010–15). Written by the Conservative peer, Julian Alexander Kitchener-Fellowes, *Downton Abbey* was widely seen as being sympathetically attuned to the conservative–liberal fusion at the time.[39]

Evolutionary adaptation is the central theme of the narrative constructed around the British monarchy. When Albert became King George VI, his eldest daughter Princess Elizabeth became the heir to the throne. The year 2016 brought her 90th birthday, and her 64th year on the throne. It was an opportunity for the conservative–liberal journalist Matthew d'Ancona to write an article in the London paper, the *Evening Standard*, which recycled many of the tropes of uncritical adoration that the media routinely pumps into the public sphere like an anaesthetic.[40] The article was accompanied by a picture of the Queen with President Obama at Buckingham Palace from his state visit several years earlier. This judiciously selected image bathed the Queen in whatever reflected sheen of 'progressivism' was still to be culled from the first Black (neo-liberal) President of the United States. A picture of the Queen standing next to, say, the King of Saudi Arabia who visited in 2007 or the Emir of Qatar from a 2010 state visit, would have stirred less pleasant connotations. Yet while a photograph of a beaming Obama next to the monarch places the latter in the positive light of establishment progressiveness, it also helped the article make a more subtle argument that the Queen's hereditary and unelected position – the embodiment of an anti-democratic ethos – was a great boon because it ensured 'continuity'. While prime ministers come and go, the Queen's undemocratic position as head of state, her insulation from public accountability, is re-framed as that necessary link to the past that allows us to make sense of where we have come from and the endurance of 'British values' (which turn out to be highly selective aristocratic ones, such as inherited service to the State). The Queen floats above mere party politics just as she transcends its humdrum temporality of ever changing faces subject to such quotidian pressures as democratic elections. Her permanent occupation of the role is celebrated by the writer as aligned with the trend towards living longer and a rebuff to the 'cult of youth' that dominates contemporary politics. It is a masterpiece of rhetorical opportunism.

Continuity, however, is combined with a pragmatic adaptive capacity that is central to conservative political culture. 'Conservative by temperament, she is no reactionary. She understands and welcomes change for which society is ready' argues d' Ancona. Of course within this conception it is conservatism that decides what change society is ready for. Nevertheless, that conservatism does have a 'liberal' wing open to selectively embracing progressive change does mark an important cultural fissure between traditional conservatism (here framed as reactionary) and a 'liberal' conservatism of the kind championed by the *Evening Standard* under the ownership of the Anglophile Russian millionaires Alexander and Evgeny Lebedev. This liberal conservatism (which *émigrés* from more repressive conservative nations have often been attracted to) is the product of a long shuttling of ideas and personnel between conservatism and liberalism. It plays the important role of detecting when things must change so that everything can stay the same.

For Tom Nairn, the Crown sits at the centre of a national identity dominated by an undemocratic State moulded around the principles of hierarchy, deference and hostility to popular sovereignty. '[O]ne [is] forced to recognise the virtually total triumph of a conservative political order' he suggests.[41] For Nairn, the fondness for 'archaic pageantry' (reproduced at university graduation ceremonies as well as within the Houses of Parliament) speaks of a deep culture of conformity, an unhealthy attraction to power and prestige and the successful imposition of an unrepresentative and undemocratic class as the vehicle of national consensus and unity.[42]

The link between culture, representation and State apparatus certainly underscores the pressing importance of the issues at stake, but once again what we have here is I think better conceptualised as an ornamental rationalisation of undemocratic structures whose origins are thoroughly capitalist and modern, rather than pre-modern. The radical Labour MP Tony Benn argued that as the absolute power of the monarch passes to the prime minister (the so-called royal prerogative), an anti-democratic 'aristocratic' culture is also evident in the dominance of the executive (PM and cabinet) over the legislature (parliament).[43] Royal prerogative gives the prime minister power on a range of issues (such as making or breaking treaties, declaring war or in one case calling off Serious Fraud Office investigations into allegations of corruption between British Aerospace and the Saudi royal family[44]) that supersede the House of Commons.[45] Coupled with a winner-takes-all voting system for parliamentary majorities, prime ministerial fiat can certainly exercise wide dictatorial powers. The abolition of the Labour-led Greater London Council and six metropolitan county councils in 1986 by the Thatcher government and the transfer of much of their powers to quangos and Whitehall was indicative of the vulnerability of democratic political rights to a centralising government with virtually unlimited power and the will to use it. The absence of a written constitution means that even the right to vote has no formal status in Britain. For this reason Benn advocated a written constitution that protected not just political rights but also, unlike the more liberal constitutional reformists such as Charter 88, social and economic rights.[46] More recently the prime minister's monarchical power was once again an issue over whether Prime Minister Theresa May had the power to trigger article 50 to begin British withdrawal from the European Union without a vote from the House of Commons, following the 'Brexit referendum' in June 2016. Theresa May indicated that she would use the Royal Prerogative to trigger Britain's exit from the EU, but that was legally and successfully challenged in the courts. The judges ruled that since such a withdrawal would require existing laws and treaties to be changed, only parliament could begin the process of re-negotiating Britain's relationship with Europe.

Like Nairn, Benn argued that the anti-democratic 'feudal values of British capitalism'[47] are responsible for its economic decline as well as the culture of deference to power. But unlike Nairn, Benn's discourse was more ambivalent as he also identifies capitalism as a major obstacle to deepening democracy. We may wonder whether the disciplines of the labour market or the education system, and the establishment in both of an economic-liberal culture of 'entrepreneurialism' are in fact more responsible for a culture of conformity and the cramping of democracy than the spectacle of the British monarchy. The idea that an 'aristocratic' culture is largely responsible for the top-down politics of a capitalist State and undemocratic executive power that seems typical across the world is the unconvincing conclusion of a position that begins by seeing conservatism as a political culture that is backward, archaic and antithetical to capitalism. Alex Callinicos summarises the essential political conclusion:

> All the major bourgeois democracies have particular features reflecting their historical development, internal social relations, and external position. What they have in common, however, is a set of structural

limits whose effect is to prevent popular participation in control of the state. These limits are both a consequence of, and help to maintain, the capitalist character of these states. The British state is in no sense exceptional in this respect. Democracy is circumscribed in Britain because the state is capitalist, not because of its peculiar, 'patrician' nature.[48]

'Backwardness' is built into capitalism, and not just British capitalism. Culturally, America's love affair with frontier culture, evident in its bizarre gun laws that are responsible for thousands of deaths annually, looks fairly 'archaic' to most other nations. Yet the frontier culture plays an important role in fostering an ideology of individualism and global expansionism and exceptionalism that is still very serviceable to American capitalism. The strange and irrational religious strands that are active within America today suggests again that this most modern of capitalist economies has profoundly archaic cultural formations within it – and necessarily so. Conservatism flourishes as a political culture not in spite of but *because* of the dynamics of capitalism. Capitalism has a split temporality, furiously modernising, transforming and liquefying its own foundations and just as desperately shoring up 'traditional' value-systems (although often 'reinvented' or re-functioned from older cultural-ideological elements) for the purposes of national identity and unity, ideological cross-class identification, hierarchical containment of democratic possibilities and so forth. The philosopher Walter Benjamin understood well that rational capitalism and irrational mythology were deeply and dialectically intertwined.[49]

The State-nation, ethnicity and class

For Tom Nairn, nationalism emerges as a response to capitalist uneven development that gives political and economic power to a minority of powers in Europe – especially Britain and France – and forces the rest to try and respond to that power on pain of being simply absorbed or permanently marginalised by it.[50] Nineteenth century nationalism in Germany, Italy, Greece, Ireland, Poland and so on involved the mobilisation of the masses or the people by the intelligentsia and the native bourgeoisie as a response to uneven development and the threat of economic and/or political power from elsewhere.

In contrast to this forced popular mobilisation against imperial power, Britain is an imperial State or 'State-nation' rather than a nation-State. A

State-nation is one in which one nationality or region acquires ascendancy in the late-feudal period and through the machinery of the absolutist monarchy begins absorbing the other nations surrounding it into its hegemony. In the case of the United Kingdom, the State subordinates a number of nations to itself (England, the 'home nation', Ireland, Wales and Scotland) before embarking on an imperial projection of power that helps cement the subaltern nations within itself (in the case of Scotland and Wales, but not of course Ireland, which largely viewed itself as the victim of colonialism rather than a coercively arranged but beneficial partnership in colonialism). To keep Wales and Scotland integrated into a hegemonic project led by England, meant that these nations could not be openly subordinated to *English* rule, but instead all nations had to be component parts of some entity larger than a mere English nationalism. That larger more capacious entity was Britain. This means that Britishness is constructed around a State rather than a particular people. For which people could that be in the British case? In addition, this State is composed of a number of fairly hierarchical, unaccountable and undemocratic elite institutions (Parliament, House of Lords, the monarchy, the army, the Church, the BBC, etc.).[51] In the State-nation it is the State that appears as sovereign rather than the people. The nation or nations are subordinated to the centralised and undemocratic supra-national State that was forged through military conquest and buttressed by economic and military power projections abroad. This was not a State that emerges from the struggles of the people (e.g. wars of liberation) but a State where the dynamic is almost entirely the other way round. The State was forged from wars of conquest, binding its people into a deeply conservative narrative. The romanticism which Nairn suggests is so important to the formation of national identity, in the British case, revolves around a deep mysticism invested in the elite institutions of the State and the elite, narrow (and White) civil society of rural England.

The sleight of hand was that, while apparently transcending any one national identity, Britishness was, as everyone knew, overwhelmingly the product of, and culturally dominated by, the English[52] (but the 'English' under the hegemony of the ruling hegemonic class bloc). This has become increasingly felt in Scotland and to a lesser extent Wales in the contemporary context.[53] For Tom Nairn, the nationalisms on the Celtic fringe of the British State, could do a better job at modernising their capitalist economies than the 'hopeless anachronism' that is the British State, which is why he looked forward, in the 1970s, to the 'break-up' of Britain, which now seems not only plausible, but likely on current trends, at some point in the near future.[54]

National discontent with the reactionary romanticism of Britishness also had a left-wing socialist manifestation against the ruling hegemonic bloc. Veteran socialist Labour MP Tony Benn argued that England was just as much a colony of the British State as Wales and Scotland[55] and it is a theme that has been popularised by the singer/songwriter Billy Bragg. Here Benn alluded to a submerged alternative popular history of struggle for democracy against many of the institutions of the British State which conservatism had made its own. This is the history excavated by communist historians such as E.P. Thompson, Raphael Samuel and the History Workshop movement or articulated in more popular forums by radical heritage museums such as the People's History Museum in Manchester or the people's social history recounted at the Beamish open-air museum in Durham.

In the conservative conception of national identity, the many differences that characterise the nation – whether differences merely in terms of the sheer diversity of people in what Defoe called 'the mongrel race' – or differences in terms of antagonistic social interests – are subsumed into a mythological and seamless class unity and ethnic purity. Given that nation building was driven by the dominant classes and that this economic elite are also the least culturally heterogeneous strata in society, it is hardly surprising that national identities are typically defined in terms of a mono-ethnic group. This dominant class tendency towards ethnic homogenisation plays an important role in helping to form hegemonic cross-class identification based on cultural similarity, often motivated by fermenting fears and anxieties around cultural or national differences. Aside from this political role of ethnic unity and purity, homogenisation is reinforced by the modern characteristics of nation building which capital accumulation requires. These typically involve the formation of a single national language, single currency, common legal system, clear territorial boundary formation over which the State exercises legitimate power and a common culture, all of which provides the predictability and level of standardisation that facilitates capital accumulation within the national territory. Such material processes no doubt facilitate the popularity of the conservative version of national identity, with its strong impermeable boundary concept of the nation, which both resists difference and potential sources of change from the outside.

From one perspective then, it is easy to see Britishness as dominated by a conservative political culture that has control of the coercive and ritualistic-ideological State apparatuses and which is tacitly encoded as ethnically 'White' (whiteness here is a construct, it did not for centuries in this Anglo definition include the Irish, for example, as full 'White' citizens or indeed the English working class).[56] However, the ambivalence of hegemony, like empires, is that as it extends itself, it risks overextending itself in the field of signification as it has to find some place within it for the very heterogeneity of the identities it simultaneously embraces and denies. A number of recent liberal theorists have contested the idea of a conservative closure on British identity and have worked to open up the concept of identity as having a more permeable border. These theorists suggest that the very supra-national and even imperial basis of Britishness helped uncouple it from a mono-ethnic self-definition.

For Robert Young, the colonialising and imperial projection of Englishness into Britishness and Britishness into empire (including Australia, New Zealand, Canada as well as the Black and Asian territories which Britain conquered), actually lays the basis for a discursive proliferation of Englishness under the banner of a multi-ethnic Britishness that is global and without firm borders.[57] Following this idea, Kenny suggests that Britishness can be seen as 'a more capacious and civic form of nationality which extended beyond the core traditions and cultural assumptions of any single nation.'[58] Krishnan Kumar picks up on this idea to suggest that Englishness need not be embarrassed by its domination of Britishness, since it is in any case a far more inclusive and cosmopolitian identity than is often realised. He defines 'nationalism' as the 'assertion of separateness and the search for an independent political roof.'[59] Kumar argues that 'English nationalism is the dog that did not bark'[60] since it was happy to accommodate itself to a supra-national identity. All this is not far from the establishment position that Britishness is above nationalism, and that other nations who are obsessed by it signal their smaller parochial mentality.[61] British aloofness, disdain for nationalism, its patrician confidence that it is not itself a kind of nationalism, is the sign of the imperial victor over other nations. But Britishness has felt compelled to speak the language of nationalism itself. The assertion of a *mono-ethnic* separateness in the post-Second World War period, following mass inward migration from the former colonies, and/or the search for political independence in the recent history vis-à-vis the European Union, can hardly be discounted as minor features of a certain version of English and/or British nationalism. There is the risk of complacency in these liberal re-readings of Britishness as a civic rather than ethnic identity because these positions tend to uncouple the redefinition of this Britishness which its imperial entanglements have wrought, from the real struggles of political cultures that achieved those re-definitions.

Formally, of course, Britishness is a civic form of identity, not ethnic, precisely because of its supra-national institutional basis. Historically the Labour Party has tended to emphasise this non-ethnic civic definition of Britishness grounded in law. Citizenship allowed not only the easy inclusion of the Celtic nations into Britishness but it was also the basis for that multicultural citizenship offered to the Commonwealth countries after the 1948 British Nationality Act paved the way for mass migration to make up for the shortfall in domestic labour power. This inclusiveness, however, existed formally and legally, but it came up against a mono-ethnic definition of Britishness that was strongly Anglo-centric and which fed into racism and at the extremes, fascism. Conservative political culture usually finds that the State and its mono-ethnic culture reinforce one another. Yet as British Labourism forced its way into the life of the State as a legitimate player and occasional occupier of government power, this was not always the case. The 1948 British Nationality Act is an example where the inclusiveness latent within the concept of Britishness could be activated by an alternative political culture. In cases where civic identity and law are turned against conservative culture, conservatism can appeal instead to the field of culture and its version of a mono-ethnic civil society as the true repository of national identity. Here conservatism often recoils from anything which suggests that the State is involved in the *making* of culture in the here and now (a reflex that conveniently steels it against contemporary democratic change). The idea that cultural identity can be produced in part by laws entitling citizenship is anathema to a political culture that prefers to think of institutions disappearing into the mists of time. This is one reason why the European Union is particularly unappealing to conservatism; it is simply too recent, too new, too obviously made and assembled, the traces of its history have not yet had the opportunity to fade into legend and myth. To conservatism, the European Union still looks like a *bureaucracy*, whereas to conservatism, British State bureaucracy – at least the parts which it most favours (the coercive and ritualistic-ideological departments) – has the austere face of moral discipline or the colour of pomp and pageantry (reactionary romanticism). Similarly, racists such as Conservative MP Enoch Powell argued from the 1960s onwards, that merely legal, formal citizenship awarded to Black and Asian citizens from the former colonies did not constitute *real* belonging, since it was *culture* that truly made formal entitlements substantive identities.[62]

This was half right; Powell was just one-eyed on the model of culture he thought *must* underpin Britishness. The 1948 British Nationality Act was the juridical moment of the State (the classic liberal moment) which made a multicultural Britishness possible. But as Stuart Hall noted, the notion of a pure civic national State that is cultureless, is a fantasy of liberal universalism. 'Every civic nationalism I know requires belongingness on the part of its citizens; it requires identification … It has to be embedded … in an imagined community.'[63] We know too from Gramsci that for the State to rule by consent, as well as the force of juridical power, it must be combined with the formation of consent on the terrain of civil society (the 'private fabric' of the State). And it was indeed on the terrain of culture in civil society that Powell's mono-cultural version of national identity was challenged and a new multicultural identity became substantively lived and accepted. This, however, was not built into the 'idea' or high institutions of the British State. History was made from below and it required anti-racist and anti-fascist action in which community groups, the broader British labour movement and the extra-parliamentary Left combined, played key roles. Here was Gramsci's 'private fabric' of the State, making formal citizenship real and substantive and often in opposition to some of the public institutions of the State. For the British Asians and anti-fascists who defended the Southall community in 1979 against the National Front and the police in a major confrontation, English nationalism certainly *was* a dog that both barked and bit.

Yet not much more than a decade later, the idea that one could be Black and British, or Asian and British, had very largely been won. In the early 1980s, one could still hear the BBC entertaining arguments about possible voluntary repatriation of Black and British citizens back to the Commonwealth countries, while this argument was even more common and forcefully articulated within the right-wing press.[64] A decade later this argument could no longer be voiced within respectable political and media circles. A major contradiction for Thatcherism was between its meritocratic capitalism (regardless of ethnicity or background) and internationalist commitment to capitalism (welcoming Japanese capital to invest for example) versus its regressive conservative, implicitly White and straight nationalism. This contradiction was wonderfully explored by Hanif Kureishi and Stephen Frears in their landmark film *My Beautiful Laundrette* (1985) but also more recently in Shane Meadows' reflections on Thatcherism in *This Is England* (2007). The latter film is very much about how loss and absence can be mobilised according to different imagined communities, as represented by Woody's version of the skinhead gang that is tolerant and inclusive against Combo's version, which is aggressively nationalistic and racist. Combo skilfully dislodges Woody's leadership of the group using his masculinity, threatening presence, cajoling and appeals to a regressive version of 'England' that is closely affiliated to the fascistic National Front. Both Woody and Combo invest symbolic significance in the presence of young Sean in the group: for Woody as a sign of the group's ability to provide him with friends and a sense of genuine comradeship, for Combo, as a sign of his ability to manipulate Sean's sense of loss (his father died in the Falklands War) for his own political purposes. Played out against archive footage of the Falklands War, this is clearly at one level an allegory of Thatcherism and how it offered the 'losers' in her two-nations strategy the compensation of a regressive cultural identity. Made in 2006 however, *This Is England* was also speaking to its own contemporary moment, as this strand of regressive conservatism was once again flourishing and about to achieve a further boost in the context of the global capitalist crash in 2008.

Stuart Hall, writing in 1987, rightly cautioned against thinking that the contradictions of Thatcherism would necessarily unravel it:

> We are all perplexed by the *contradictory* nature of Thatcherism. In our intellectual way, we think that the world will collapse as the result of a logical contradiction: this is the illusion of the intellectual – that ideology must be coherent, every bit of it fitting together, like a philosophical investigation. When in fact, the whole purpose of what Gramsci called an organic (i.e., historically-effective) ideology is that it articulates into a configuration, different subjects, different identities, different projects, different aspirations. It does not reflect, it *constructs* a 'unity' out of difference.[65]

This is an important corrective and Hall is right that a politically effective project can weld different projects, constituencies and identities together despite tensions. As Robert Eccleshall noted: 'conservatism has always consisted of diverse strands whose consistency, either internally or in relation to one another, does not necessarily match standards of intellectual rigour.'[66] Yet at the same time, when the contradictions are or become very fundamental, they can *over time* contribute to the exhaustion of a political project, to the fraying of the unity of different projects and the reception of people to new emergent political projects. This is what happened in the case of Thatcherism's ethnic exclusivity and nationalism in a world of global capitalism. By the late 1990s, the Conservative Party *leadership* had officially disavowed Thatcherism's model of national identity at the social and cultural level. As Kevin Davey remarked: 'Even the Conservatives now recognise that the idea of a singular and unchanging heritage is untenable and ethnocentric, and, perhaps more importantly, a barrier to a growing and differentiated Black and Asian vote'.[67]

This remarkable shift, however, was not just the victory of the Left, the labour movement and Black and Asian communities in particular. What made this victory potentially more ambiguous than it might have been is that it was made not just from 'below' as it were, but from 'above' as well. But this 'above' was less the British State – for reasons that we have seen – than it was the rapid changes in global capitalism in which international flows of finance, culture and people made the discourse of a defensive national identity seem increasingly problematic and un-related to empirical experience.[68] While on the one hand this exposed the growing contradiction between global capitalism and its historic *national* organisational base, it also opened up the prospect of uncoupling the question of cultural difference from class and re-articulating cultural difference to a new, apparently progressive, because cosmopolitan, form of capitalism, which social liberalism took advantage of. From New Labour to cultural studies, multicultural ethnicity was disarticulated from class relations. This uncoupling of Black, Asian and Minority Ethnic (BAME) groups from class spoke little to the empirical evidence that class inequality and race discrimination remain significantly interconnected. Unemployment for example remains significantly higher for Black African, Black Caribbean, Pakistani and Bangladeshi groups than for White people.[69] The same groups are far more likely to live in low-income households than White people,[70] and unsurprisingly are far more likely to be in poverty than White people.[71] Racial discrimination significantly inflects class, and conversely, the working or the unemployed or underemployed working class remain ethnically heterogeneous (of course this is inflected again by the uneven geographical spread of ethnic minorities in the UK). Yet as *multicultural ethnicity* was uncoupled from the working class in the dominant discourses of the day, so both liberal and conservative political cultures worked hard to re-articulate the working class to a *mono-majority ethnicity*, namely *whiteness*.[72] On the right of the Conservative Party conservatism mobilised whiteness around a resentful nationalism as part of its anti-European Union project and desire for a different State policy agenda that encompassed not only immigration but a new political economy based on a fantasy that Britain could return to its nineteenth century identity as a global trading power. A new party organisation also emerged on the flanks of the Conservative Party to press this case more vigorously: the United Kingdom Independence Party (UKIP). Yet even UKIP had to at least officially insist that its hostility to immigration was not focused on the British citizens whose parents had arrived from the Commonwealth countries after the Second World War, but on the unregulated inward flow of immigration from within the European Union and this meant that the discourse even attracted some Black and Asian support. Yet when the Black comedian Lenny Henry suggested that there should be more Black and ethnic minority people in the creative industries, a UKIP council candidate tweeted that Henry should emigrate to a 'black country'.[73] This was only one of numerous examples where UKIP's official position was either not understood by its membership and representatives, or, its official position was understood only too well as a necessary fiction until such a time as its real instincts on race and national identity could become 'acceptable' again.

There was a potentially overlapping Labour Party version of this conservatism but it was not articulated against the EU project, but instead its mediation through a different party-political vehicle gave it a different set of concerns. This was the so-called 'Blue-Labour' project, in which New Labour belatedly tried to reconnect with the working class it had abandoned but only on the basis that the working class was essentially culturally (and politically) conservative and so had to be appealed to in terms not a million miles from traditional conservative constructions of the working class (namely submerging class difference and antagonism into the conservative mythology of national unity and cultural homogeneity). If conservatism crossed party lines in this period, liberalism's key party vehicle between the mid-1990s until the 2010 General Election was New Labour. Liberalism mobilised negatively around the image of the resentful ethnic majority working class as the basis for a liberal State policy that defended 'openness', 'tolerance' and 'internationalism' (i.e. global capitalism with its need for cheap immigrant labour) against the ignorance and racism which apparently characterised (for the liberals) the White working class. With both conservatism and social liberalism aligned to economic liberalism, there is little prospect of a permanent defeat of conservatism's more regressive nationalist and racist sentiments, but nor is there any prospect of social liberalism developing sufficient self-reflexivity to recognise economic liberalism as the engine of ill-liberalism that it is.

5

The oscillations of liberalism

Introduction

The changing relationships of liberalism to conservatism, to economic liberalism and to the working classes have been indicative of the role liberalism has played in facilitating particular outcomes in terms of those coalitions of classes whose relationships and 'terms of settlement' set the agenda for an epoch. Gramsci called such settlements 'historic blocs'. Liberalism has been central to their formation while its critique of conservatism has allowed this political culture to pose as a more progressive force than its hegemonic role within these blocs suggests that it is. We can identify three historic blocs that have shaped politics in Britain in the last two hundred years or so. The first represented an alliance which had crystallised by the early nineteenth century between the conservative landed aristocracy (represented politically by the Tories) and the slightly more liberal sections of the gentry, the commercial, mercantile and banking groups (represented politically by the Whigs, who later transformed into the Liberal Party). By the 1830s, industrial capital was sufficiently powerful to help broaden the franchise to include the new urban bourgeoisie and their growing professional middle-class support base.[1] The decomposition of this historic bloc took a lifetime (between the late nineteenth century and the 1930s and 1940s), such is the sometimes glacial rate at which change in a society fiercely resistant to progressive change takes place. The driving force of this decomposition was undoubtedly a one hundred year or more struggle by the newly formed industrial working classes (between the 1830s and the 1940s) to change the terms of their position within British society. This change required a transformation in the composite national identity and national cultures, a transformation which culminated in the 1930s and

1940s with a new acceptance by the dominant classes of the centrality and importance of the working class to British society. This was a struggle of enormous sacrifices, against a repressive State–capital nexus that was saturated in anti-working-class sentiments and prejudices. The working classes had to force their way into the political life of the country, demanding social and economic rights that broke up the old historic bloc and produced a new one and with it a new component part of the national identity. The oscillation and transformation of liberalism in the decay of one historic bloc and the formation of a new one, was critical. Liberalism moved away from its initial identification with economic liberalism (the free market as the solution to all social and economic ills) in which it posed itself as a 'radical' reforming politics in opposition to a conservative dominated State that was seen as a threat to individual liberty. Instead the free market itself became identified as a source of social problems and the State came to be seen as the necessary body that could transcend piecemeal reforms and establish the nation-wide changes required for society at large. Social liberalism uncoupled itself from economic liberalism, entered an informal alliance with the labour movement and again as such, but on different terms, posed itself once more as a 'radical' reforming political culture.

The motive force for this change came from without as a response to the organised working class and the political competition for the working class vote which the gradual extension of the franchise required in the last quarter of the nineteenth century. Liberalism though was to provide the philosophical and policy bridge between the working classes and the owning classes that would eventually establish the terms of the second historic bloc around social democracy. While the political struggle was the primary determinant in shaping this transformation of liberalism, there was a cultural dimension that helped facilitate this new set of class alliances. That cultural dimension can be located around the cluster of images, values, sense of purpose and progress invested in 'the industrial' by both liberalism and Labourism from the mid-nineteenth century. In this chapter I develop the argument that the cultural fissure between conservatism and liberalism on the question of industry became significant precisely because it provided a resource for a new set of class alliances. This was the main effect of conservatism's relative indifference to an industrial culture. As we saw in Chapter 3, British capitalism was more powerfully determined by the economic groove which its own historical development had established (the priority of commerce and finance within an imperial framework) than by any cultural bias against industry (although that certainly existed). The normative investments of writers such as Anderson, Nairn and Weiner in a thwarted industrial development have paradoxically led to a downplaying of the extent to which liberalism and industrialism have *actually* been present within the dominant hegemonic blocs that have shaped British national identities. Economic historians such as Cain and Hopkins, and Rubinstein have alternatively not presupposed a normative framework in favour of industrialism and pointed to the empirical evidence that commerce and finance were always the dominant partners in the British economy. The argument that industrialism played a smaller role in the British economy than commerce and finance and that that outcome was either a thwarting of the proper development path of British capitalism (Anderson, Nairn, Weiner) or was in line with the prior groove of development (Rubinstein, Cain and Hopkins) does threaten to marginalise the important *political* and *cultural* role industrialism nevertheless played despite its relatively smaller weight as a capital formation.

The cultural fissure within the hegemonic bloc between conservatism and liberalism played its part in helping to peel liberalism away from conservatism and position it closer to the rising labour movement. The resulting class alliance around a new political culture (social democracy) was certainly efficacious socially, politically and even economically (at the level of some modest redistribution of wealth although not in terms of changing British capital's underlying investment priorities). Yet with the decomposition of the social-democratic bloc in the 1970s and 1980s, social liberalism re-converges with economic liberalism once more. The cultural and industrial imaginary that underpinned social democracy is reworked into a more entrepreneurial, commercial and service sector direction with the cultural industries playing a significant part of the new liberal imaginary. This lent a generative dynamism to capitalism belied by its narrowing social base and expanding crisis tendencies. This chapter will chart liberalism's oscillations in a series of snapshots.

Classical liberalism and the working-class public sphere

Liberalism began life as the philosophical expression of the new dynamic capitalist mode of production that had established itself by the eighteenth century. Political economy was its science. For Adam Smith, if the pursuit of individual interests were rational then why would such pursuits not add up to a rational and beneficial outcome for all of society? The 'hidden hand' of the market brings about such positive social outcomes 'unconsciously' even more effectively than when people act with the express and conscious intention of benefitting society and the common good rather than the self. Smith was a complex figure but he was certainly the founding philosophical thinker for a very contemporary cynicism towards the State as a means of addressing systematic problems. Bentham, in the same vein, declared that the motto of government should amount to being quiet since individuals, not government, know their interests best. Ricardo at least noted that when the market price for labour falls beneath the value it needs in wages to survive, great hardship ensues. Yet human misery could not trump the rational laws of the market. 'Like all other contracts', he wrote, 'wages should be left to the fair and free competition of the market and should never be controlled by the interference of the legislature.' Ricardo recommended that what the poor needed was to learn 'the value of independence, by teaching them that they must look not to systematic or casual charity but to their own exertions for support, that prudence and forethought are neither unnecessary nor unprofitable virtues.'[2]

In its fierce defence of private property and its ignorance of the violence of asymmetrical economic power and wealth, liberalism overlapped significantly with conservatism's investment in the capitalist social order. Yet conservatism, as we have seen, has always maintained a strong belief that the market must be embedded in relations of social hierarchy, in relations of State power (both repressive and ritualistic-ideological) and in the small-scale (rural) civic community, to offset the potentially disintegrative consequences of the 'free market'. Liberalism on the other hand leaned more towards the rational autonomy of the individual as its moral compass and this necessarily brought it into a degree of political and cultural conflict with conservatism. Individual autonomy was the basis for its Enlightenment values (against conservatism's reactionary romanticism) and its sporadic agenda to reform the State which conservatism saw as the bedrock of its powerbase. In its classical phase, before its growing disenchantment with the failures of the market, liberalism believed, in a way that conservatism could not, that the pursuit of private interests would add up to harmonious social outcomes because the social was no more than an agglomeration of individual interests. With its Enlightenment rationalism, liberalism invested heavily in the educative experience of the market economy to teach people the

Ricardian virtues of economic rationalism, responsibility and civilised obedience to the laws of contract. It also invested in formal education as a means of socialisation that was more rational than the conservative predilection for relying on State power and the mysticism of State institutions.[3] As part of the repertoire of political management it was less ready, at least at a rhetorical level, to reach for the sword as a means of maintaining oligarchical rule. Shortly after the Peterloo Massacre in 1819, Earl Grey made a speech to the House of Lords noting that 'the employment of force increased discontents: these would demand the exercise of new powers, till by degrees they would depart from all the principles of the constitution.'[4] As Thomas Macauley warned in 1831 in the debates running up to the Great Reform Bill that would widen the electoral franchise to include industrial capital and a wider pool of the middle class: 'Reform that you may preserve'[5] and this may be taken as liberalism's core dictum.

Yet when it came to the crunch, defending class interests often trumped abstract appeals to social and political reform or individual autonomy. Hence the line separating the Tories from the 'liberal' Whigs in the early nineteenth-century parliament was often difficult to discern in actual policy terms. Despite their competing cultural and political orientations, (Bentham spoke of the 'sinister influence' of the aristocracy)[6] conservatism and liberalism were the differentiated faces of an integrated post-Civil-War power bloc. And despite their dominance in matters of the economy, classical liberalism was something of a junior partner in terms of political culture. This has puzzled historians such as Anderson and Nairn who wondered why the most advanced capitalist economy, had a political culture less liberal than their normative model, France, after the 1789 Revolution. Yet this is no paradox. Precisely *because* England was at the cutting edge of capitalist change, it needed a hybrid political culture more calibrated and cautious than unadulterated liberalism, which had, in matters of governance, to accept its place within the division of labour in the management of this still novel form of society. As Robert Eccleshall puts it:

In order to quell any unruly conduct flowing from the inequalities produced by the market, economically successful groups needed access to an adequate power structure. Yet, having made an absolute of private judgement in order to erode aristocratic privilege, the liberal doctrine was not geared to legitimating the coercion required for political actors to exercise tutelary supervision of the subordinate class. This was why propertied groups were so quick to elaborate a conservative version of the capitalist market.[7]

The economic basis of liberalism in individual autonomy had to be folded into a more Burkean image of natural hierarchy, obedience to the existing social structure and its laws, the inevitability of inequality of outcomes sanctioned by the Divine and all presided over in the here and now by the wise judgement and statecraft of those elites who had proved by their success (or the success they had been born into) to be the superiors of the common unruly masses who lacked the refinement needed to appreciate the virtues of private property.[8] 'We know', wrote Burke confidently in the face of the French Revolution, and its Third Estate, with its unseemly mix of common middle-class professionals,

> that the British House of Commons, without shutting its doors to any merit in any class, is, by the sure operation of adequate causes, filled with everything illustrious in rank, in descent, in hereditary and in acquired opulence, in cultivated talents, in military, civil, naval, and politic distinction that the country can afford.[9]

The division and convergence between conservatism and liberalism on the 'sure operation of adequate causes' involved the latter tutoring the former to accept contained reform when necessary. This is nicely illustrated in their positions on the Stamp Duty for newspapers. Introduced in 1712, the tax was increased by 266 per cent between the start of the French Revolution in 1789 and 1815. The express intention was to increase the cover price in order to make newspapers unaffordable to the poor.[10] As Engels pithily observed some decades later, 'the bourgeoisie has little to hope, and much to fear, from the education of the working class.'[11] Yet the unstamped and therefore illegal press was, by the 1830s, massively popular, despite the fierce repression meted out to publishers, editors, printers and vendors. *The Poor Man's Guardian* sold between 12,000 and 15,000 copies per edition in the early 1830s although sales dropped to between 5,000 and 7,000 thereafter.[12] In London the total readership of the unstamped press is estimated at more than two million.[13]

While conservatives tended to want to rely on coercive State power to repress the radical working-class publications, this offended liberalism's sense in the rational autonomy of the individual and the capacity of the market and civil society organs such as education and the media, to teach people how to be good (capitalistic) citizens. Liberalism was less supportive of the Stamp Duty, which in any case by the 1830s, clearly was not working, and was often critical of it (without rushing to abolish it). The liberals hoped that if the tax was reduced and then abolished, the market would be taken up by a profusion of capitalist publications that would wean the working classes away from the dangerous politics they were currently being exposed to. With a high Stamp Duty in place, only the illegal and therefore usually radical press had access to working-class readers. The 'respectable' middle-class press was out of their price range. Once again this nicely encapsulates liberalism's belief that the rationality of the market as an economic mechanism fitted snugly with ideological preferences congruent with private ownership of the means of production. The hesitancy with which they pursued the abolition of the Stamp Duty (finally achieved in 1855) is indicative of liberalism's internal contradictions and its need to work in tandem with the conservative political culture (and vice versa). Together they offered the political repertoire within which challenges to the social order could be navigated. The Stamp Duty was reduced in 1836 (a liberal measure) but this was coupled with even more repression for those who violated the law by printing without paying the tax (a conservative outcome). Thus the new Stamp Duty had the effect of making the middle-class press cheaper and the working-class press – which could not now avoid the tax – more expensive.[14] By the time the Stamp Duty was fully abolished a powerful capitalist press that could attract more advertising revenue than the radical press (why would advertisers advertise in the pages of newspapers criticising capitalism?) did in fact capture the working-class mass readership as Chartism went into decline. Press 'freedom' as James Curran notes, was no story of liberation, but the elimination of a range of voices outside the liberal–conservative consensus. An advanced capitalist media market helped eliminate a working-class public sphere just as a well-developed capitalist market for labour power helped atomise working-class consciousness and encourage narrower 'bread and butter' economic objectives.[15]

If liberalism was an important part of the political-social power bloc, the seeds of a later transformation in its role were being laid outside liberalism. The people who owned and worked in the radical working-class press in the 1830 and 1840s, the years of Chartism's greatest influence, were either organic intellectuals from the working class or organic intellectuals from the middle class whose political outlooks and beliefs had been shaped by long involvement in working-class politics.[16] The term 'organic intellectual' is Gramsci's and, as discussed in Chapter 2, has two essential components: firstly it speaks of an organic connection between a class and its intellectuals, a deep bond of interest and familiarity. Secondly, and just as importantly, the organic intellectual synthesises economic interests with broader moral-political analysis of the social order, touching on every and any issue of the day and making it explicable from the perspective of a coherent worldview or philosophy. The organic intellectual is an organiser of opinion and action, which means not only that individuals are organic intellectuals but so too are the organs of their coming together, such as in the form of civic bodies, movements, parties and media.

The working-class radical press met all the cultural rights which Graham Murdock identifies as essential for meaningful participation in the political debates that shape policymaking that in turn affect people's lives and opportunities. Murdock identifies four key communication rights. The first is access to information about the consequential activities of powerful political and economic actors. However, information alone is not enough to participate autonomously in the active formation of political cultures. People also need 'knowledge rights', which refers to the explanatory frameworks available to interpret the factual information that is put into the public sphere. Different frameworks will – within limits – shape that information in different ways, pronounce different diagnoses of the problems the empirical facts allude to, and offer different possible solutions. Therefore it is important that citizens have access to a wide range of competing and even conflicting frameworks for making sense of the world. The third communication right is the right of representation – which refers to the normative goal of having the experiences, lives, perspectives and values of different social groups recognised as legitimate subjects of media attention and debate. Finally, the right to participate in and be a producer of media representations, and not just a consumer of representations produced by other social groups, is also an important enabler in establishing and exercising citizenship.[17]

The radical press helped construct a nascent genuine working-class public sphere according to these principles and one that had a national reach. The *Northern Star* in particular conceived itself as a *national* paper and was the focal point for the working-class radical reform movement, Chartism. 'The *Star* was the most important agency for the integration and transformation of disparate local radical agitation and organisation into the national Chartist movement'.[18]

The paper brought a national context to local struggles and made struggles and leaders in the localities national figures within the working-class movement. As such, the *Star* and other papers like it played a crucial role in developing the cultural–political level of working-class consciousness and its efficacy as a political force. The radical press of the 1830s and 1840s marked a significant development in the critical analysis of society from an earlier generation that had remained firmly within the terms of a liberal critique of the aristocracy and the corruption of the oligarchical State.[19] By the 1830s, the more radical parts of the working-class press could see clearly that *neither* the 'landlords' *nor* the 'cotton lords' represented the interests of their readers. Although Anderson thought that the English working class were hamstrung in this period because socialism was hardly available to them as a 'structured ideology',[20] the radical press displays a critique of the social order that laid the foundations for the subsequent more systematic critique developed by Engels and Marx in the subsequent decades.

An article in *The Poor Man's Guardian* from 1832 outlines a labour theory of value in moral and social justice terms. It is laced throughout with a religious imagery that articulates a powerful denunciation of the social evils of capitalism, 'far worse than Egyptian bondage'. Its philosophy of free trade which sacrifices children to profit is a 'pestilential and blasting influence'. The 'Manufacturing System' is 'accursed' for the benefits it brings to the capitalist and the barbarism it brings to labour. Turning liberal philosophy on its head, the author declares their agreement that property ought to be protected, only to point out that: 'It has never been protected. Labour is the foundation – the only foundation of all human property. How then can property be secure – how ought it to be secure – while its very foundation is left unprotected …?'[21] Taking a swipe at the skewed priorities of the closeted capitalist public sphere that excludes working people, the author notes that the dominant classes 'theorise on subjects that none are interested in but themselves'. Perhaps this sounds familiar?

Both wings of the capitalist class sought to enlist the support of the working classes in their conflict over the corn tariffs. These were charges added to imported corn designed to artificially inflate the price so as to protect the domestic landlords from foreign competition. While this suited the capitalist farmers and their aristocratic landlords, the 'cotton lords' thought it impacted on their ability to compete in international markets because they had to pay wages to their workers that could cover the inflated cost of this basic staple food. The industrial capitalists raised the flag of liberal free trade against the protectionism of the aristocracy and their capitalist tenants. In their petition to the House of Commons drawn up by cotton manufacturer Richard Cobden, the Manchester Chamber of Commerce tried to raise the spectre of the workers turning against the establishment because of the Corn Laws:

> The continuance of the loyal attachment of the people to the established institutions of the country can never be permanently secured on any other grounds than those of universal justice. Holding one of these eternal principles to be the unalienable right of every man, freely to exchange the results of his labour for the productions of other people, and maintaining the practice of protecting one part of the community at the expense of all other classes, to be unsound and unjustifiable, your petitioners earnestly implore your honourable house to repeal all laws relating to the importation of foreign corn … and to carry out to the fullest extent, both as it affects agriculture and manufactures, the true and peaceful principles of free trade, by removing all existing obstacles to the unrestricted employment of industry and capital.[22]

The Northern Star was unmoved, however, by the liberals' appeal that the working classes join the Anti-Corn Law League set up by Cobden and John Bright in 1838. The liberals they declared were 'cheap-bread brawlers and cheap-labour seekers'. Yet the paper did not merely hurl insults but displayed an acute historical perspective by which to relativise the philosophical principles of the free-traders. Pointing to the historical specificity and relative novelty of the principles underlying classical political economy was of course to be a key feature of Marx's critique. The *Northern Star* article refers to an Act of Parliament passed in the reign of Henry VII which obliged landowners to keep as much land in cultivation (and not let it go out to pasture) as was required to keep the local peasants in 'wholesome and necessary employment'. Thus the Act recognised that those who had nothing but their labour to sell, were 'entitled to employment from those who monopolise the property and capital of the country.' This social obligation from the past is contrasted with the current situation where the 'millowners' throw labour out of work and deny the workers the only means they have of feeding themselves and their families. Application of the 'wholesome principle' found in past law to the contemporary situation would lead to the 'practical abolition of the infernal New Poor Law'. In attacking the liberals' overtures to the working classes, the paper was not naïve enough to believe that the contemporary capitalist landlords would be 'any more willing than the cottonlords' to concede the principle that was once a part of the English constitution. The article describes both sides in terms that Marx would later use, as 'Vampires' feeding off the labour of the working classes. 'In order to attain this position [labour rights] the people must fight their own battle against both – they must accomplish their own measures – they must assert their own rights – and, above all, and before all, the right of being represented.'[23] While political representation was rightly seen as crucial, throughout this period, both rulers and ruled knew well enough that change might come or have to come through some revolutionary convulsion as well as political reform.

None of this is to say that there were no traces of liberal philosophy within working-class political culture of this time. In fact the radical press did draw on liberalism's natural rights theory and even utilitarianism, an especially meagre philosophical justification of economic liberalism that emphasised happiness in terms of self-interest and hard work rather than communal solidarity and collective culture. Yet in drawing on these philosophical resources and in combining them with an emergent socialism, liberalism itself was transformed.[24] Natural rights theory was used to make the argument that the land ought to be nationalised, freeing it from the sectional interests of capital, monarchy and church and laying the basis for the kind of harmony for which nature itself was seen as the model. Utilitarianism's argument that happiness and the avoidance of pain should guide normative principles was used to make the argument that the extension of the vote to the working classes and therefore political representation was essential for improving their appalling condition. Hence 'there was an almost definitional relationship in numerous working-class publications between the greatest happiness for the greatest numbers and manhood suffrage.'[25]

What this appropriation and reworking of liberalism showed was not that the working class remained trapped within classical liberalism but that they were working with a hybrid mix of intellectual resources and weaving them into a distinct coherent perspective that spoke to the needs of their class. If 'socialism' as a fully structured philosophy had yet to emerge, they were laying the essential foundations for it. It also showed, however, that liberalism could be more radical than it was prepared to be if its principles were transferred to a different class base exercising a counter-hegemonic politics. What the working class achieved by re-functioning liberalism within an emergent socialist perspective, liberalism itself would subsequently discover over the next few decades as its class base did indeed shift but largely onto the heterogeneous and expanding *middle-class* professions while industrial capital, as represented by the Manchester Chamber of Commerce, for example, shifted towards conservatism. But in the 1830s and 1840s, there was no basis for a dialogue between the working class and classical liberalism. The latter's unquestioned commitment to the freedom of those who own productive forces to dispose of it as they wished within a system of free competition, made an alliance between the liberals and the working class impossible, even as the latter reworked classical liberalism into their own distinct political discourse. Industrialism, however, would provide one resource that would help mediate a future convergence between a more radical liberalism and a more tamed socialism prepared to work within the constitutional status quo.

Modernity and the concept of service

As an engineer who designed railways, bridges and steamships, Isambard Kingdom Brunel (1806–1859) was instrumental in developing the means of circulating goods and people. He was in the tradition of James Brindley (1716–1772) who built canals, John McAdam (1756–1836) who developed road construction, and George Stephenson (1781–1848), who built locomotives and railways. In contrast to the question of circulation, the high point of a fusion between science and the factory – the point of production – was of course James Watt's (1736–1819) steam-driven engine that mechanised and amplified productive power in Matthew Boulton's (1728–1809) factories. But thereafter we may say that British capital investment was more orientated towards the circulation of goods than research and development in productive technologies. Of course circulation was crucially important in order to profit from the British Empire and its trading connections. Yet it may be that Brunel's engineering feats in the field of circulation can stand as a symbol for a tilt towards circulation that came at the expense of research and development in production and higher productivity. This contradiction between circulation and production within British capital made it

vulnerable to its competitors. By comparison the German engineers of
the late nineteenth and early twentieth century were tightly integrated
into manufacturing and were often industrialists as well as engineers,
such as Ferdinand von Zeppelin, Gottlieb Daimler, Rudolf Diesel and
Karl Benz. They helped lay the basis for the productivity gains that began
to erode even the colossal advantages that the empire gave to Britain in
terms of protected markets and trade networks.

Yet even with the centre of gravity of British engineering moving
towards circulation, we can discern the potential of an industrial and
machine culture to develop something of a fissure with the conservative
imperial culture within which it developed. Industrial production was
inherently 'revolutionary' – constantly uprooting established social
and cultural relations and producing new relations, new habits, new
practices, new values and new products. Even with an emphasis on the
circulation of goods rather than their production, something of this
industrial ethos was necessarily part of the growing professional classes
tied to an advanced capitalist economy. This is evident in Brunel's
instructions to the captain of *The Great Eastern* steamship which he
had designed and which was built during the 1850s. It was, typically of
Brunel, a project conceived on a vast scale and at its launch was by far
the biggest ship ever built, designed to take émigrés to Australia (with a
passenger capacity of 4,000).

In his instructions to the captain, Brunel describes *The Great Eastern*
as a 'machine we are about to set afloat' and reminds him that the
financial fortunes of the investors depends on the 'skilful management'
of what is 'nominally a ship'. This management requires setting aside
'most of the habits, feelings, and sensations' which sailors would have
acquired crewing 'ordinary ships'.[26] The personal instinct and skill
which sailors take pride in to 'get out of a scrape in time' should be
subordinated to a more methodical and systematic approach that is
more suited to the power and speed which the science of locomotion
has increasingly introduced to vessels. As Brunel puts it: 'The man who
takes charge of such a machine, in which is embarked so large a capital,
must have a mind capable of setting aside, without forgetting, all his
previous experience and habits, and must be prepared to commence as
an observer of new facts, and seize rapidly the results'.[27]

The captain of the ship must thus adopt the stance of a quasi-scientist
insofar as he should observe the new 'facts' which this engineering feat
produces, and change behaviour and practice accordingly. The captain's

concern should be overseeing the 'general management of the whole system' and they should not be drawn into 'frivolous pursuits and unimportant occupations' to do with passengers and cargo. The captain is not in charge of a 'vast hotel' and should avoid 'attending to the hours and the forms of a large society'. Rather than the interpersonal social relations that a more aristocratic concept of service might have prioritised, for Brunel, the captain's main concern is with the 'perfect working of a highly methodical pre-arranged system'[28] which is in turn at the commercial service of a large mass public. Brunel it seemed did not want to be thought of as the engineering arm of an aristocratic culture.

Brunel's instructions speak of a discourse alert to how industrial machinery and techniques change the culture of work and the roles the captain and the sailors perform as they manage this vast apparatus. The concept of 'service' that underpins this discourse is very different from the one that shaped the aristocratic model of leadership. There, service is conceived largely in relation to the State where it is much easier to imagine the continuities of roles rather than emphasise ruptures with past practices, as Brunel envisages. With the State as the main terrain of aristocratic service, the values of duty, obligation, honour, self-sacrifice to the Monarch, to the Country and to the Military, were primary. The aristocratic concept of service is also based on being born to serve, on hereditary credentials rather than professional ones. The cult of the amateur has been strongly associated with aristocratic ideal of service because the amateur is not someone who has learned a profession, studied theories and wants to introduce change, but instead studied the classics at private school and knows how to value tradition rather more than scientific innovation.[29]

Brunel's discourse by contrast is all about how science and the technological changes it generates demands a professional, quasi-scientific attitude in which *The Great Eastern* is no pleasure cruiser but something like a seaborne factory. This represents a professional middle class cultural challenge to the older aristocratic ideals and a reconfiguring of the concept of service that prizes utility, efficiency, method and work. Here service is linked to the use values produced by the modern industrial age, instead of the abstract ideals of State power or the frivolous pursuits of the leisure classes (the ship is not a 'vast hotel'). The complexity and scale of modern industrial forces as well as the revolutionary changes they unleash, also puts a premium on a culture of systematic planning. To some extent this middle-class professionalisation of service in the direction of modern utility and planning represents a democratisation of the concept, relative to its aristocratic definition. It fosters an enquiring stance ready for, open to, and expecting change. Yet it is service attached to exchange value and Brunel is highly concerned that there are important capital investments at stake (as well he might be as the building of the ship was a troubled one and it never really made a profit for its owners). It would take a further shift in class values to democratise the concept of service still further, uncoupling it from profit and the class stratifications of the market and linking service to social provision based on need provided by new organs of the social State.

Brunel's discourse shows industrialism to be highly multi-accentual, to use Voloshinov's term. It can be inflected in radically different directions depending on historical conditions. In America, it would develop in the early twentieth century in the direction of the time-and-motion studies pioneered by F.W. Taylor and represent the power of capital to appropriate modernity to enhance its own power against labour. Here planning is conceived primarily at the level of the factory or industrial corporation, although this restructuring of work has broader social implications. As taken up on an industrial scale by Henry Ford, Taylorism and Fordism represented for Gramsci, 'the biggest collective effort to date to create, with unprecedented speed, and with a consciousness of purpose unmatched in history, a new type of worker and of man.'[30] In Russia and Germany and other parts of Europe after the 1917 Russian Revolution, industrial modernity was appropriated as the sign of the working masses entering history and shaping the future in a socialist direction. Typically perhaps, Britain's conception of industrial modernity and State planning was somewhere in-between these oppositions. It had neither the sense of an industrial transformation led by an ascendant capitalist class as pioneered by Henry Ford in America, nor the sense that industrial modernity released the productive forces that the working class would harness for their emancipation from capitalism. The historical moment when something like an industrial modernity came to be accepted as part of the national identity of Britain, in the 1930s and 1940s, was one where a social-democratic alternative to American capitalism and European revolutionary aspirations were seeded. A reformed liberalism met working-class aspirations for progressive change on the ground of an industrial society that accepted the necessity of some planning at the level of the social State, but with limited intervention into or coordination of private capital. In the 1830s and 1840s, there was little enthusiasm for the industrial age from the working class, so appalling had its consequences been up until that point. Yet gradual reforms led to improvements in working and living conditions that made a more positive identity between worker and industry possible in subsequent decades.

The new liberalism and industrialism

In his discussion of the new liberalism that developed in the second half of the nineteenth century, Michael Freeden prioritises the internal conceptual development of liberal thought at the expense of its wider historical conditions, including its intense dialogue and contestation with socialism in this period. 'The point to be made is not that liberalism was uninfluenced by socialist theories external to it, but that such influence was not essential to the rise of social-liberalism.'[31] For Freeden, liberalism already had within it the resources and the motivation for a conceptual morphing that dis-identified it with economic liberalism. He argues that the traditional liberal attack on monopolies and restrictions on free trade that represented an 'unearned increment' meant that 'it required no great intellectual effort to advance to an attack on the whole myth of freedom of contract itself.'[32] Yet the critique of protectionism hindering free competition (as with the Corn Laws) is qualitatively different from a critique of the unequal relationship between labour and capital in which capital *itself* becomes a monopoly whose profits must be seen as more than a private resource. Here the solution is not free competition but State intervention and regulation. As we have seen this critique of capital was pioneered by the working-class press and learned subsequently by liberalism, which required a substantive change in its philosophy and political commitments. This is inexplicable as merely an internal 'conceptual extension',[33] but it is typical of liberalism to disavow its dependence on the labour movement for whatever progressive credentials it accrues. With the widening of the electoral franchise following the 1867 Reform Act, liberalism and the Liberal Party which emerged in this period, had every reason to try and win working-class male votes by recognising the limits of the market.[34]

At a municipal level, the development of a public services ethos was driven by the anarchy of market provision in the sphere of exchange and the 'primary contradiction of capital accumulation during the nineteenth century ... the physical destruction of living labour power.'[35] With the labour force suffering extreme degradation and the massive expansion of the industrial cities posing the acute problem of providing the infrastructure that would enable large numbers of people to live together without mass diseases and epidemics, liberalism developed a philosophy of State coordination, regulation, oversight and later some selective ownership of key utilities such as gas, water and sewage, following Chamberlain's reforms in Birmingham.[36] Economic recession in the 1880s and a growing, organised working-class militancy helped push liberalism away from merely recommending moral reform for the subaltern classes as Ricardo suggested. The State was going to have to take on a larger role in wealth redistribution. As Robert Eccleshall notes: 'It was during this period that material abundance became a respectable economic objective.'[37]

The Yorkshire-born philosopher and radical T.H. Green (1836–1882) provided a key philosophical re-orientation for liberalism with his distinction between negative freedom and positive freedom. Negative freedom, the freedom from constraint associated with freedom of contract, was he argued only a 'means to an end'. That end was 'positive freedom', which he defined as 'the liberation of the powers of all men equally for contributions to the common good.' This was an assertion of the normative priority of the social good over individual property rights. Green was clear that the older cherished values of liberalism that Adam Smith had articulated, such as 'enlightened self-interest' and 'unlimited freedom of contract' could *not* deliver the conditions that are compatible with 'the free development of the human faculties.'[38] In *The Principles of State Interference*, the Scottish born philosopher D.G. Ritchie (1853–1903) sought to refuse the antithesis between individual freedom and society, rehabilitating the State in liberal thinking by developing the Hegelian argument that the State was a more rational and trusted organ for the public good than the free market. It was not the role of the State to directly promote moral goodness but it could, argued another new liberal philosopher, L.T. Hobhouse (1864–1929) 'provide for it [i.e. moral goodness] the most suitable conditions of growth.'[39] This meant that the individual's moral autonomy was retained but a more realistic account of the material conditions that made moral autonomy possible, was now accommodated.

The new liberalism broke from laissez-faire because it could see that in a complex and interdependent society, individualism and free-market competition could have deleterious consequences. The market was no longer synonymous in the minds of the new liberal philosophy with the rational. When a single employer can undercut other employers willing to adopt measures to strengthen health and safety or raise wages, then some appeal to social organs above the market become necessary. State intervention at whatever level (municipal or national) comes to be seen as providing the necessary 'enforced uniformity' (Hobhouse) that prevents selfish and irrational forces from triumphing.[40] The State thus becomes a 'supervisor' to protect the more expansive notion of positive freedom and the images which helped feed this new philosophical imagination are drawn from the same 'industrialism' that saw Brunel recast the role of the captain of the Great Western as also one of 'superintending' a complex interdependent system in which everyone has a function and therefore everyone fulfilling a role has a value. As L.T. Hobhouse writes, for example: 'A society in which a single honest man of normal capacity is definitely unable to find the means of maintaining himself by useful work is to that extent suffering from malorganisation. There is somewhere a defect in the social system, a hitch in the economic machine'.[41]

Here the problem of unemployment is no longer the fault of the individual, but a problem which has both social causes ('malorganisation') and a normative claim on society to do something about it because society suffers from this inability of a 'single honest man' to find 'useful work'. The culture of industrialism and the industrial enterprise worked as a model from which inferences could be drawn as to what a better performing society looked like and provided liberalism with the imaginary resources to break from its earlier identification with the individualistic model of free competition. Instead liberalism could assert the values of rational planning based on the actual and ethical interdependence of all within the social 'system'.

Industrialism, then, functioned as a conceptual metaphor. The cognitive linguists Mark Johnson and George Lakoff have argued that metaphors are built into our everyday conceptual tools. Metaphors help us structure one 'domain' of experience (what they call the source domain) in terms of another domain of experience (what they call the target domain). Typically, the move from source to target domain is a move from the perceptually concrete to the more abstract, but the 'inferential structure' of the source domain is preserved in the more abstract-in-itself, difficult to grasp, target domain.[42] Thus the inferential structure of industrialism that I have been exploring (large-scale complex interdependent systems made up of many moving parts that need to be observed and supervised with great care and attention in order to assure their necessary coordination) could be transferred to the more abstract (target) domain of society in liberal philosophy to imagine the social in a way that classical liberalism could not. Industrialism thus functioned as a partial de-reification of capitalist social and economic relations.

Industrialism was not the only conceptual metaphor that liberalism had to hand in facilitating this transition in liberal philosophy. Michael Freeden focuses on the role of organicist metaphors in liberal philosophy especially in the work of the Derby-born liberal thinker J.A. Hobson. Organic metaphors steered evolutionary biology away from social Darwinism and instead captured the inference of a teleological drive for change and adaptation for a project of social reform. In doing so we see how the polysemic potentialities of conceptual and cultural resources are dependent on their wider social and historical conditions. Within the paradigm of the new liberalism, the organism as a totality of parts working on behalf of the reproduction of the whole could be recruited to a less individualistic model of the social.[43] Yet Freeden's prioritisation of organism as a conceptual metaphorical resource is perhaps part and parcel of his determination to play down how inextricably the new liberalism depended for its internal conceptual modification on a political and inter-discursive dialogue and contestation with socialism. Industrialism seems to me the more efficacious of the two conceptual metaphors, and for at least four reasons:

1 It helped provide a bridge between liberalism and the industrial organised working class upon which a political alliance could be built to sustain liberalism and the Liberal Party (at least until its eclipse by the Labour Party after the First World War). It could also, even more fancifully but nevertheless effectively at a rhetorical-political level, suggest a cross-class alliance between the 'producing classes' (i.e. labour and industrial capital).[44]

2 Industrialism helped sharpen the new liberalism's traditional critique of the aristocracy/landed wealth by counterposing 'good' industrial productive wealth against the 'bad' parasitic capitalism represented by the land, the City and empire. While not entirely irrational by any means, this evaluative distinction is problematic, leading to an overly rigid compartmentalisation between different capital formations

that in reality were and are more complexly interlinked, as we saw in Chapter 3. However, this old but now transformed new liberal critique of aristocracy went on to be overly influential on the Left (as in the Nairn/Anderson thesis).

3   Industrialism helped depoliticise problems that arose from the antagonistic structure of social and economic groups within capitalist society, by suggesting that there were technocratic solutions at hand which middle-class professionals had a key role in implementing. By drawing on the value-neutral ideology of science which industrialism was associated with, liberalism could present the professional middle classes as the intellectual and management elite who could save society from the class conflicts advocated by conservatism on one side and socialism on the other.[45]

4   Industrialism was a far more potent and prevalent image than organism as it correlated with the observable social and economic changes going on within British society. It could thus be translated into an idiom that connected with people's lives and experiences in a way that made it politically relevant.

The importance of industrialism as a conceptual metaphor in shaping the developing alliance between liberal philosophy and the labour movement can be seen in J.A. Hobson's analysis of the 1910 General Election results. The election was called because the Liberal government's plans to raise higher taxes on the rich had been blocked by the hereditary House of Lords, causing a constitutional crisis. This question, along with the issue of whether import duties should be imposed to protect some British employers from foreign competition (a Conservative proposal) dominated the election debates. The Liberals under Asquith were returned to power with just two more seats than the Conservatives (274) and had to form an alliance with other parties to govern. The recently formed Labour Party increased its representation by 16 to 40 MPs. The 1906 election had resulted in a landslide for the Liberals, conversely, the 1900 election, which the Conservatives had fought, whipping up nationalism around the Second Boer War, had been handsomely won by them. The 1910 election was notable in the way the even split between the popular vote and the seats won had a pronounced geographical distribution. Although there were caveats to add to nuance the picture (such as the usual criticism of the way the losing political preferences within a constituency do not appear to have any political representation within that constituency) it was clear, Hobson noted, that the majority of Liberal and Labour seats were to be found in the north while the majority of Conservative and Unionist seats were to be found in the south, with London reproducing this split from east to west. This split corresponded to regional political economies Hobson argued. The 'great productive industries of manufacture and mining' produced Liberal and Labour majorities while the agricultural and small manufactures of the south, along with the coastal pleasure resorts, tended to produce Conservative majorities.[46]

In the north the 'textile, machine-making and mining constituencies' not only produce Liberal and Labour majorities in the big cities, they also influence 'the semi-agricultural constituencies in their near neighbourhood.'[47] Likewise, the solidity of the economic and cultural domination of conservatism in the south shapes the opinions and views of unorganised 'servile and ill-paid labour' in the south.[48] This question of influence and the relationship between economics and political cultures gives Hobson's analysis a distinctly Gramscian quality to it, at least at a methodological level, even if the methodology is inserted into a rather different political framework. Thus Hobson speaks of this geographical, economic and political cultural split resulting in 'two Englands', which he describes as a 'Producer's England and a Consumer's England'. It is worth quoting the following passage at length, both because it is a fine passage in itself and because it provides a synoptic account of these fissures and their evaluations (from a liberal/Left perspective) that would shape political life in England and therefore Britain for decades to come:

> ... one England in which the well-to-do classes, from their numbers, wealth, leisure and influence, mould the external character of the civilisation and determine the habits, feelings and opinions of the people, the other England in which the structure and activities of large organised industries, carried on by great associated masses of artisans, factory hands and miners, are the dominating facts and forces. The Home Counties, the numerous seaside and other residential towns, the cathedral and university towns, and in general terms, the south, are full of well-to-do and leisured families, whose incomes, dissociated from any present exertion of their recipients, are derived from industries conducted in the north or in some over-sea country. A very large share, probably the major part, of the income spent by these well-to-do residential classes in the south, is drawn from possessions or investments of this nature.

The expenditure of these incomes calls into existence and maintains large classes of professional men, producers and purveyors of luxuries, tradesmen, servants and retainers, who are more or less conscious of their dependence on the goodwill and patronage of persons 'living on their means'. This class of 'ostentatious leisure' and 'conspicuous waste' is subordinated in the north to earnest industry: in the south it directs a large proportion of the occupations, sets the social tone, imposes valuations and opinions. This England is primarily regarded by the dominant class as a place of residence and a playground, in which the socially reputable sports and functions (among which churchgoing, the theatre, art, and certain mild forms of literary culture are included), may be conducted with dignity and comfort. Most persons living in the south certainly have to work for a living, but much of this work is closely and even consciously directed by the will and the demands of the moneyed class, and the prestige of the latter imposes habits, ideas and feelings antagonistic alike to useful industry and to democracy.[49]

Hobson's 'Gramscian' critique, which emerges out of the New Liberal paradigm is the key bridge to Nairn and Anderson's later work on the impediments to the rational development of British capitalism. Hobson's analysis of the two Englands, the producers and consumers, the north and the south, an emerging Labourism versus the already historically sedimented conservatism and its geo-economic powerbases in civil society, in retail, in the City, in empire and in the resulting deformations of the British State (such as militarism and oligarchy)[50] is undoubtedly attractive to a Left critique. Like Gramsci, Hobson's starts with a very concrete moment: the 1910 General Election results, and then deciphers that in a larger context of deep-seated and developing trends and conflicting political cultural projects, that may break out into a new historical conjuncture. As a mapping of political cultures, Hobson is evidently describing significant swathes of life in twentieth-century Britain. It has potential explanatory power in accounting for political developments as well as the lack of developments (conservative barriers to progressive change). It seems to be an indispensable map for thinking about a good deal of cultural politics and aesthetic practices, for example the limited extent to which modernism of one sort or another could find a toehold in British culture. It also demonstrates the moral-exhortatory power of industrialism as a conceptual metaphor with its contrast between the parasitic non-productive south and 'earnest' industry in the north. In 1910, and a decade later, the largest occupation for the working class was in fact domestic service.[51] But the prospects for organising workers to demand change were far better in industry than in domestic service for obvious reasons, and this is why although it was a quantitatively smaller part of the economy as an occupation, industrialism was an increasingly potent image of the need for change. Apart from the practical difficulties of organising workers in the domestic service sector, it was also culturally less fertile territory for a new political discourse seeking to make workers a central *productive* and *modern* force in the British imaginary. While industrialism can be highly technocratic, in the emergent social-democratic context that Hobson's 1910 essay can be situated in, industrialism could also nourish a more democratic political project. Here it is seen as part of a project that the working class itself makes possible through its labour. There is a sense that the political maturation of the industrial organised working class is absolutely central to the prospects of developing a democratic society in which the majority had a say in the conditions which shaped their lives. Hobson fully expected and broadly welcomed the fact that industrial muscle would translate into political influence. He articulates here a fairly radical and less than usual paternalistic species of liberalism:

> The intelligence of associated labour is less likely to be led astray by sophistry or sentimentalism than the more cultivated but more individualised intelligence of the scholar, the professional man, or the member of that swell-mob commonly termed 'Society' ... From the will of such a people proceeds a constructive political energy ... learning the art called democracy.[52]

Around the same year that Hobson was remarking on the low level of political consciousness among the dis-organised southern working class hegemonised by the 'prestige' of the 'moneyed class', Robert Tressell was finishing his posthumously famous socialist novel, *The Ragged-Trousered Philanthropists*. Based on his experiences working as a painter in Hastings, the novel sets its drama in the house-renovation business – that form of wealth based on property values being one of the quintessential pillars of conservatism's economic base, then and now. The novel has been widely celebrated as a socialist classic, although its view of the English working class as passively accepting their condition and hostile to the socialist perspective represented in the lead character Frank Owen has been less widely remarked upon or critiqued[53] But had Tressell lived and worked less than two hundred miles north he could not have written the same pessimistic book, because he would have left one England and entered another. Of course this is not to say that as a political culture conservatism had no purchase in this other England, but the whole tone of the novel is marked by the complete isolation of the socialist hero from any support culture, and the absolute confidence his workmates have in treating him and his didactic lessons with contempt. This tone could not have been reproduced had Tressell been shaped by or set his story in that other England.

The moral and political supremacy of this other England compared to the conservative one in the south and south east, was the basis of Hobson expecting some redistribution of wealth. This would involve rebalancing some of the resources currently monopolised by the consumer's England to expand the consumption power of the producer's England. Yet while industrialism worked very well as political rhetoric it was less perspicacious as economic analysis. The two economies of England were far more intermeshed and inter-reliant than the somewhat dichotomous political cultures that they gave rise to. Each of those cultures depended on the capital formations they denigrated quite as much as the capital formations they celebrated. Industrialism was a powerful and for progressives, undoubtedly and rightly a preferential image, both morally and in terms of political efficaciousness, to the southern consumer's England. It would come to be a moral-political orientation for much of the English intelligentsia and especially the cultural intelligentsia within the next two decades.

Industrialism, the working class and political communications

We have seen that the early historical emergence of capitalism in England and Scotland meant that the form that capitalism took was one whose wealth was very largely based on land, on a rural proletariat, on slaves, on imperial subjects' cheap labour, on rent, property and later on financial transactions. Industry was certainly part of this mix, but it could be a culturally subordinate one because of all these other revenue streams available to British capital. Even the composition of industry reflected its position within the broader hegemonic bloc, with agricultural derived food, drink and tobacco based investments prioritised more than chemicals, engineering and electronics.[54] Weiner makes the mistake of thinking that conservative indifference to industry is synonymous with a hostility to the profit motive. Nothing could be further from the truth.

166 · ENGLAND'S DISCONTENTS

British conservatism is rapaciously interested in the profit motive but its exploitation model is different from the dynamic of technological change driving productivity gains to give competitive advantage in the market place. For Marx this was the core image of advanced capitalism, accounting for its dialectic of progress and barbarism. It is one of the great ironies that the centre of gravity for this cutting-edge capitalism had already moved away from England, his main empirical case study by the time *Capital* was published. For the new liberalism there is more progress than barbarism under capitalism but under pressure from the labour movement, it now conceded that rationality could not be fully embodied in the free market but also had to be embodied in the State, which had to develop new responsibilities, new organs and new priorities. This kind of industrialism was also anathema to Weiner since while it is industrial it does not place the unalloyed profit motive at the head of every decision. 'The purpose of industry' Weiner complains of mid-twentieth-century Britain, 'was seen less and less as primarily that of producing goods efficiently; industry had overriding social obligations'.[55] Weiner's position is therefore rather curious in a British context. He is an economic liberal but one who is invested in *industry* rather than the more traditional repository of the English conservative imaginary: the culture and free-market economics of rentier capitalism. This historically peculiar combination (Weiner's formation within an American context is important here) makes his book both richly fascinating as a critique of Britain's dominant political culture, but also weak on political history and critical political economy.[56] In particular he over-homogenises the political cultures of the dominant bloc, seeing the conservative south as having the status to absorb and neutralise the 'spirit' of industrial capitalism located in the north.[57] Yet that reflected the convergence of political interests between northern industrial capital and southern rentier capitalism. But by the 1930s, industrialism had a new firmly established class base – the fusion between the intelligentsia and the labour movement that underpinned the emergence of the social-democratic historic bloc.

The struggle to establish this new social-democratic political culture, which had the working classes and industry as a legitimate component part of national identity and by extension new organs of the social State, can be seen in the field of political communications. In this field, we see the fusion between the new liberalism and the labour movement shift from the realm of philosophy and education in the works of Hobhouse,

Hobson, etc., to the realm of practical organisation and direct intervention into State institutions. A key figure here is John Grierson, the man who established, for a time at least, a particular conception of British documentary filmmaking as part of the State's political communications with its citizens. I want to re-frame the usual discussion around Grierson as the 'father of documentary' and instead situate him as a political communications advocate who had to take on and get the old nineteenth century conservative and laissez-faire dominated political culture of the State to cede some ground to the emergent social-democratic political culture he identified with. Grierson's project helped seed and anticipated the fuller change in the British State brought about by the 1945 victory of the Labour Party. Before that, at least some of the debris of the nineteenth century State had to be cleared out.

In establishing a new conception of political communications Grierson was nothing if not ambitious. 'History is determined', he wrote, by 'building new sentiments. It was clear that we had to learn to make our building deliberate.'[58] Grierson was writing here of his work at the Empire Marketing Board (between 1930 and 1933), the first State body which he persuaded to invest in documentary filmmaking with the help of a sympathetic civil servant, Sir Stephen Tallents. The new sentiments he refers to was the attempt to transform popular perception at home and abroad of empire as a matter of domination to the notion of empire as a commonwealth. This location of Grierson's work in the State apparatus makes it easy for him today to be dismissed as an uncritical propagandist of the State. Yet behind this explicit brief a more interesting and subversive political project – with a new and different conception of the State at its heart – was emerging.

Grierson was primarily a producer figure who gathered documentary filmmaking talent around him, but his first film, *Drifters* (1929) was designed to demonstrate the power and potential of this new genre of filmmaking, which for Grierson, was differentiated from mere actuality newsreel footage by its dramatic and aesthetic ambition. The film, about the Scottish fishing industry, linked the aesthetic modernism learned from Russian revolutionary cinema, to an emergent social-democratic validation of the dignity and importance of labour: 'the shots were massed together, not only for description and tempo but for commentary … One felt impressed by the tough continuing upstanding labour involved, and the feeling shaped the images, determined the background and supplied the extra details which gave colour to the whole'.[59]

The theme of documentary for Grierson was 'the ardour and bravery of common labour'[60] and while it is easy now to identify the limitations and potential paternalism of this perspective, we should not underestimate what was at stake in the production of a new component part of national identity. This was a cultural and political battle very evident to the participants at the time.

> When the posters of the Buy British Campaign carried for the first time the figure of a working man as a national symbol, we were astonished at the Empire Marketing Board to hear from half a hundred Blimps that we were 'going Bolshevik.' The thought of making work an honoured theme ... is still liable to the charge of subversion.[61]

Work and its association with the industrial working class, the basis of much of the wealth of the country, could not be openly acknowledged or accepted by the dominant conservative political imaginary at that time. Grierson recalls how he struggled to convince the cinema exhibitors that a film about 'an industrialised fishing fleet might be as brave to the sight as the brown sails of sentiment'.[62] That is an interesting phrase of course because 'the brown sails of sentiment' – as featured in many paintings by nineteenth-century painter Joseph M.W. Turner – would have been the traditional high-status racing yacht or commercial vessel – both of which were redolent of a certain upper-class aristocratic or mercantile identity. The industrial fishing fleet, however, spoke to a very different representation of British national identity and one that had not been given such positive prominence since perhaps the time of the Chartist press. Grierson's writings are a fascinating trace of a cultural and political battle to reshape the British State and the British national identity. As with Hobson, and despite the social-democratic framework, Grierson's thinking is strikingly comparable to Gramsci's in its understanding that political change must win on the cultural terrain and in the field of feeling and sentiment. This requires self-awareness that the task to implement change is difficult because it has to in part be conducted by people like himself, who have been 'rotted through' with the old individualism. He admits that deep down he is still receptive to appeals of 'personal initiative and personal right' and aesthetics is not unconnected to such political imaginaries: 'I still find the greatest image in rhetoric is the single man against his horizon, seeking his destiny'.[63] To this day, such auto-critique is extremely rare within the British intelligentsia. Evidently though, Grierson was part of a wider shift for this stratum of society. The filmmakers he gathered around him, such as Arthur Elton, Basil Wright and Stuart Legg were very much part of the traditional dominant class, privately educated, Cambridge, with substantial private incomes to subsidise what was a relatively poorly paid job at the Empire Marketing Board (EMB) compared with the commercial film industry.[64]

Grierson's next film *Industrial Britain* (1931) was 'cheered in the West End of London. The strange fact was that the West End had never seen workmen's portraits before – certainly not on the screen.'[65] In fact *Industrial Britain* is a visual document of the conflicting national identities at play in this moment. The film was produced by Grierson but directed by Flaherty, the latter was far more drawn to the images of traditional Britain with which the film begins: the windmill, cotton wheel, haystacks, canals, swans, clippers with their sails against the backdrop of the sky (no industrial fishing fleets here). For a film about industrial Britain, this opening is symptomatic of a set of anxieties about industry that we have seen were deeply embedded into a conservative culture. The new order is one of 'steam and smoke' powered by coal and the voice-over is clearly ambivalent about this state of affairs. Under Flaherty's direction there is a concern to discover the continuity of craft skills still present within this industrial Britain, hence the focus on glass blowing and pottery which are celebrated for the continuity of methods that stretch back in time and which depend on the individual expertise and knowledge of the workers who are featured. These workers might, we are told, be 'Venetian glass-masters of the sixteenth century'! There is something of a shift in tone later as the film moves onto the more Griersonian territory of a steel furnace and the individual recedes as industrial processes and scales come to the fore. But even here as the finished steel is checked for imperfections, individual observation and skill is then reintroduced by the film and linked back to the historic tradition of craftsmanship by the voice-over.

For Grierson, the individual and tradition were far less important than the collective endeavour and the modern situation. Documentary film raised the question of developing knowledgeable citizens who can participate in the running of things – their community, their union, their workplace, their government and country. These documentary films provided at one level information about how things were run, what the processes were involved to make specific goods or services and their centrality to the modern way of life. But these were never merely 'information films'. The centrality of the citizen-identity requires dramatisation, a bringing of issues to life, to move away from a static and undemocratic pedagogy that Grierson feared dominated the education system, in which the bare minimum of structures and rules is taught but with no sense of the citizen as a living participating presence in the civic life of things: 'The life of the thing is missed. It has not been made to enter for good and all into his imagination.'[66] Here then is the substantive heart and connection between citizenship and modernist aesthetics or the formal creative dramatisation of actuality material in the documentary that differentiated it from the more routine standardised newsreel: the role of dramatisation is to bring civic life, responsibility and participation *alive* and make it a vivid part of the imagination. It is important to recover how new this democratic sentiment was as a feature of State political communications. Film, for Grierson, can awaken the interest of the viewer in things beyond their immediate experience through interpretative dramatisation and thus widening knowledge, imagination and perhaps political possibilities.

Grierson's political communications theory was a response to the pessimism that the world was too complex for ordinary people to understand, implying that it would be better to leave the running of affairs exclusively to specialised elites.[67] Grierson's response was that 'a dramatic apprehension of the modern scene' by using the new technologies of the mass media could meet the educational, political and citizenship needs for a democratic order. The documentary film became an instrument of 'civic enlightenment'.[68] The whole concept of service which had been partially democratised by a middle-class liberal professionalism in the latter half of the nineteenth century, now became further democratised by linking it not only to modernity, science and work (all still susceptible to a undemocratic liberal rationalism) but the needs of the community which the workers above all were meeting by their work. It was only a short step from here to then justify the public funding of such goods and services. This is how culture seeds political change.

Industrialism helped progressive forces identify themselves with that powerful (but also problematic) trope of modernity. Grasping the modern world meant a transformation of those old habits that rested in the English case, on an assumed gentlemanly cultural superiority. Protected by empire markets, the commercial wing of British propaganda was notoriously complacent and slow in coming to grips with marketing and advertising for example.[69] The assumption that

English 'craftsmanship' speaks for itself the world over was widespread. But for Grierson this meant that 'the Englishman never quite got round to studying the other fellow's point of view and the special requirements of the market.'[70] Note here the affinity between Grierson's mindset and Brunel's nearly a century earlier. Both recognise the need to scientifically study what is required and to break the complacency and habits that no longer suit revolutionary changes in the modern world. Grierson displays an impatience with a cluster of attitudes that were widely prevalent in the British State and civil society and that threatened to undermine Britain's ability to survive the economic crisis of the 1930s and the war years of the 1940s. Grierson embodied that broader conflict with what we have called for the sake of summing up an entire political economy in a single image, the southern-consumer-rentier England of the conservative political imaginary. The success and the lack of success of establishing the documentary tradition in Britain speaks to the extent to which conservatism was neither exclusively hegemonic (as many have assumed) while still nevertheless being sufficiently entrenched to provide the internal obstacles against which Grierson fought and perhaps eventually lost (he went to work in Canada in 1939). He would lament, for example, that his experiments in political communications did not lead to similar documentary units being set up in the departments looking after agriculture, health, transport and labour. Instead the documentary film was forced to go to commercial and municipal sources of funding especially after the Second World War ended in 1945. In a remark that probably sums up much of British industrial development, retarded by an elite that was cautious, conservative, complacent and anti-democratic precisely because it could be and get away with it economically for so long, Grierson notes: 'It seemed at the time a pity that others should reap the full benefits of a medium which the government service discovered but which it was not inspired enough to mature'.[71]

During the war years, however, the British State could not do without the documentary-film movement and located it from the General Post Office where it had been since 1933 to the Ministry of Information. The kind of State organisation which the Second World War required and the new mentalities which it engendered, were explicitly linked by Grierson to a rejection of nineteenth-century laissez-faire. Total war meant total effort.[72] The systematic planning and effort at coordinated organisation involves a transformation in sentiments and habits to re-work relationships with one another and with the State, just as industrialism did for Brunel's first captain on *The Great Eastern* ship where vast forces of human and material energies were at work. 'Total war may yet appear as the dreadful period of forced apprenticeship in which we learned what we had hitherto refused to learn, how to order the vast new forces of human and material energies to decent human ends'.[73]

There is in Grierson's discourse an implicit link between coordinated systems and effective *action*, the sense of a collective working together to achieve results on a large scale. This requires a critique of an out-of-date style of organisation that lacks the rythmn of the industrial age. For the Scottish born Grierson, steeped in Calvinism's work ethic, the modern world necessarily calls into being the active, practical, doing capacities of people – against the more languid, restful, pleasurable and individualistic structure of feeling associated with gentlemanly capitalism and indeed southern (Anglican) England. For Grierson, there is a clear geography in the class divisions that have hampered British political and cultural development. The 'social and aesthetic leadership' of England 'has long lost that proud contact with simple labour which characterises the younger countries, and particularly America'.[74] This distances artists and intellectuals from social reality which is then, he suggests, better explored by the Irish, the Scots and the northern English.

Reflecting on his own upbringing in a Scottish village and thinking about the work of his schoolmaster father, Grierson saw an object lesson in the transformation of the intellectual vis-à-vis the working class. His father, who thought of himself as a conservative was also in practice a liberal of the old type. He was deeply invested in the power of education to change the lives of individuals from modest backgrounds. His father's efforts to bring the wider world to the village, using film and a book repository specialising in Carlyle and Ruskin were, in his way, progressive. Yet he saw the workers' education as refining their individual tastes, to make 'every workman to be a gentleman in a library'.[75] But social and economic developments were to smash his father's 'idyllic viewpoint'. The village was based on both agricultural labour and coal mining and developments in the latter were decisive. The education the working class received produced not 'gentlemen' in the library, but a knowledgeable working class less and less deferential to the employers, who in turn, through amalgamations of ownership, grew ever remoter from the direct life of the village, until the class conflicts between the miners and capital depended on 'massed unions and massed corporations'. As the 'motivating powers were abstract and unseen' and on vast colossal scales, so the purpose of education came less and less to be something primarily concerned with the honing of an individual sensibility. Leadership in education passed, says Grierson, to the working class itself as the political landscape shifted and as the Labour Party became the dominant agency for a desired socialist Britain.[76] However, this historic moment, the formation of a new historic bloc in which the working classes came to be accepted as a legitimate constituency of national identity, also occurred against the background of a historic defeat. The collapse of the 1926 General Strike, led by the miners, almost certainly allowed for a wider receptivity among the middle class to the claim for working class inclusion. After 1926 this claim could no longer be seen as a fundamental threat to the economic order, but rather inclusion on terms heavily mediated by the middle-class intelligentsia, such as Grierson himself.

Fast-forward several decades and even this history is in danger of being forgotten. Contemporary liberal conservatives like the broadcaster Jeremy Paxman, are quick to bury the memory of a 'northern' Britain as ever rivalling or achieving hegemonic parity with the south:

> The intriguing question is why this rock-solid powerbase did not result in a new idea of England. After all, not only did most of the people now live in conurbations, but they possessed in the Labour Party, a coherent focus for their ambitions … [Yet] they failed to invent an alternative to the roses-round-the-door, thatched cottage and village-green impression of England …[77]

But the social-democratic alternative to conservatism and economic liberalism was British rather than exclusively English, a distinction that allowed two rather different political imaginaries to cohabitate by exploiting the ambiguity between distinct national identities and their conglomeration into the composite supra-national identity of Britishness. When the social-democratic identity of Britishness began to break down in the 1970s and was rolled back in the 1980s under Thatcherism, the old conservative identity of England that had never gone away but had accommodated itself to the social-democratic identity of Britishness could now reassert itself unchecked on the terrain vacated by social democracy. At the same time, economic liberalism required a complex combination of conservatism and *social* liberalism to secure its rule at the level of electoral legitimation.

Liberalism after social democracy

In comparison to the nascent working-class public sphere established by the Chartist press, the Griersonian project looks like a diminished one. Judged against what came after social democracy and its associated political and cultural communications policy agenda, the Griersonian project looks distinctly better. In any case it casts an interesting light on the subsequent oscillation of liberalism away from social democracy in the 1990s and away from working-class culture. The decisive party-political vehicle for social liberalism to return to its original identification with economic liberalism was of course 'New' Labour (itself a rebranding exercise), under the leadership of Tony Blair. Blair had hoped to formalise the new political ascendancy of liberalism by bringing members of the Liberal Party into cabinet after the 1997 General Election. In the event, Labour's victory over John Major's Conservative Party was by such a wide margin that there was no basis for a formal partnership between the parties. It did not matter, however, because 'Blairism' was intellectually hegemonic within the Labour Party and in alliance with the old centre-right of Labourism which was more culturally conservative but happy with or (in the case of Deputy Leader of the Labour Party, John Prescott), acquiesced to New Labour's enthusiastic embrace of free-market capitalism. Both New Labour and the old centre-right shared a conservative predilection for using the State's 'educational' apparatuses and coercive power to discipline the working class legally and morally into accepting the new order of economic liberalism. This internal party alliance was a party inflected microcosm of the spectrum of hegemonic political cultures across the dominant parties.

The ascendancy of a socially liberal economic liberalism in the form of New Labour accepted the Thatcherite settlement of a State ever more receptive to opening up markets for capital. Hence making the Bank of England 'independent' (i.e. outside democratic political influence), the refusal to renationalise the railways, the use of private finance initiatives (PFIs) in health and transport, refusing to deflate the private housing bubble by building publicly owned housing on the scale necessary to meet demand, extensive outsourcing of State services to private corporations, creeping privatisation of health and education and as the logical extension of this domestic economic liberalism, a cataclysmic alliance with US imperialism abroad at its most dangerous and destructive (the Bush–Cheney 'axis of evil'). With the a priori acceptance of the ascendancy and superiority of markets, the biggest political question was already answered and that meant a style of political communications characterised by centralised control, the politicisation of civil servant press officers and the bullying of media outlets that did not play ball.[78] In its relationship to the public, New Labour eschewed a style designed to re-politicise and re-engage the public in a politics open to deliberation, but instead tried to control perceptions and treat the public with something approaching contempt. This was wonderfully skewered in the BBC television series by Armando Iannucci, *The Thick of It* (2005–2012).

Yet, as in the past, New Labour's liberalism continued to differentiate itself from conservatism in order to give itself that all important sheen of progressivism which liberalism depends on for its identity. Cultural differences were to be key signifiers of liberalism's progressive credentials as well as the old bêtes noires of liberalism, going back to the late eighteenth century, the struggle against inherited wealth and long-accumulated status hierarchy. All this was symbolically rendered by New Labour's renaming of the Department of National Heritage to the Department of Culture, Media and Sport. As with nineteenth-century liberalism, the substantive differences at the level of economic structure between liberalism and conservatism were tiny and tactical. New Labour certainly was not even a radically reforming liberal project of the kind envisaged by Will Hutton, whose 1995 bestseller *The State We're In* was essentially a more mainstream version of Tom Nairn's call for a 'second bourgeois revolution'.[79] For Hutton this meant reforming British capitalism away from its historic bias towards the City with its short-term thinking and overseas focus and institute major constitutional reform, revitalise Britain's productive base with an investment programme, and regulate the market back to social responsibility. New Labour, though, was not that kind of project and Hutton's call for reform failed to recognise that the political mobilisation that it would require could not be contained within the safe confines of a top-down technocratic delivery by the great and the good of the parliamentary system and liberal elite.[80] A classic liberal, Hutton feared any change that had an untamed labour movement in a leading role.

For Grierson, the cultural struggle against conservatism had been part of a middle-class alignment with the industrial working class in a project to democratise the British State. Social liberal neoliberalism had a very different cultural project and a very different class alignment, in which commercialisation rather than democratisation was paramount. Industrialism continued as the basis of a narrative about the future, the basis of an alliance between class forces and as an orientation for policy. But in each of these respects, the meaning of industrialism was radically changed. In New Labour's policymaking agenda, the culture of the industrial working class was displaced in favour of the elite strata of the professional 'creative class' working within the cultural industries themselves, a move that helped detach the Labour Party from its historic class roots.[81] Now the role of the middle class was to mediate primarily between themselves and capital. So complete was the victory of capital over labour in the Thatcher years that a liberal mediation between capital and labour was no longer desirable or necessary.

We have seen that industrialism was a potent component in the social-democratic political culture and imaginary, but it was fundamentally reconfigured by New Labour. After the physical reduction of manufacturing as a significant part of Britain's political economy (de-industrialisation) and the political, cultural and moral depletion of the working class as a key agent within 'industrial Britain', New Labour needed a new narrative to cast its policy agenda at the forefront of modernity. The cultural industries were perfect in so many ways to fill the gap – at least at the level of ideology, if only partially at the level of reality. The cultural industries were at least *industries*, retaining a residual commitment to manufacturing within a political economy that New Labour readily accepted would continue to be dominated by the City. Likewise, the cultural industries were envisaged as orientated for international export markets and selling Britain as an attractive and modern place for inward investment. Culture then was perhaps a word too freighted with certain expectations for what New Labour had in mind, as Blair himself made clear: 'The next century will be dominated by brain, not brawn. Creativity and knowledge will be the key tools. And Britain has always been a world leader in creativity and innovation'.[82]

Cultural theorists were quick to spot the implications of the terminological shift from culture to 'creativity'. As Toby Miller observed, creativity facilitated an emphasis on inputs into processes rather than something as definite as an output that could bear the classification of being 'cultural'. Instead, creativity of inputs made it 'possible for anything that makes money to be creative'.[83] The terminological shift to the 'creative industries' expanded the concept of culture and media so that it could be articulated to the more economically orientated boosterism of information society debates and policy agendas.[84] Blair's references to 'brain' power, 'knowledge', 'tools' and 'innovation' are some of the key buzz words of a discourse that looks forward to a new high-tech industrial revolution that will power capitalism to the next stage of growth and profitability. This positive story of growth and wealth generation was captured and inflected by New Labour around the cultural/creative industries, although they needed to include the information technology, software and computer services sectors to make these industries sufficiently large for a quasi-plausible story around their importance to the economy to stick. According to recent figures the IT, software and computer services sector accounts for 43.5 per cent of the creative industries gross value added, with advertising and marketing accounting for another 15.8 per cent.[85] While some software production around games design could certainly qualify as both creative and cultural, it is sobering that these two sectors account for nearly 60 per cent of the gross value added (GVA) of the UK's so called 'creative industries'. The temptation for many cultural producers has been to accept economic value as a key measure of value because that is the measure of value that policy-makers seem to recognise as most valuable. The reality though is that this economic value is inflated by cohabitation with sectors that have precious little to do with cultural production. It is a cohabitation in which culture lends the business of making money some 'esteem' and in return has its genuinely cultural characteristics penetrated by commercial imperatives. In terms of institution building, this conflation of the cultural with the IT sector saw the creation of the Office of Communications (OFCOM) a light-touch, market-friendly regulator designed to open up public service television to the long term penetration of the new international giants of the telecommunications industry, consumer electronics manufacturers and global (Hollywood based) content providers.[86]

Not only did all this amount to a very limited cultural policy, it also amounted to a very limited industrial policy. For two economists this substitute for a more substantive set of institutional reforms and investment programme was of a piece with the 'hallucinations' of Blair's 'bullshit Britain'.[87] Elliott and Atkinson argued that the real 'service' economy that characterises employment in the UK is less the high-tech creative sector than the more menial low-paid jobs in call centres and those working in a servant economy employed to do the cleaning, cooking, childcare and gardening of the well-off (around four million people, many from Eastern Europe).[88] And even within the cultural or creative industries, a policy agenda high on public relations but low on workers' pay and conditions meant that beneath the idealised promotion of the creative industries, sociologists of cultural labour noted that work in these sectors for the majority was becoming harder, less secure and less well-rewarded.[89] The next great high-tech revolution rests, it seems, on driving down labour costs and externalising risk.[90]

The convergence of social liberalism with economic liberalism and the tacit differentiation of this alliance from the alliance between conservatism and economic liberalism sets the perfect political backdrop for the widely noted appropriation by capitalism of culture's 'artistic critique' of the system in the name of authenticity and freedom.[91] The romantic model of the artist as self-directed, 'passionate' about their work, innovating, living on their wits, living precariously but investing their freelancing mode of life with the moral hue of freedom and authenticity, was appropriated and rolled out as the template for all subjects under economic liberalism.[92] A new internationally prevalent discourse meant that job insecurity was now discursively repackaged as an exciting opportunity to multi-skill and avoid being stuck in the same 'boring' job for years. Social liberalism, more attuned to new trends and generally more comfortable with the important youth market, was far better placed than conservatism to achieve this subtle cross-fertilisation between culture and the labour market.

As capital appropriated culture it also tamed it, hollowing out the substance (the artistic critique) leaving only an empty clever marketing sign in place of real culture. As Jim McGuigan notes: '"Cool" is actually the dominant tone of capitalism today. Corporations have incorporated counter-cultural traditions and deployed signs of "resistance" in order to market their wares'.[93]

Cool capitalism and cool social liberalism need a certain version of conservatism against which to define their own supposedly progressive politics. 'I make no apologies' wrote Blair, 'for wanting Britain to be a nation characterised by merit, not privilege or stuffiness.'[94] The creative industries were a perfect vehicle for the ideology of meritocracy, since it is one of the great myths of the cultural sector that 'talent' will find its way to the top irrespective of material conditions.[95] In fact, as has become increasingly apparent, 'talent' has become very homogenised from what was already a pretty narrow base, as the middle class colonise opportunity and congratulate themselves on how 'creative' they are.[96]

The culture of the working class, linked in Grierson's time to modernity, were now seen by New Labour, the creative industries and the middle class, as an anachronism that individuals should leave behind as quickly as possible. Films like *The Full Monty* (1997) and *Billy Elliot* (2000) and television programmes such as *X-Factor* and *Britain's Got Talent* extolled the supposed social mobility unleashed by the performing arts. As in the nineteenth century, social liberalism's new alliance with economic liberalism has drastically limited its ability to think critically about the economic consequences of deregulated capitalism, or indeed to think about socio-economic determinants at all. The seeds of 'Cool Britannia', the admittedly short-lived marketing hype that connected Blair to British pop music in the late 1990s, can today be found flourishing in the phenomenon of 'art washing'. Here the dreams of urban regeneration through culture have long since degenerated into something far more sinister: a kind of class cleansing. Artists are now the advance guard of property developers and asset strippers, colonising the inner city and transforming what was initially said to be valued (the multi-cultural location) into a different kind of value (economic in nature) and a more homogeneous, generally whiter and certainly more middle-class location in the fullness of time.

Social liberalism's alliance with economic liberalism had significant consequences in the political cultures of Britain. Its electoral hegemony and cultural agenda wounded a traditional, even reactionary conservatism, that fought a rear guard battle against what was framed as a liberal metropolitan elite whose value systems were out of touch with the majority. The Countryside Alliance (what else?) which was formed in the same year as New Labour's General Election victory, mobilised around a defence of fox hunting (which New Labour 'banned' in 2004) and 'country living' more generally. Later the centre of gravity for the political right moved to UKIP, which combined economic liberalism with a Thatcherite model of British identity that was anti-EU, anti-immigration and Atlanticist. This conservative counter-attack was to be expected, but the problem was that social liberalism aligned with economic liberalism built the conditions for a reactionary conservatism to win new recruits to illiberalism among the most disadvantaged. New Labour effectively abandoned the working class whose communities, industries and cultural organs had been devastated by the 'mark one' model of neoliberalism under Thatcherism and then Majorism. This abandonment led to the electoral decline of New Labour over time (five million votes were lost between the New Labour victory in 1997 and the General Election defeat of 2010). Centre-right Labourism tried belatedly and dismally to offer the working class cheap cultural and State solutions to material insecurity (on immigration, on national identity, on strong 'law and order', etc.) in response to their weakening electoral prospects. This makes sense for the centre-right, as cultural compensation (and pumping up State coercion) is less threatening to neoliberalism and class inequalities than a real redistribution of wealth. But the 'Blue Labour' crowd or Gordon Brown's risible 'British Jobs For British Workers' slogan, could always be outflanked by UKIP and the anti-EU ultras in the Conservative Party. The weakening of New Labour and the lack of credibility which its leadership cadres had after 2010 represented a significant weakening of social liberalism and this was the backdrop for two referendums: one in 2014 and one in 2016 that represented a deepening of the crisis for the entire historic bloc. It is to these two referendums that we now turn.

6

Geopolitical discontents: a tale of two referendums

The immediate consequences of the stagnation of the socially liberal neo-liberal project were for alternatives to emerge around possible geopolitical reconfigurations offered by two referendums. In Scotland the sentiments for a return to social democracy had, despite little party-political representation, survived among the population and began to be captured by the Scottish National Party and tied to their independence project. This led to the 2014 referendum on whether the future of Scotland should be as part of the UK or as a separate independent nation. This referendum represented the aspirations for a new policy direction and irrespective of the reality of the SNP's policy agenda, constituted a popular grass-roots challenge to *economic liberalism*, and *not* just a cultural differentiation of the same economic project. The latter, as we have seen, has constituted the limits of political debate in the dominant political and media institutions of the UK since the 1990s. Beyond Scotland, in the rest of Britain and in England especially, the exhaustion of New Labour's socially liberal version of economic liberalism, led to a renewed conservative challenge to the *cultural* model of economic liberalism pursued by New Labour and the coalition government of Conservatives and Liberals between 2010 and 2015. But this was no challenge to economic liberalism itself. The fault line along which this political mobilisation occurred was (as with the Scottish referendum) geopolitical, this time concerning Britain's membership of the EU. This allowed conservatism to mobilise a reactionary nationalism around the 2016 referendum on Britain's continued membership of the EU, while social liberalism mobilised an equally uncritical defence of the EU, in which the neo-liberal character of its policy objectives and the lack of democratic accountability over its institutions, received little scrutiny. It is to these two referendums and the struggle between the political cultures and national identities that lay at their heart that we turn to in this chapter in order to explore the current fracturing of the historic bloc.

The north-south divide

The decline of the Conservative Party in Scotland as measured by General Election results developed over several decades. In the 1950s it shared broadly equal number of seats with its main rival, the Labour Party. But from the 1960s onwards, Labour pulled ahead, winning roughly double the number of seats in successive General Elections. The decline of empire hit the party most associated with it harder than it did the Labour Party, which was rightly seen as the architect of the new social democratic settlement. With the decline of sectarianism, the skilled Protestant working class shifted its electoral allegiance from the Unionist Conservative Party to the party of labour.[1] But if these transformations halved support for the Conservative Party in Scotland, the new politics of economic liberalism, meant worse was to come. Following Margaret Thatcher's General Election victories of 1979, 1983 and 1987, the Conservative Party's break with its own 'one nation' accommodation to the social democratic settlement, was complete. For the Tories, there was now a 'two nation' project in which the 'productive' part of the nation was deemed to be all those who were thought to live successfully and independently in the market place for labour power and goods, apparently (but not in reality) with minimal State support, while all those who depended on public spending or benefits were cast as 'parasitic', requiring a bloated public sector to survive that cultivated a distinct lack of moral fibre and dragged Britain down in terms of economic competitiveness.[2]

While this fantasy ideological narrative won sufficient support to achieve successive General Election victories for the Conservative Party with around 40 per cent of the popular vote, the explicit abandonment of one-nation Toryism led to a further deterioration in the party's electoral fortunes in Scotland. In 1983 they won 21 seats in Scotland but this dropped to ten seats in 1987, although it should be noted that because of the blunt first-past-the-post system of counting votes this drop in *seats* happened on the basis of a loss of *fewer than* 100,000 votes.

Nevertheless, following the 1987 General Election victory this collapse in seats initiated the beginning of a debate about whether the Conservatives had democratic legitimacy to run Scotland from Westminster. It also accelerated the debate about a north-south divide within the country as a whole, with Scotland, Wales, the north-east and west of Britain and Yorkshire and Humberside constituting a relatively less well-off north and the south (starting from the Midlands) constituting the relatively more prosperous regions benefitting from the Thatcherite revolution.

The split was glaring in terms of electoral support for the Conservatives and Labour. After the 1987 General Election: 'of the large northern cities containing three or more constituencies, Glasgow, Manchester, Bradford, Hull and Newcastle upon Tyne were represented only by Labour MPs and no Conservatives were returned in Liverpool; while the Conservative hold on the south remained virtually unblemished'.[3]

Social scientists cautioned that the north-south divide was a somewhat crude metaphor painting a picture in broad brushstrokes. The Conservatives and their ideologists in the media dismissed it altogether. But the social scientists also found that while potentially simplistic because there was poverty to be found in the south and prosperity to be found in the north, some sort of material fissure along spatial lines was taking place. Overall, across significant variables, such as health, house prices and above all employment opportunities, regional inequalities that had been diminishing in the post-World War Two era of functioning social democracy, were now growing. '[O]n a wide range of economic measures a fuzzy line drawn between the Severn and the Wash shows marked differences between those regions above and those below it.'[4] Pre-1974, when full employment was achievable within the context of global capital's expansionary phase – public spending on road building and housing as well as direct employment in public administration, health and education, compensated for any potential regional employment downturns.[5] But once the Conservatives abandoned full employment as a policy goal in order to transform British capitalism and weaken the trade union movement, economic divergence between regions opened up. The winding down of the coal industry following the traumatic defeat of the Miners' Strike in 1984–5 and the contraction of heavy industry and manufacturing especially in the early 1980s, hit the northern regions – where it had been especially concentrated – particularly hard. Scotland's economy had depended on iron ore, steel, shipbuilding and coal, but such industries could no longer count on government support strategies. 'An industrial shutdown on an unprecedented scale has been taking place' wrote Andrew Gamble in 1987.[6] Cuts in public spending exacerbated the problems in the north where there was less compensating growth in private sector jobs than in the south. Thus unemployment and long-term unemployment rates were consistently higher in the north than in the south.[7] Employment growth occurred most strongly in the private sector in the south, in such areas as banking, insurance, finance, business services, and property related services.[8] The traditional hegemony of a power bloc located in the south, in the non-productive finance sectors and orientated towards international investments had reasserted itself. These were the heartlands of neo-liberalism. But this spatial structuring of inequality had a significant fault line in a multi-nation State where borders could still be the basis of mobilising national consciousness for a political challenge to the British State as such.

Neo-liberal devolution

In the early 1990s a cluster of civil-society groups organised themselves into the Scottish Constitutional Convention which took the initiative to press for devolution and drew the initially reluctant Labour Party (that feared it could be a step towards independence) and the SNP (that feared that devolution would satisfy the Scots and kill off independence) into its wake. A system of proportional representation for a new Scottish Parliament was conceived that would make it highly unlikely that any one party could achieve a majority, thus seemingly preventing the nationalist SNP ever being in a position to pose a referendum on Scotland's independence. The Labour Party saw itself as the beneficiaries of the new parliament, running it in coalition with the Liberals (which had been the plan for the Westminster Parliament as well). In 1997 the Conservatives were wiped out completely in Scotland, winning no seats in the General Election and with a now sharper fall in the share of the vote (less than 500,000 compared to 800,000 in 1983). Labour formed the government at Westminster and following the setting up of the new Scottish Parliament (after a referendum), Labour and the Liberals dominated it between 1999 and 2007. As Neil Davidson argued, devolution is not incompatible with economic liberalism, rather it functions as a 'strategy of delegation … responsibility for implementing anti-reforms is spread beyond governing parties and central apparatuses to elected bodies whose policy options are severely restricted both by statue and reliance on the Treasury for most of their funding'.[9]

Yet for the neo-liberal consensus to hold, party competition ought not to lead to any openings back towards social democratic policy formulations. But the Iraq War and Scottish Labour's devotion to following the neo-liberal agenda of the Labour Party at Westminster, lost it support. The SNP appeared to occupy the centre-left ground of social democracy abandoned by New Labour and it became a minority administration in 2007. Of course the SNP has been criticised by both the right and the Left for trying to square commitments to social equality with neo-liberal policies on low corporation tax.[10] The issue at hand here though is less the adequacy of the SNP's policy agenda than the popularity of its modest social democratic policies such as free tuition at higher education, free personal care, free bus passes, abolition of bridge tolls, free prescription charges and so forth. For the neo-liberal hegemony it was a significant fracture when this policy agenda helped the SNP win an absolute majority at Holyrood in 2011.

The inconceivable had happened, but Scottish Labour continued to doggedly follow the neo-liberal devolution agenda storing up trouble in the future. Scottish Labour leader Johann Lamont denounced free tuition fees in 2012 as 'not viable' and in danger of making Scottish universities 'lose ground' to international competitors. Lamont even went so far as to suggest that publicly provided higher education was symptomatic of a 'something for nothing' culture.[11] So ingrained had New Labour's contempt for its voters and values become, so dogmatic its equivalence of economic liberalism and civilisation, that Scottish Labour had forgot to check if those voters really had – as in England – no alternative party of power to go to. While in England the conversion of New Labour to neo-liberalism had left the sizeable constituency for social democracy without political party representation and leadership, this was no longer the case in Scotland. In articulating the question of independence to a social democratic politics, the SNP had also moved substantially away from a culturally and ethnically defined nationalism, although their opponents refused to register this.

After their 2011 victory, the Holyrood government was pressed by the British government (the Conservative–Liberal Coalition) to name a date for the referendum. The Unionists were extremely confident that they would win. It was agreed to hold a referendum on whether Scotland would become an independent nation in September 2014. Unionist confidence would turn out to be misplaced in the first of a number of indicators that 'mainstream' political and media thinking were hardly 'mainstream' at all. The social democratic challenge to neo-liberalism articulated with the independence agenda meant that Scottish politics was in a very different place to the neo-liberal consensus. The political cultural integrity of the British State was about to be severely tested and the first real breach in the hegemony of conservatism, social liberalism and economic liberalism, was about to occur.

Clash of national identities

In the 1970s Tom Nairn famously argued that it would be the rising nationalisms from the subaltern nations that would rupture the British State rather than the class-based revolutionary convulsion that the Left hoped for. The nationalisms of the Celtic fringe, he argued, could do a better job at modernising the capitalist economies than the 'hopeless anachronism' that was the British State.[12] By 'modernisation' Nairn meant a State-led (re)industrialisation project that the old regime of laissez-faire capitalism with its languid aristocratic cultural leadership had signally failed to achieve. In order to make his case for the uninterrupted continuity of the archaic State, Nairn had to downplay the composite and contradictory make-up of the political cultures that constituted the British State. In particular, Nairn assimilated social democracy into the status quo since according to him it had never seriously challenged the 'underlying nature'[13] of the archaic State. A lot depends on what one means by the 'underlying nature' of the British State of course. The welfare state was for Nairn a distraction from the main order of business and worked to integrate the working class into an 'antique form of bourgeois society and constitution'. This 'pacification' view of the welfare state, popular on the Left at the time, failed to appreciate that social democracy and the welfare state were actually thorns in the side of a capitalism in crisis, a residue of a past compromise it could no longer afford. For Nairn, if it was a thorn, it was a regressive one because it stifled 'individualistic, mobile but more egalitarian social relations'.[14] That hymn to an American-style model of capitalism where individualism is equated with egalitarianism reveals unfortunate affinities between social liberalism and the then rising tide of economic liberalism. Nairn's call for a 'second revolution of the state'[15] was about to be answered by Thatcherism's regressive modernisation project (i.e. economic liberalism coupled with a reactionary cultural defence of Britishness).

When the 2014 referendum posed the question of the break-up of the British State, Nairn's analysis turned out to be only partially prophetic. For it was a defence of social democracy that was the main driver threatening Britain with a loss of 32 per cent of its landmass if the Scottish people voted Yes to independence. Social democracy was not seen as antithetical to constitutional and industrial reform, but integral to it. The SNP Government's referendum document, *Scotland's Future*, sums up the key problems of the 'Westminster' system (the neo-liberal political economy, essentially). These include an economy orientated overwhelmingly towards London and the south-east, Westminster's indifference towards manufacturing, its attacks on public services, the anti-democratic imposition of Westminster policies rejected by Scottish voters, the lack of a written constitution, ongoing attacks on the Welfare Benefits system and the growing and unnecessary inequality associated with neo-liberalism: 'Under the Westminster system, Scotland is also locked into one of the most unequal economic models in the developed world: since 1975 income inequality among working-age people has increased faster in the UK than in any other country in the OECD'.[16]

Scotland's Future also proposed a national conversation after a Yes vote for Independence on a new constitution. Emerging from a democratic process, a new constitution would reflect the different political culture in Scotland from an England dominated UK, namely that 'the people, rather than politicians or State institutions, are the sovereign authority in Scotland.'[17] It was envisaged that the new constitution would include an entitlement to public services and a ban on nuclear weapons, which would close the Scottish location for Britain's nuclear submarine base at Faslane.[18] The former underscored the threat posed to public services in the rest of the neo-liberal UK while the latter represented a potentially serious problem for British self-identity as a military nuclear power.

The national case that the SNP Government was making was cast strongly in terms of a civic-based national identity and this was an argument for independence that both Whitehall and the Conservative Party in particular were unfamiliar with.[19] Rather than nurturing ancient grievances, or asserting essential ethno-cultural characteristics of the Scottish, the case for independence was made primarily in terms of a different set of *political* values grounded in a desire for social justice that the Westminster dominated UK could not deliver.[20] The dominant tone of the independence campaign seemed a good translation into practice of what some philosophers have been calling a 'constitutional patriotism' or 'civic nationalism' in which cultural exceptionalism is abandoned in favour of a discourse built around an explicit set of social-justice, human-rights, and democratic guarantees.[21] The ambiguities of the popular-Romantic re-imagining of history, culture, myths and narratives that was the model for nationalism for two centuries or more, has been subject to increasing critical scrutiny in an age of perceptible and necessary cross-border flows of people, goods and cultures. Essentialising community on the one hand and outsiders on the other, while diminishing popular understanding of international economic, political, legal and other kinds of interdependencies, has left a once powerful conservative version and vision of national belonging on the defensive. This is not to say that it cannot acquire traction, as the triumph of Donald Trump in America shows, but it is ever less adjusted to the real world and therefore more prone to pathological outcomes. Liberalism and the Left would agree with this critique of a conservative inward orientated national identity. However they part company in their respective stances towards the economic structures that are criss-crossing and eroding the old Romantic nationalisms of the past. Whereas liberalism, in its present convergence with economic liberalism, reifies the structures as inevitable, rational and progressive, the Left adopts a more critical stance vis-à-vis the actual operational viability of this order, the validity of its normative claims and the necessity and inevitability with which it cloaks itself.

Confronted with an unfamiliar civic nationalism contesting the ability of the British State to meet social justice goals, Unionism continued to characterise the independence movement in the conventional terms that Britain's State-centric supra-nationalism has always cast subaltern nationalisms: as petty, small-minded parochialisms, narrow and mean compared with the supposedly grander and loftier aims of Britishness. As Étienne Balibar noted 'dominant or oppressive nationalisms are generally 'invisible' as nationalisms, at least to themselves'.[22] In the second television debate between SNP leader Alex Salmond and the leader of the 'Better Together' Unionist campaign, Labour MP Alistair Darling argued that while his own 'first priority is to build a fairer and better society' Salmond's was to 'create a separate state no matter what'.[23] Here the apparent narrowness of the desire for Scottish independence is craftily coupled to the notion that independence is an egotistical project of one man: Alex Salmond. This theme in the Unionist campaign was often uncritically recycled by the media. Writing in *The Guardian*, columnist Martin Kettle could not but concede towards the end of the campaign that the vibrant Yes to independence movement had been a massive boost to democratic participation, but at the same time Kettle warned that Scottish independence was 'divisive' because nationalism was intrinsically divisive.[24] This liberal critique of nationalism, however, represses the fact that Britishness is itself a form of nationalism. On the day of the referendum, Scottish Labour MP Douglas Alexander, writing in *The Daily Telegraph*, cast Scottish nationalism as introverted, fixated on 'putting up borders' and associated with dark dictatorial political forces (Vladimir Putin and Korean dictator Kim Jong-Un were the only world leaders who wanted Yes to succeed).[25] Again there was that sense that Unionism could not quite engage with the actual model of civic nationalism that was being proposed. Instead Unionism remained remarkably stuck in a set of arguments that it had been recycling since the 1970s at least, when calls for Scottish independence first really began to achieve a wider reception. As Nairn noted at the time, the size of the State unit one belongs to was taken as a sign of the value of the national identities on offer, a conflation that conveniently favoured the larger supranational State of the United Kingdom.[26] An editorial in *The Evening Standard* during the referendum replayed this trope, arguing: 'Scotland in the Union has a larger and more ambitious destiny than it would as a small independent state. Its place in the world is that of a global player, since Britain is still one of the great economic powers'.[27]

No doubt lurking beneath the self-confident assertion of Britain's role as a 'global player' was the anxiety that such a role could be fatally wounded by Scotland's departure from the Union. This concern, however, was displaced onto Scotland's smaller 'destiny' should it vote wrongly. In the television special *Scotland Decides: The Dimbleby Interviews*, Alex Salmond was asked, revealingly, whether Scotland would be happy to 'leave the world stage'.[28] With Tony Blair's calamitous Iraq adventure still vivid in popular memory, Salmond denied that was what Scotland would be doing. Instead a different model of what being involved in the world meant was on offer and this was contrasted with Britain's military/imperialist history. Here as elsewhere, the Scottish referendum was opening up perspectives on what sort of country Britain had become which the conservative–liberal hegemony would have preferred not to have to address.

Britain as a political unit that had achieved great things by combining the 'family' of nations together was another way in which it was implied independence meant a smaller future for an independent Scotland. Labour tended to define the virtues of the Union very much in terms of the social democratic settlement that came out of the Second World War, although this raised uncomfortable questions about New Labour's erosion of the self-same institutions which they extolled as a benefit of staying in the Union. Conservatism predictably appealed to a longer history less charged with contemporary political contestation (e.g. the Enlightenment). Prime Minister David Cameron declared that if Scotland voted to leave the UK he would be 'heartbroken'. This was part of a very deliberate campaign decision to stress the *emotional* case for Scotland staying in the Union.[29] This strategy is an example of Britishness mobilising classic nationalist rhetorical strategies, such as the nation as family, the nation as a shared history, and the nation as a deeply sentimental bond of affection.[30] But if Cameron led the conservative battle to keep the Union intact, there were other voices within conservatism, albeit in a minor key, that suggested that even within this political culture, support for the 1707 settlement that joined the Scottish and English Kingdoms together, was eroding. Unionists questioned whether Scotland on its own could afford the social justice agenda that Yes campaigners were advocating as part of a future independent Scotland. The argument was that Scotland could afford its social conscience only thanks to the subsidies it got from the Treasury in the form of a block grant (the Barnett formula). For some Conservatives, Scottish desire for independence began to rankle as a sign of impertinent ingratitude. Austerity in England, it seemed to these voices, was being made worse by public subsidy scroungers who could not pay their own way. This of course was a familiar Conservative refrain but now it was being applied to a whole country. 'Why', asked Conservative MP Nadine Dorries, 'are we paying them to eat deep-fried mars bars when we can't even get decent health care in this country?'[31] It seemed that faced with the prospect of addressing the stresses and strains that were endangering the Union or continuing the direction of travel mapped out by economic liberalism, conservatism was beginning to acclimatise itself to picking the latter over the former. This new emergent structure of feeling within conservatism amounted to a remarkable collective shrug when faced with the prospect of losing the three hundred year Union. As *Daily Mail* columnist Richard Littlejohn put it: 'Out here in Daily Mail Land, most people value the Union and want it to endure. But increasingly I get the impression that if the Scots do vote to split, it would be greeted with a collective shrug of indifference'.[32]

Here we see two very characteristic features of conservatism: firstly, and oddly for a philosophy that prizes *individual* responsibility, its reluctance to confront its *own* responsibility as a political culture for a given set of outcomes. As a result it needs to instead find explanations using displacement mechanisms (here a view of Scottish ingratitude which displays an almost Nietzschean *ressentiment* against subalterns for using morality to try and curb their power or agenda – here neo-liberalism).[33] The second characteristic feature of contemporary conservatism revealed by Richard Littlejohn's observation is that the commitments to economic liberalism generates negations of conservatism's own moral-political universe and that the impulse to *conserve* is trumped by the impulse to maintain the most expansive room for manoeuvre on behalf of capital.

Contradictions of political communications

Ever since Jürgen Habermas's groundbreaking work *The Structural Transformation of the Public Sphere*, the tacit assumption underpinning analysis of political communications is that in formally democratic situations, the State as a power over a territorially defined unit (the nation) could be made accountable to the public through various communication channels, debates and the exercise of political choices on the basis of rational opinion formation.[34] The 'national' media are envisaged by public sphere theory as one of the central organs and sites for communication, debate, public opinion formation and the means by which to exercise accountability pressures on State functionaries and sometimes private sector actors when they are perceived to be making negative consequential decisions for the wider public. Yet for a *multi-nation* State, this requires the State to have legitimacy in relation to the nations over which the State has ultimate sovereignty. Internationally, globalisation of economic liberalism has tested this as nations submerged into bigger nations and regions have increasingly sought to position themselves differentially from their nation-state vis-à-vis the global flows of capital, goods, labour and culture that are going on 'above' the nation-state. In the case of Scotland, legitimacy conditions broke down as the political cultural unity of Britain was put under tremendous stress by the deepening of inequality caused by economic liberalism. Devolution, or rather neo-liberal devolution was seen as the solution to this problem by Unionism, but it immediately opened up questions concerning which 'nation' political communications implies as its addressee – Scotland or Britain? That there might be tensions in trying to address one or the other or both simultaneously is already implicit in the fact of devolution. As Philip Schlesinger was quick to note, devolution means that 'the dominant model of the nation-state as a unitary political community, as a stable locus in which we speak to ourselves about politics and public affairs, is breaking down.'[35] How far, for example, could the British 'national' media based outside Scotland but influencing media within it, acknowledge for a Scottish audience, Scotland's perceived identity divergence from the rest of the UK?[36] How far could the rest of the UK have a political communication system that could inform publics outside Scotland what was happening inside Scotland?

For a British broadcaster such as the BBC, the new relative political autonomy which devolution brought Scotland, opened it up to contradictory pressures as to which 'nation' it prioritised. For example, BBC Scotland's attempts to develop a Scottish *News at Six* in 1998, was blocked by BBC headquarters in London and the Labour cabinet who opposed it.[37] It seemed that the Labour Party chiefs, who had green lit devolution were fearful that a Scottish *News at Six* would fan the flames of nationalism.[38] This liberal fear that it was *cultural* and *symbolic* forms that might foster a national consciousness that could not be contained within devolution, rather than the consequences of economic liberalism producing that feared end-game, is deeply revealing of liberalism's blind spots. The squashing of a Scottish *News at Six* became a major political story and by the end of the row, some 70 per cent of Scots supported the idea of a specifically Scottish news broadcast at that time of the evening.[39]

Although in 1999 Mark Thompson, Controller of Regional Broadcasting stated that the BBC was 'not a unionist organisation in the sense of favouring any one constitutional settlement over another',[40] this view would likely be challenged by many favouring independence. During the 2014 referendum the BBC's role in reporting on the debates was controversial for many, with protests outside BBC Scotland over reporting by the BBC's then chief political editor Nick Robinson. Academic research suggested that the BBC's reportage did tend to follow the press in reducing the independence question to the SNP leader's individual ambitions.[41] Conversely, how far did British national media organisations help the public outside Scotland understand the debates going on inside Scotland? The first debate between Alex Salmond and Alistair Darling was broadcast live on STV in Scotland, but the ITV network which STV is a part of, showed *Alan Titchmarsh: Love Your Garden* to the rest of the UK instead.[42] This decision rather implies that the referendum was a 'local' affair to do with the Scots, rather than a debate that could lead to the break-up of the British State as we know it. In other ways parts of the national press operate in ways that make the divergence between the political cultures of Scotland and the rest of the UK self-evident. For example, *The Sun* gave radically different recommendations to readers in Scotland and the rest of the UK (but primarily England) in the run-up to the 2015 General Election. On 30 April the Scottish edition of *The Sun* had the new SNP leader Nicola Sturgeon photoshopped as Princess Leia wielding a light sabre. Along with the headline 'STUR WARS: A NEW HOPE' went the advice that Scottish readers should vote for the SNP to represent them in Westminster. Thus *The Sun* positioned itself as 'British' with a Scottish identity seen as being in close and legitimate proximity to that identity (i.e. the SNP would fight for the interests of Scotland *at Westminster*). The Scottish edition of *The Sun* is not an advocate for independence, but tries to negotiate the tensions implied by the hyphenated identity: Scottish-British. Those tensions, however, are vividly revealed by *The Sun's* English/rest of the UK edition on the same day. While *The Sun* had been able to situate Nicola Sturgeon as a political leader wrapped in the garb of popular culture, no such option was available to it when it wanted to endorse old Etonian David Cameron as the leader of the Conservatives. So instead they had David Cameron, in a weird photoshopped image, swaddled in a blanket as a new-born baby. Along with the headline 'IT'S A TORY' went the advice that English voters should vote for the Conservatives, in order, among other things, to stop the SNP from 'running the country'. Here the paper positioned itself as British – perhaps even English – with Scotland and its elected representatives at Westminster viewed as distant and threatening rather than friendly and proximate to the core values of 'the country'. Opinion poll research suggests that this message which was pushed relentlessly by the Conservatives in the final week of the 2015 election, was devastatingly effective in securing a victory for David Cameron's party, something Scotland's *The Daily Record* for one, had an item on.[43]

The press and independent media in the referendum

Within media studies, Habermas's concept of the public sphere has been used as a normative stick with which to critique/beat the civic-citizen performance of existing media. Gramsci's concept of hegemony offers an explanation as to why the media systematically fail to meet the normative criterion that they themselves appeal to in their self-identification as the 'fourth estate', supposedly holding power to account. One advantage which Gramsci's concept of hegemony has is that it stresses the contingent nature of political power and leadership. It is something that has to be constantly re-secured and cannot be guaranteed. Although Yes supporters in Scotland's independence campaign were deeply unhappy about the role of the press in particular,[44] there is evidence to suggest that in parts of the press, there was some heterogeneity in the views and voices that were articulated and some mitigation of an un-reflexive Unionism.[45] Unionism was far from seamlessly hegemonic even in the dominant media. This is important since any account of how hegemonies can be broken must be able to explain how and why the media, which has a powerful role in shaping public opinion, can find its authority, power and ability to shape perceptions and attitudes, checked and frustrated.

There was certainly a strong Unionist defence made by the British national press, the majority of which are unambiguously on the right of the political spectrum. The two biggest selling mid-market titles, the *Daily Express* and the very popular *Daily Mail* have Scottish editions but felt no need to do anything other than speak to a conservative constituency in terms of defending the Union. In the General Election of 2010 the Conservative Party won 412,855 votes, i.e. 16.7 per cent of the vote and just one MP. While this is electorally disastrous, the numbers indicate that conservatism as a political culture remains substantial enough to support conservative mid-market and broadsheet titles. Yet while this may help explain why ideologically there was little difference between the Scottish *Daily Mail* and its English (or rest of the UK editions), this was not true of *The Sun*.

The Scottish Sun occupies an indeterminate position between the London-based titles and the 'indigenous' Scottish based titles. *The Sun* launched its Scottish edition as far back as 1987, but apart from sport, much of the Scottish edition duplicated the edition for the rest of Britain. However with devolution *The Scottish Sun* properly 'editionised' with a 'printing plant and substantial editorial presence in Glasgow' and engaged in a vicious price war with the Scottish paper, *The Daily Record* (owned by Trinity Mirror) for the working-class market.[46] However *The Scottish Sun* was not in a position to duplicate the ideological position of its London-based counterpart, for the simple reason that its readership had long abandoned conservatism for Labourism, but until the referendum had remained steadfastly Unionist. Yet it was also clear, since the 2007 Scottish Parliament election, that the working-class vote was no longer habitually bonded to New Labour and was shifting to the SNP, not only as a party of government but on the ultimate question of independence. This fault line between the nation-states of Britain had to be negotiated by both *The Sun* and its tabloid rival *The Daily Record*.

The Labour-supporting *Daily Record* was also far from monolithically hostile to the Yes campaign – nor could it afford to be. Leaking readers to *The Scottish Sun* it would have been aware that the Unionism of Labour's working-class base was crumbling. In this context the already wounded *Daily Record* could no longer unreflexively polemicise on behalf of Labour, despite a very long history of close ties with its patronage networks, including even financial donations to the Scottish Labour Party.[47] For example, the paper took the innovative decision to give the leaders of the two campaigns, Alex Salmond and Alistair Darling, editorial control of the paper for an issue each, so that they could lay out the arguments over the first seven pages of the paper. *The Daily Record* also had multiple opinion columns every week by a former journalist and SNP Member for the Scottish Parliament, Joan McAlpine.

The middle class indigenous Scottish press also felt obliged to register the strong grass-roots campaign for independence that went well beyond the SNP's party-political base. Neither *The Scotsman* nor *The Herald* supported independence, but they were both critical of the lacklustre campaign waged on behalf of the Union and both papers included a minority of items that discussed independence as a legitimate position and therefore without the kind of hysteria that could be found in the *Mail* or *Express*. Of course *The Sunday Herald*, the sister paper to *The Herald* did come out in favour of independence and as a result saw its circulation boosted in the last six months of 2014 by 35 per cent, an astonishing figure in an age of almost relentless decline across the board for press titles. We should also note that Scotland has important 'city-state' papers such as Dundee's *Courier* and Aberdeen's *Press and Journal*.

These papers actually have larger readerships than the 'national' Scottish press, but are classed as 'local' papers because of their content. Yet these papers could not and did not ignore the referendum, and again, being more embedded in the Scottish political culture than the London-based papers, had to register voices on both sides of the debate (Dundee for example voted 57 per cent to 43 per cent for independence).

So for a variety of reasons, relationship with readers, economic pressure on titles, perceptible shifts in public opinion, the relative merits of the two campaigns and so forth, the press, while undoubtedly not neutral on the question of independence, were not in a position to be uniformly hostile. There was another reason why they could not afford to be, and that was the emerging counter-power of the independent and social media.

The dominant media, including the broadcasting news media, have indexed their perspectives to the discourses and institutional practices of an increasingly out-of-touch political elite, and on major political issues of the day, risk in turn their own legitimacy with their audiences as a result.[48] The Scottish journalist, Iain MacWhirter, who wrote for the pro-independent *Sunday Herald*, detected a substantial 'degree of alienation from the press, shared by hundreds of thousands of Scottish voters' following their performance during the referendum, and concluded that this 'should be causing alarm, not just in editorial offices, but in the political parties which are losing their ability to communicate.'[49] This is what Gramsci would call a crisis of hegemony. Accompanying and exacerbating this crisis in the persuasiveness of established political communication are alternative media practices that were organically linked to a vibrant grass-roots campaign.

Clearly talk of 'Twitter revolutions' and the like forget that, to be effective, new media communications must be articulated with genuine political organising. In the case of the Scottish referendum this was indeed the case, so it is not a form of Left cultural romanticism to highlight the progressive role of social media in this instance. A plethora of civil-society organisations were set up, providing the backbone to bottom-up political canvassing, often with no connections with either the SNP or the official umbrella organisation coordinating the independence campaign, Yes Scotland. Digital media and the more 'liquid' forms of organisation and leadership they facilitate[50] give new life to Gramsci's thinking about civil society as a loose network of 'molecular' initiatives.[51] Using Twitter, Facebook and websites to coordinate their activities, groups such as National Collective – which ran an imaginative artistic campaign promoting Yes, and the left-wing Radical Independence Campaign, which engaged with an alienated working class in a voter-registration drive, showed how the organisational capacities of a dynamic civil-society campaign could be facilitated by digital media. Websites such as Wings Over Scotland, Bella Caledonia, Newsnet Scotland and The National Collective were particularly popular where a virtual mediated public congregated that would have had a much more limited means of extensive self-constitution without the social media. National Collective's 'Yes Because' twitter campaign for example was seen by three million.[52] Elizabeth Linder, Facebook's politics and government specialist suggested long before the dominant media realised it that the vote would be close, based on Facebook chatter and the fact that network friends were potentially more influential than communication channels of the big vertical media companies.[53] Once again this would have been recognisable to Gramsci who was alert to the importance of peer influence, with his argument that everyone is a philosopher in some way, with their own conception of the world.[54]

Post-referendum research suggested that 54 per cent of people got information about the vote from social media, compared to 60 per cent for the press. That is a considerable achievement with virtually zero capital outlay (but some success in crowd-funding) compared to the huge resources the corporate media have at their disposal.[55] The research also found that the social media were more influential in forming voting decisions than the press (39 per cent to 34 per cent).[56] In the end the No campaign won the referendum by 55 per cent to 45 per cent, but over the two-year campaign, the constituency for independence had grown from the low 30s to the mid- 40s, despite the range of establishment forces against it. While it would be premature to draw any fixed conclusions about the long-term potential of the digital independent media to counter the hegemonic framing of debates by the dominant media in all circumstances, in the circumstances outlined here, there is evidence that they can be efficacious for progressive causes and that the dominant media was struggling to 'hold the line'. The big over-arching circumstance in this instance is the fracturing of the current historic bloc. The deepening crisis of economic liberalism manifests itself as the weakening capacity of the two major political cultures with which it is allied – conservatism and social liberalism – to always define the main terms of the debate.

Brexit

On 23 June 2016 Britain voted in a referendum to leave the European Union by 52 to 48 per cent. The political dynamic of the referendum on Britain's membership of the European Union (popularly known as Brexit) was very different from that which drove the Scottish referendum. In the Scottish case the referendum was driven by – and opened up a further space for – both social democratic and, to the left of the SNP, socialist political perspectives to get a real hearing in Scotland's public sphere. By contrast the British referendum was debated almost wholly within a spectrum that ranged from nationalistic but neo-liberal conservatism (that wanted to Leave) and liberal conservatism (best represented by Prime Minister David Cameron and the Chancellor George Osborne) and social liberalism (that wanted to Remain). The ability of these political cultures to keep the negative consequences of economic liberalism, both at home and across the EU, out of the public debate certainly testifies to their continued resilience. As Vivien A. Schmidt noted, neo-liberalism is 'so pervasive that it is hardly recognized as a major source of the disenchantment that lends support to the Leave campaign.'[57] The invisibility of economic liberalism as a creed, doctrine, ideology and set of policy orientations that shape lives is extraordinary. The journalist George Monbiot has remarked: 'Imagine if the people of the Soviet Union had never heard of communism. The ideology that dominates our lives has, for most of us, no name.'[58] Despite the consensus on the inviolability of economic liberalism, the referendum signalled a very deep and fundamental conflict between the two political cultures as they fought for intellectual and moral leadership of economic liberalism. The depth of the disagreement is itself symptomatic of the fact that the historic bloc is in deep trouble despite the difficulty non-consensus voices had breaking into and disrupting the terms of the debate. Because economic liberalism could not be called into question by either of these political cultures, the referendum was a debate driven less by reason and critical scrutiny than a defence of the shibboleths which each political culture has invested in, namely: a fantasy return to a quasi-imperial national identity of the past (for the reactionary conservative political culture) or the EU as a totemic embodiment of liberal intergovernmental cooperation, cultural cosmopolitanism and guarantee of open markets rather than a feared collapse back into national protectionism. In fact, within the referendum period itself, the debate on UK television news bulletins was even narrower than this because the key representatives of the Leave and Remain camps were overwhelmingly drawn from *within* the Conservative Party.[59] Only the Conservative Party would have been allowed by the media to be seen as sufficiently representative of the nation as a whole for what was essentially their own internal party dispute to stand in for the range of opinion and interests of the country (England or Britain?) at large.

The 52–48 split in the outcome left the disunited Kingdom divided along clear geographical lines (with Scotland and London voting overwhelmingly to Remain and much of the rest of the country stacking up voting majorities to Leave). Commentators were also divided as to how to interpret the vote, how to divine its meaning. Some on the Left saw it as a 'carnival of reaction' in which chauvinism and racism had been unleashed.[60] Others saw it as a democratic revolt against 'the business and banking oligarchy';[61] the Right also saw it as a 'peasants revolt' against the elite, but here the 'elite' in question was less the capitalist class (which the political right are quick to airbrush out of sight) than the social-liberal political culture that invests in 'detached cosmopolitan institutions' and detests the *culture* of the working class which helpfully, from a right-wing perspective, is essentialised as a coarser patriotic version of right-wing elites.[62] As if to confirm this right-wing critique of social liberalism, there was indeed coming from that quarter much in the way that suggested that people who voted for Brexit were a stupid, racist bloc who voted against their own economic well-being. In other words, each perspective saw what they wanted to see in Brexit. Conservative Party strategists for example saw a constituency that brought together the conservative south and the Labour voting north and thought that constituency could be recreated in a 'Brexit' General Election, which the new Prime Minister Theresa May duly called one year later. Things did not quite pan out as the Conservative Party strategists hoped and that perhaps indicates that the 'meaning' of Brexit is contradictory and its implications were not set in stone but a site of struggle in exactly the sense that Gramsci would have understood.

The different interpretations or readings of Brexit also pose a methodological problem – can we construct an account of Brexit that could synthesise the partial truths found in the different interpretations of Brexit in a coherent way? One reason some on the Left may have read the result as a working-class revolt against capital is that quite clearly the majority opinion of the capitalist class was against a Leave vote.

For the City of London, it threatened to jeopardise financial services done in Euro-denominated assets. For British manufacturing with any significant trade with Europe, leaving the EU threatened to make that trade more difficult and costly. For international capital investing in Britain as a bridgehead to Europe, the Leave vote raised questions as to future investment decisions.[63] Meanwhile, cutting EU immigration, the main stated purpose of leaving the EU from conservative Leave campaigners, risked robbing the Treasury of a net gain in tax receipts from working migrants, to say nothing of the impact that cutting the labour supply would have on various public services. Yet this only poses a challenge to Marxist explanations of political outcomes that stress the economic interests of capital as the primary adequate causal forces to be mapped in any and all explanations. For Brexit is an example of the relative autonomy of the political, an example of the political as a rupture from the trends set by the dominant economic interests that are prevailing – and on which any revolution in fact depends. Except in this case it was primarily, at least in terms of the moral-political leadership that made the running in the mainstream, clearly a 'revolt on the right'. A Gramscian perspective is well prepared to explore how cultural identities and differences could be mobilised and articulated to specific political projects, even ones like Brexit that disrupt certainly the majority opinion and quite possibly the majority *interests* of the dominant classes.

Conservatism and Brexit

Conservatism as a political culture has long had an ambivalent relationship with Europe. In the eighteenth and nineteenth centuries conservatism did not see itself as a European power – that was too small an ambition for a country with imperial holdings spread out across the world. Instead conservatism saw itself as a global power – with its Navy providing the military underpinning to its commercial interests. Conservatism retains strong residues of latent suspicion and even symbolic aggression towards the two main European powers – France and Germany – with whom Britain has had serious military conflicts. The conservative vision of Britain following any withdrawal from the EU is a return to Britain as a global trading power, exploiting its links with its former colonies as in the days of old and securing bilateral trade deals in which the supplicant status of the British would be concealed behind nationalist rhetoric.[64] The most important partner would of course be North America. In the twentieth century, conservatism has been attracted to a certain version and vision of America: America as the global superpower with whom Britain (here conceived by conservatism as an equal partner and not *very* junior lieutenant) is allied in protecting 'democracy' around the world; America as a far more deregulated free-market capitalist power in which the rights of private property to do as it wishes have been historically more extensive than in Europe for much of the twentieth century; America as the global capital of consumer capitalism, the nation that best sells the benefits of capitalism and the system of free enterprise to the world (while keeping out of sight the vast inequalities and poverty in the country); and America as Britain's progeny, sharing a history, culture and language. Of course there are other versions and visions of America that are active within British popular culture, but the above are the ones that are of most interest to conservatism's Atlanticist leanings.

In the 1980s as the political and economic integration of Europe began to gather pace, old conservative instincts about Europe were compounded by the apparent threat which social democracy on the western side of the continent might pose to economic liberalism, which had begun to consolidate itself under the Thatcher revolution.

In 1988 Jacques Delors, then President of the European Commisssion wooed British trade unions with a speech to the TUC conference at Bournemouth, with the promise that the construction of an internal EU market would be coupled with a social market offering EU-wide workers' rights and protections. Defeated at home, the trade unions thought they might bolster their domestic position with the help of the integration project that Delors was enthusiastically touting. Conversely, the conservative right saw the EU as an emerging super-state that threatened the autonomy and powerbase of conservatism's newly resurgent economic liberalism within its own borders. To the Thatcherites, the EU 'reflected a mushy, even effeminate European notion of social solidarity and soft communitarianism.'[65] A couple of weeks after Delors' speech to the TUC, Margaret Thatcher gave a now-famous speech in Bruges that was subsequently seen as a hardening of her opposition to the direction of travel within Europe. After affirming the importance of Europe to Britain and even more perhaps, the importance of Britain to Europe, Thatcher indicated that Europe must remain a collection of individual nation-states working together. Europe she argued must not 'try to suppress nationhood and concentrate power at the centre of a European conglomerate'. Instead Spain as Spain, France as France, Britain as Britain, 'each with its own customs, traditions and identity' must be preserved and not dissolved into an 'identikit European personality'. In affirming British identity and sovereignty Thatcher noted: 'We have not successfully rolled back the frontiers of the State in Britain, only to see them re-imposed at a European level with a European super-state exercising a new dominance from Brussels.'[66]

Others within the Conservative Party were more supportive of the EU precisely because in their assessment, which proved right, the balance of power within Europe was shifting towards economic liberalism and away from the 'social' Europe which the British Left hoped could be secured at supranational level. Yet even though there would be greater convergence between the neo-liberal political economy of Britain and that of Europe as both entered the twenty-first century, conservative suspicion of Europe did not abate. As is evident in Thatcher's speech, what also worried conservatism was anything that might diminish the actual and symbolic power of the British State in which conservatism had invested so much and over which it had secured such an entrenched and powerful position. Anything that diminished the British law, British Parliament, the British judiciary and the monarchy, diminished the ritualistic and ideological power of State institutions which conservatism saw as virtually identical with itself. Brussels as the location of many of the EU's key institutions came to be known as 'Brussels bureaucracy' within conservative discourse, primarily because it was felt not to be 'our' bureaucracy. There was, however, one element in the conservative critique of EU overreach which the 'bureaucracy' tag highlighted that had a more legitimate basis, and that was the democratic deficit in the EU institutions. For example, the EU Parliament has no independent legislative role but is instead subordinate to the Council of the European Union, the EU Commission, and the European Court of Justice which is dedicated to protecting markets from political interference, as well as, increasingly, the European Central Bank. As Wolfgang Streeck has argued, this supra-state apparatus looks to be the realisation of the dreams of neo-liberal theorists such as Schmitt and Hayek: a politically constructed apparatus designed to insulate market failures in the terrain of social justice from popular democratic correction.[67]

Of course conservatism's critique of the democratic deficit within the EU is highly selective in its framing of the issue. Conservative discourses identify the threat of the burgeoning EU 'super-state' but not the economic order that that apparatus is designed to advance. Similarly, for conservatism British sovereignty is not felt to be threatened by powerful global corporations, financial markets or American economic and political power. This is significant because the conservative nationalist dream of recovery of sovereignty is more accurately the preserving of the appearance of *political* sovereignty while *economic* sovereignty continues (through nation-states or the EU) to be transferred to transnational capital (finance and corporate). At least the appearance of political sovereignty – now hollowed out by economic power – does not directly erode conservatism's own domestic institutional powerbase from which it can build powerful bonds of loyalty from and to the conservative nation.

Splits within the Conservative Party over Europe had weakened and helped topple Margaret Thatcher and they also went on to badly damage the electoral prospects of the party under John Major. These internal fissures seriously weakened the traditional party of British conservatism as an electoral force and so gradually the political dynamic of hostility to Europe moved outside the Conservative Party and into UKIP in the noughties, which sought to revive Thatcherite suspicion of the EU in the face of the liberal ascendancy that New Labour represented. Three key developments helped UKIP remobilise a traditional and reactionary conservatism in this period. Firstly, following the 2001 attack on America by al Qaeda, the declared 'war on Terrorism' by George Bush and the 2005 London bombings by Islamic terrorists, UKIP were able to link up a whole range of conservative fears around the apparent threat which a multicultural society posed to 'Christian' Britain. A binary discourse of 'our' values and culture and 'theirs' revived a typically conservative model of simple polarities between a White nativist population and alien others (no matter how long those others had lived in Britain). Secondly, net migration increased dramatically from 2004, especially from the EU as ten more countries became members of the EU; eight of them former communist states. Although this meant eventual commitment to the free movement of labour, Britain, unlike Germany, France and most other EU countries, waived the option of transitional controls until 2011. This was in part because the New Labour leadership wanted to align itself closely with the former communist states as a counterweight to the traditional Franco-German axis within the EU, a continuation of the centuries-old British policy of trying to prevent the emergence of a single dominant force on the European mainland.

204 · ENGLAND'S DISCONTENTS

The third and decisive development was the economic crash in 2007–8. This allowed UKIP to tie immigration to the feelings of economic insecurity which both the crash and austerity orientated responses to the crash would produce. By 2009, in the European elections, UKIP came second with nearly 2.5 million votes (16.5 per cent), pushing the Labour Party into third place. With the formation of the Conservative–Liberal coalition government in 2010 committed to austerity politics that marked a return to the crude Thatcherite methodology of cuts to public services, it was easy for UKIP to opportunistically connect under-pressure services such as doctor surgeries, hospitals and schools as well as the falling real value of wages to the increased numbers of immigrants and asylum-seekers. In a further conflation, Islamic terrorists could be bundled into this generalised threat and then conflated again with the already existing long established Muslim community in the UK, producing a toxic stew of condensations (a Muslim, immigrant, asylum-seeking, terrorist, EU multi-headed Hydra) and displacements. This image of a loss of control of borders mixed in with threats to the sustainability of public services and security fears and linked back to membership of an enlarged EU and the transfer of power and control to 'Brussels bureaucrats' does have for many people a very powerful resonance, one that links the psychological to the social, the individual to a national identity, both apparently threatened with disintegration.[68] A classic and deeply irrational displacement strategy had been facilitated by the conservative–liberal consensus on economic liberalism, arguably to the detriment of British capital, unarguably against the majority weight of opinion within the British capitalist class.

Further to the right of UKIP was the right-wing version of the new anti-party horizontal politics to be found on the Left, with the English Defence League mobilising not just the 'populist' discourse of UKIP but an openly racist and Islamophobic, culture-war politics expressing itself in street demonstrations. Ethnographic work by Winlow, Hall and Treadwell on this brand of English nationalism provides a very rich and suggestive evidence base on the dynamics of politics and sentiments. They point to the degradation of material well-being that once structured the ontology of the working-class lifeworld as a significant factor in the rise of White working class anti-Muslim feelings. Yet even more important than this directly material decline is the sense of political betrayal and the breaking of a tacit compact that made this degradation possible. They identify a major source of anger and hatred with the unilateral 'severance of the relationship they once had with the Left-identified liberal class that once pushed itself uninvited into their lives *in loco parentis*.'[69] Unable to find a place within a new set of political narratives from which they were deliberately excluded as archaic leftovers, there are layers of the working class that have become receptive to the moral-intellectual leadership of the right, including the fascist right. The discourse of their respondents reads like a tick-box list of grievances carefully nurtured and amplified by the right-wing press, which together with the political parties functions as the 'intellectual High Command'[70] of conservative nationalism. Islamic terrorism, fundamentalism, preachers of hate, paedophile rings of Muslim men, immigration, overpopulation, and foreign cultures resistant to assimilation, an 'English' culture under threat from Sharia law, and multiplying mosques, all loom large and all overseen by out-of-touch political elites in Westminster and the even more remote institutions of the EU.

In January 2013, the Conservative Prime Minister David Cameron promised a referendum on Britain's membership of the EU if his party won an overall majority in the 2015 General Election. He planned to put to the electorate a new renegotiated relationship with Europe prior to any referendum. This was an attempt to protect the party's vote from further incursions from UKIP, which by 2013 was registering between 11–18 per cent support in the polls. And it was an attempt, just as importantly, to neutralise the issue within the Conservative Party where a significant minority of Conservative MPs, possibly around a third (one hundred) were not just Eurosceptic but Europhobic Leavers.[71] This phalanx of Conservative Party MPs functioned to give the anti-EU discourse establishment legitimacy and ensured the presence of a right-wing critique of Europe within parliament. They functioned in a tacit alliance with UKIP. While Conservative MPs tended to focus on the constitutional issues and thus to secure legitimacy for anti-EU discourses within elite circles, UKIP's discourse was more right-wing populist, aimed at winning wider electoral support for leaving the EU based on fear and displacement strategies. UKIP out of parliament and Europhobic Conservative MPs in parliament constituted an informal alliance. The right-wing media which dominated debate within the public sphere typically presented the EU as being either a foreign apparatus subordinating British sovereignty to its will or a bargaining forum in which the interests of the Franco-German axis always prevails.[72] Certainly this represents another contradiction in the political communications of the nation-state, as it tries and fails to properly make sense of a supranational apparatus based on multilateral compromises and negotiations. However, this is a failure that is not intrinsic to the nation-form as such but of the specific political culture we are discussing and its domination of the media. On the other hand, liberal critiques of conservatism's inability to think in intergovernmental terms, lacks conservatism's pragmatic intuition that there are real world exercises of power and individual nation-state interests being deployed under the cover of multilateralism, which liberalism, in its attempts to promote a 'rational' institutional framework for capitalism in a global age, underplays. Beyond the relative blind spots of the conservative–liberal framework for political communications, the fundamental contradiction is this: political legitimacy, such as it is, remains fundamentally a resource of the national, but transnational capitalism operates with limited accountability above and below the nation-state.

The national press, especially those that have any investment in conservative nationalism, also have little incentive to wish the British nation-state to pool sovereignty to a supranational level along the lines of the EU project, since, while that is a pro-capitalist project, it diminishes the distinctive ideological power of British conservatism and with it their own ability to influence public debate on key policy issues and pursue their own corporate interests (e.g on media regulation and ownership) vis-à-vis a political class that is easily frightened and bullied by the power of the press to make or break careers.[73]

There is little doubt that it was rising conservative support in England that was the main driver for the referendum and the result (although a 52.5 per cent majority in Wales also voted to Leave). If UKIP's support base was initially mapped onto the electoral strongholds of the Conservative Party, it also gradually began to eat into the Labour Party's support, especially after the 2007–8 crash. In 2010 UKIP got approximately 919,000 votes but in the 2015 election this jumped very significantly to just under four million, with much of this increase coming from former Labour voters in the north of England. Scotland, where as we have seen, something like a social democratic politics had re-emerged around the independence movement, voted 62 per cent Remain against 38 per cent Leave. It is deeply ironic that Scotland's civic nationalism continued to be framed by Unionists as having dark, extreme, intolerant undercurrents during the independence referendum debate. Yet it was clear that if the classic reactionary nationalist model of the past was to be found anywhere, it was in England. Unlike Scotland, discontent with economic liberalism in England had nowhere else to go than to a political culture that was feeding off the discontent generated by economic liberalism but which offered only a different cultural identity or cap to top off the same neo-liberal economy. Unlike Donald Trump's populist right-wing presidential campaign in 2016, British conservatism made no gestures towards economic nationalism that might have brought it into conflict with economic liberalism's globalist agenda. Anti-EU conservatism only offered an even more intensive contradiction between cultural and political nationalism and an economic policy premised on further rounds of de-regulating workers and consumer rights, driving down corporation tax and attracting international capital on the basis of high profits and low social obligations. Nostalgic conservatism saw Britain as a buccaneering island-state operating in the high seas of free-market transnational capital like Singapore or Hong Kong, both small former island colonies from Britain's long gone era of empire.[74]

Liberalism, class and Brexit

Perhaps the evident nostalgic fantasy of the 'little Englanders' persuaded liberalism that it had little reason to fear defeat in a referendum on EU membership. Yet this was a rationalist hubris that forgot how capitalism, as an engine of economic insecurity, stokes irrational politics and a stew of not so irrational discontents. With the culturally reactionary wing of conservatism now deeply antipathetic to the EU, the deep bonds of loyalty to the British State could be mobilised against the thin attractions of an abstract ideal that had progressively lost its lustre throughout the 2000s, with even the French refusing to ratify a new Constitution for Europe in their 2005 referendum. Liberalism, which has always played second fiddle to conservatism when it comes to 'owning' the symbolic identity of the State, actually had few strings to its bow. The major one, that it was economically beneficial to stay in the EU, had taken a significant knock with the Eurozone crisis after the global 2008 crash. The New Labour governments decided that it was politically difficult for them to drop the British pound and join the Eurozone, although they dressed this up as a set of five economic tests that had to be met before joining the monetary union. As well as deferring to conservatism on questions of the State (such as that most resonant and symbolically loaded question of currency) liberalism also left the field of battle in terms of the question of class. As we have seen, conservatism can in fact accommodate some version of working-class consciousness and identity within its culture, as long as it is primarily cast in terms *of* culture and that the right (i.e. conservative) *forms* of identity and *objects* of identification are cultivated. Liberalism too offers an idealised model of culture as part of its sense of identity and narrative of the past, present and future, and in the contemporary period it is one that is evacuated of a class dimension. New Labour signed up to the EU's social chapter, giving minimum guarantees of workers' rights, but they certainly were not going to roll back nearly two decades of Conservative government trade union legislation that would help give not only the right to trade union representation but the ability to have *effective* trade unions that could substantively counter the ongoing employer offensive.

Cultural studies is more symptom than cause here but we can certainly illuminate this evacuation of class in this highly meta-theoretical sub-system of liberalism. Writing at the end of the 1990s and evaluating the first two years of the New Labour government, Kevin Davey was critical of the timidity and superficiality of its refashioning of British identity. Yet the terms of his critique were themselves problematic, since Davey wanted a more robust confrontation with what he saw as the cornerstone of conservatism within New Labour:

> A residual white Englishness, which has long struggled to shore up its fractured identity, must be helped to unlearn its privilege, to adjust to the global flows and circuits of capital and culture, and the transnational social forms that regulation will increasingly take, and to construct new relationships, real and imaginary, with its cohabitees and neighbours in England, in Europe and across the globe.[75]

Being told you are 'residual' (out of date, fading from history, on the wrong side of modernity, etc.) must be a candidate for the top prize of encouraging a counterproductive cultural defensiveness. Who really is supposed to embody the 'privilege' of 'white Englishness' is never explicitly articulated; a subtle coding which is itself revealing. For to have explicitly named the real subject here as the White working class would have perhaps raised two queries in the mind of any curious reader: firstly, could this group, which had been on the receiving end of a sustained class assault since 1979 really be described as privileged? Secondly, to frame this group in terms of 'White Englishness' instead of part of a multicultural working class, a cross-cultural group that have *together* suffered material deprivation, might be thought to have already foreclosed on at least the *possibility* of a different kind of political project. It is clear though what kind of political project is on offer from Davey, one in which adjustment to 'the global flows and circuits of capital and culture' are a given. One has to wonder what kind of new relationships this liberalism imagines is likely to be produced with local neighbours, let alone across Europe and the globe, for people whose opportunities for doing anything more than surviving are growing smaller, not larger and more expansive.

Confronted with the idealism of conservatism, liberalism offers not cultural materialism but another version of cultural idealism. Of course, theoretically it is a more progressive cultural model but its idealism means that in our current circumstances, it has little critical reach into the non-cultural conditions that could sustain this progressive cultural model. On the contrary, by bracketing off the socio-economic conditions that make cultural diversity the object of a displaced fear and anger, liberalism ends up reinforcing the culture it says it wants to critique and negating the culture it claims it wants to flourish. More broadly, this cultural idealism nestles within what Gramsci criticised as a 'bourgeois cosmopolitanism' that reflected the remoteness of the Italian intelligentsia from their own national conditions.[76] This in turn opened up a political space for 'a frenzied chauvinism which linked itself to the glories of Rome'.[77] Structurally, we are analysing a similar dynamic in our present conjuncture.

Within the British intelligentsia there is an extraordinarily uncritical investment in the EU as a symbol of internationalism and cultural tolerance against the reactionary nationalism that framed the anti-EU referendum. Liberalism has been very successful in equating any opposition to the EU with the reactionary conservatism that opposed it. Compared to the 1975 referendum after which Britain entered what was then the European Economic Community, a socialist critique of the EU's current institutional, economic and political setup has been effectively silenced. Two examples of recent EU policymaking indicate that the absence of a Left critique from the debate about the EU diminishes collective understanding of its leading trends. Firstly there is the brutal assault which the EU (and particularly Germany's political class), the European Central Bank and the International Monetary Fund has conducted on the Greek economy, politics and civil society since the 2008 crash rippled across the Eurozone. Where was the 'internationalism', the European solidarity, the economic benefits, the dedication to democracy, the Europe with a 'social conscience', the tolerance and other worthy values that the European Union is supposed to symbolise? A punitive, extreme, economic liberalism has been meted out to Greece, in which debt has been mercilessly used as a weapon to drive a privatisation, cuts and deregulation agenda that has pauperised an advanced western society at massive cost to health, opportunity and well-being[78] and in the name of a northern European soberly prudent economic order disciplining the lazy spendthrift southern Europeans. Once again economic liberalism and racism are close bedfellows.

The second example of the EU's dominant tendency towards enforcing economic liberalism across the EU, can be found in the Trans-Atlantic Trade and Investment Partnership (TTIP) deal that was being conducted in secret between the EU and US authorities for three years before talks collapsed shortly after the EU referendum in August 2016. TTIP aimed to reduce protective regulations on food and standards, workers' rights, the environment and finance. The centre piece though of the plans was to build into the agreement extensive recourse to Investor-State Dispute Settlements (ISDS) which allow 'investors' to sue governments who take *any* action which corporations feel damage their interests (whether health and safety, environmental rights, etc., to say nothing of nationalisation). With TTIP the old Marxist formulation of capitalist democracy as the 'dictatorship of the bourgeoisie' has never looked less like hyperbole.

Together the Scottish referendum of 2014 and the referendum on Britain's future relationship with the EU, reveal the deepening divisions and crises of the current historic bloc. In both, profound questions of national identity, of how people think of themselves, perceive themselves and how they feel about their individual and collective circumstances, were tied up with the relationship of nation(s) to larger geopolitical entities. In the case of the Scottish referendum, conservative, liberal and neo-liberal Unionism had sufficiently exhausted the reserves of historic esteem and good will, pragmatic acceptance and institutional inertia, to endanger the United Kingdom's existence as a political entity. The emergence of an alternative in the form of independence is always a moment of significant danger for any historic bloc, since it fractures the appearance of historic inevitability and challenges the 'There Is No Alternative' narrative that has been particularly associated with economic liberalism and its hollowing out of political choices. The Scottish referendum demonstrated that the popular sentiment for and memory of social democracy as a defining characteristic of national identity remains active. This in turn widened the space for a Left current to also make itself heard within the public sphere, and social media, combined with grass-roots activism, was an important tool to facilitate that. The social democratic and left discussion of identity is different from the conservative–liberal paradigms insofar as the former reintegrate questions of culture back into political economy considerations. This is why Scotland's national independence movement was in the main driven by civic concerns, including questions of social justice and for the Left, an explicit politics based on the redistribution of wealth. Since neither conservatism nor liberalism can offer anything more than at best a feeble creaming-off strategy (meritocracy) designed to revivify the desiccated ranks of the elites with a few recruits from outside its social base, social justice and culture remain separated from each other. A significant component in any substantive attempt to address social justice questions must include social class considerations. Neither conservatism nor liberalism (in its current alliance with economic liberalism) can do this effectively. The 'economy', which certainly featured heavily in both referendums, is treated by conservatism and liberalism merely as an economic universe that may have impacts on us, if *it* is 'harmed', but not itself constituted by social and political interests and relations. In the Scottish referendum, conservatism and liberalism presented the economy as something that it is best to not disturb by changing its surrounding circumstances. In the EU referendum, liberalism continued this line of argument (a new 'Project Fear') while Brexit conservatism adopted a remarkably optimistic posture given that it was now proposing as big a transformation in political and economic arrangements as Scotland's independence movement but which it had warned could be economically devastating. In both cases the discourse rises only to the level of the economy as a set of numbers, trade, investment and so on; the 'givens' of what is taken for granted as the universal and naturalised laws of the economy. How wealth is being produced and distributed and what its implications are for political, social and cultural well-being barely enter the discussion. Conservatism and liberalism are therefore prone to cultural idealism (culture severed from the economic) and economic determinism (the economic severed from political and cultural conditions). In the case of the EU referendum, the hegemonic power of conservatism and liberalism was preserved; they framed the entirety of the debate, at least in the main public spheres. The absence of any significant major organisation such as the Labour Party or the trade unions making a critique of the EU helped squeeze out further more radical voices. Of course, below what the official public discourse can register, there were small-scale and interpersonal conversations that motivated people to vote Leave for reasons very different from dominant Brexit conservatism. But the relative absence of these conversations in the mass media organs of the public sphere meant they lacked legitimacy and were blocked from providing the moral-intellectual leadership that could have developed the arguments, make them more coherent, more robust, more replete with examples, more confident and more likely to crystallise as mapping out a different future trajectory. Instead the conservative–liberal consensus held the line and as a result the policy horizon remains dominated by the dynamic of competition between conservatism and liberalism and contradictions between them and their object of desire: economic liberalism. Both the contradictions and the competition is intensifying, but since neither of these political cultures can resolve the fundamentals, Britain remains locked into a political dynamic that becomes more unpredictable, even for the dominant classes. Every crisis, as capital knows, is always an opportunity, but not every crisis is always and only an opportunity for capital. The historic bloc is under significant pressure, the question of hegemony and counter-hegemony has never been more urgent or relevant.

7

Hegemony in question: Stuart Hall, Gramsci and us

In the 1980s, when a new historic bloc was being constructed by successive Thatcher governments, Stuart Hall was widely seen as Britain's pre-eminent Gramscian scholar. He occupied a dual role as both a founding figure within Cultural Studies and as a leading political commentator on the Left, writing in the pages of *Marxism Today*. Within Cultural Studies he argued for a Gramscian understanding of popular culture as a site of struggle and contestation and critiqued Marxist economism which 'read off' the ideological and the political from economic-class positions and relations. In *Marxism Today*, he applied these Cultural Studies arguments in a more directly political engagement by critiquing the Left's intellectual and political response to and understanding of Thatcherism. In particular, the Left, according to Hall, did not understand what was new about Thatcherism or how this political philosophy operated to change the parameters of what had once been the settled compromise between the classes. In large part, for Hall, this alleged lack of sensitivity to the novelty of Thatcherism and the changes taking place within the British political scene flowed from the somewhat static orientation which economism imposed on the analysis of political and ideological phenomena (as the almost transhistorical reflection of underlying, more or less permanently fixed economic-class forces). The two arenas of intervention (Cultural Studies and *Marxism Today*) were obviously connected but they also produced somewhat different versions of 'Stuart Hall'. The Hall that appeared in Cultural Studies seemed to flirt dangerously close to the post-structuralist positions that were then very much in vogue. In the pages of *Marxism Today* however, the Communist Party's monthly magazine that sat on the shelves of mainstream retail outlets, Hall's work was less theoretically speculative, more grounded in live political debates and more focused on the flaws of social democracy and Labourism than critiques of Marxism. Here, Hall's argument that the Left needed to take ideology and the battle of ideas more seriously, in the same way that Thatcherism did, sparked an extensive debate about the relative importance and determining power of different levels of the social, economic, political and cultural formation. Revisiting this debate can help us clarify Gramsci's concept of hegemony, its component parts and its relevance for us today, as well as Hall's own contribution to our understanding of hegemony in theory and practice.

Because Hall was asking tough questions of the Left, because it was a historical moment of retreat and defeat, because in his Cultural Studies writings he often critiqued Marxism more than any other position, because he wrote for *Marxism Today*, which has (despite the title) generally been seen as following a right-wing trajectory that influenced New Labour types, because of occasional ambiguities in Hall's own formulations and his flirtations with discourse theory and post-structuralism; because of all these and other reasons, Hall's work has often been seen as laying the intellectual foundations for the retreat from class, from critical political economy, from socialism and a headlong rush to embrace New Labour. Yet I think if one does Hall the service of actually reading the words on the page, especially the writings in *Marxism Today* during the 1980s, I think that proposition is really quite hard to sustain. Indeed I must confess that my own memory of Hall's work during the 1980s had to be revised when I turned again to his writings collected in *Thatcherism and the Crisis of the Left: The Hard Road to Renewal* (1988). I offer here then a critical re-engagement with Hall's work on Gramsci. In doing so I hope to show that Hall's Gramscian inspired writings offer a very considerable source of wisdom and relevance to our present moment, when the historic bloc of economic liberalism, conservatism and social liberalism is vulnerable and open to challenge in a way that has not been the case for around forty years.

Materialism

Hall's interest in Gramsci stems from the difficult methodological and philosophical questions entailed in the relationship that Marxism posits between economic and social-class forces and ideas, values, culture and consciousness. We have seen in Chapter 1 that Gramsci himself rejected economism, which he saw as fostering a mechanistic conception of the world, a view of necessary and fixed relations between classes and politics that induced a pacifying element into socialist politics which could afford to wait for history to unfold according to a teleological schema in which it triumphed over capitalism despite temporary setbacks. Hall detected something similar within the Left in the 1980s as Thatcherism consolidated its ascendancy. It took the form of a comforting assumption that socialist politics remains 'the natural centre of gravity' for the working class[1] and that any setbacks or incursions by the Right into that support base are inevitably temporary: 'There is a strong assumption that, in a class society like ours, where the vast majority of working people are continuously at the negative, the receiving end of the system, the social and material conditions in which working people themselves live will inevitably predispose them towards socialism'.[2]

There is, Hall insisted, no guaranteed link between the conditions of a life and the political ideas that make sense of those conditions. There is no guaranteed link that the political ideas people have do match their interests. Of course there are many complex issues here as to how 'interests' are assessed: is it just about money in the pocket or does it include whether the food you eat or the air you breath is damaging your health? Is it just about what you can purchase tomorrow or is it about something longer term? Does it include the welfare of family and friends and community? Such questions indicate that 'interests' need to be defined through a process of political and cultural struggle. They do not simply speak for themselves from the material 'facts' of social being as it were.

Hall does not, in principle at any rate, dismiss powerful tendencies of social being that may predispose individuals and groups towards a given complex of ideas, values and perspectives. Yet these are only tendencies that can be seized upon and inflected in a variety of directions by different political projects. The 'logics of ideological inference turn out to be more multivariate, the automatic connection between material and ideal factors less determinate, than the classical theory would have us believe.'[3] Whether this was being fair to the 'classical theory' is rather contentious. Marxism is nothing if it is not some kind of theory of determinate social phenomena in which economic-class relations play a powerful explanatory role. But nothing can protect any body of ideas from disciples degrading its sophistication. As the Bolshevik thinker A.K. Voronsky noted long ago, 'Marx's method in the hands of simplifiers can easily turn into primitive vulgarizing'.[4]

216 · ENGLAND'S DISCONTENTS

An anti-vulgarising materialism recognises, as Gramsci did, that different political projects can interpret social realities in different ways, in part because social reality and social being itself is deeply contradictory and a dynamic field of potentialities that can be realised in different directions. 'Materialism remains active' Hall wrote, '[b]ut its tendency is not unidirectional.'[5] Thus collective notions of identity that form around an antagonism against powerful social and economic interests, vie with the equally powerful tendency towards a 'spontaneous' atomistic consciousness encouraged by market relations, market exchanges and market discourses, of the kind that today pollute our language and representations. Hall was very aware of this 'spontaneous' consciousness and its roots in material life.

> In a world saturated by money exchange, and everywhere mediated by money, the 'market' experience is *the* most immediate, daily and universal experience of the economic system for everyone...It should not surprise us if the mass of working people don't possess the concepts with which to cut into the process at another point, frame another set of questions, and bring to the surface or reveal what the overwhelming facticity of the market constantly renders invisible.[6]

Thus social struggles and experiences have to become 'politically active' through an 'oppressor/oppressed form of consciousness.'[7] Tendencies then – whether towards social solidarity and collectivism or towards atomised market relations and conceptions – are not guarantees of any particular outcome. They are only the material prerequisites that make a form of politics possible or impossible. And an important part of increasing the efficacy of solidarity and combating and contracting atomised individualism, are the ideas in circulation that make sense of and rationalise social being and the experience of social being.

Hall wanted to avoid a mechanical materialism that made ideas merely the pale dependent reflections of more important activities going on in the economic sphere. If the subaltern classes can have their experiences inflected into different interpretive schemas, it is also the case that neither the middle classes nor the dominant power bloc are 'fixed' in their historical consciousness by the continuity of socio-economic class relations. To think that they are would, in the case of the rise of Thatcherism for example, lead one to assume that there is nothing new here; it is the 'same old same old', and that can lead to a debilitating refusal to engage in the struggle over ideas or to see what is at stake in the ascendancy of new idea formations.

Hall criticised Marx's early formulation in *The German Ideology* that 'ruling ideas' are the ideas of the 'ruling class' because it suggests a fixed and immediate relationship between socio-economic dominance and the field of consciousness: 'To say that the "ruling-ness" of a class is the guarantee of the dominance of certain ideas is to ascribe them as the exclusive property of that class, and to define particular forms of consciousness as class-specific'.[8]

It is certainly true that the 'rulingness' of a class is not a guarantee of the dominance of certain ideas. This, for Hall, required political and ideological struggle. Ownership of resources did not automatically translate into dominance in the realm of ideas and public opinion formation. There is a sense in which this argument that there is no automatic equivalence between ownership of the means of production and presence in the public sphere of ruling class ideas, can be inflected in a way that calls Hall's broader emphasis on the importance of ideas, into question. For Hall, ideas are important in shaping outcomes even if they have to be struggled for and the dominance of certain ideas cannot be guaranteed. Yet what if there is no equivalence between ownership and control and the broader circulation of ideas precisely because the latter and the legitimation it appears to afford, is not required? Some ideas of the ruling class have little general circulation but their institutions have plenty of actual institutional force simply by virtue of their control of the apparatuses of political and economic power. For example, the principles by which finance capital operates have very little penetration into the wider population outside finance and other linked bourgeois groups, yet its power to affect the value of currencies and other commodities is considerable. Thus financial news dominates the specialist press but is in effect a restricted conversation for the elites only.[9]

It may be, to follow the direction of the argument along the lines Hall was probably intending, that the ideas actually dominant in the public sphere are a more composite mix of ideas, value systems, etc. that can be sourced in a variety of classes, strata within classes and non-class groups and configured as an unequal compromise formation. Certainly I have argued that British national identity is such a composite construction of this sort, even if certain sectors have more esteem within the mainstream institutions of society than others, as one would expect in a class society.

218 · ENGLAND'S DISCONTENTS

It is also true that particular forms of consciousness are not necessarily class-specific – they can be initially associated with one group and then achieve some acceptance or consent amongst other classes for example. The whole basis of the theory of hegemony depends on this possibility. It is also the case that what may appear to be a shared set of values and ideas on the surface are in their contexts actually different to various degrees as lived by different modes of social being. Idea complexes can also be appropriated and refunctioned in the heat of ideological struggle, prised away from one set of value systems and made to work for another, in the way we saw the Chartists develop a proto socialist discourse out of hybrid sources, including liberalism, Christianity and feudalism in Chapter 5.

Despite Marx's early formulation on ideas and the role of the intellectuals as the 'thinkers' of the ruling class, his actual practice was a good deal more sophisticated. As Hall argued, if one looks at Marx's engagement with Hegel or classical political economy he did not dismiss these bodies of thought. On the contrary, he conducted the most meticulous process of synthesis and critique on which his own thought and development depended. But he did argue that there were structural limits to these systems of thought beyond which they could not go; that they could only symptomatically allude to things which they had to avoid facing full on; that there were implications they could not pursue; that they had to assume certain things and that these assumptions necessarily deformed their work. As Hall put it:

> The distortions, to be precise, within bourgeois theoretical ideology at its more 'scientific' were, nevertheless, real and substantial. They did not destroy many aspects of its validity – hence it was not 'false' simply because it was confined within the limits and horizon of bourgeois thought. On the other hand the distortions limited its scientific validity, its capacity to advance beyond certain points, its ability to resolve its own internal contradictions, its power to think outside the skin of the social relations reflected in it.[10]

On this definition, ideology refers to the limits, boundaries, silences and repressions as much as the actual content of ideas and value complexes. And these limits are systematic, linked to the social interests they cannot transcend without ceasing to in one-way or another rationalise inequality of resources, power and status.

Ideology and ideologism

In this study I have used the term 'political cultures' to discuss how ideas, values, perspectives, habits and preferences form in relation to social classes. 'Political cultures' maps nicely onto Gramsci's interest in politics as located in the State and culture as formed and developed in civil society. A potentially synonymous term might be ideology, which Hall played a key role in helping to get back onto the agenda of media and Cultural Studies in the 1970s. Here he defines ideology as: 'the mental frameworks – the languages, the concepts, categories, imagery of thought, and the systems of representation – which different classes and social groups deploy in order to make sense of, define, figure out and render intelligible the 'way society works'.[11]

By this definition, ideology is synonymous with culture. Hall argued that because we can only know the world and make sense of it through the available languages at our disposal, the struggle around which definitions and systems of representations becomes dominant, taken for granted, 'common sense', is an intensely political issue. Here contemporary theories of language seemed to connect with Gramsci's emphasis on cultural and political struggle. Hall was careful, however, to distinguish his position from post-structuralist theorists such as Foucault or the post-structuralist reading of Gramsci offered by Laclau and Mouffe. 'Society', Laclau opined, 'as an underlying mechanism that gives reasons for or explains its own partial processes, does not exist, because if it did, meaning would be fixed in a variety of ways.'[12] Here, any determinate conception of social phenomena is conflated with fixity.

Whether Hall did enough to retain explorations of the relationships between culture and agency on the one hand and broader structural conditions that do not pre-determine outcomes but are still crucial factors that make them determinate rather than random or merely the product of 'will' or discourse, is an open question. There were often crucial ambivalences in his formulations that pushed him closer to post-structuralism than he appeared to want to go. For example, discussing how discursive struggles operate by the 'articulation and disarticulation' of terms and meanings, he writes:

> outcomes, in the final result, could only depend on the relative strength of the 'forces in struggle', the balance between them at any strategic moment, and the effective conduct of the 'politics of signification'. We

can think of many pertinent historical examples where the conduct of a social struggle depended, at a particular moment, precisely on the effective dis-articulation of certain key terms, e.g. 'democracy', the 'rule of law', 'civil rights', 'the nation' ...[13]

Are the forces in struggle that Hall refers to here more than discursive? Is the 'balance' anything more than rhetorical power or is everything absorbed into the 'politics of signification'? How far did the outcomes of the struggle to advance democracy within capitalism by the working class depend on 'the effective disarticulation of certain key terms' and how far did the latter emerge from the lived experience of class conflict, which of course always had to be 'signified' in some terms to be made intelligible but which it is extremely reductive to think of primarily in the linguistic terms of 'articulation/disarticulation'. Of course Hall could argue that discursive struggles are always woven into material practices, organisations, collectives of people coming together to do something, but, there is a tendency to slide into a world of discourse in which the latter eclipses all those other factors, such as how much economic resources and political power different combatants can commit to a struggle and how that determines the scale, reach and to some extent, nature of their 'discourse'.

Yet we must admit that the question of determinations is a deep and profound methodological problem, one that confronts all inquiry with inherent complexities. Gramsci attempted to formulate the problem with his concepts of conjuncture and organic conditions. Conjuncture refers to those periods in which a certain configuration of forces struggle for ascendancy to define a new direction for future social development. This is the moment where political agency can break the mould and shift the course of events. The conjuncture is 'not a slice of time', argued Hall, although of course it requires some periodisation, elastically conceived according to what one wants to study or demonstrate for the purposes of analysis. But it is above all 'the accumulation/condensation of contradictions' such as we have analysed in relation to the referendums of 2014 and 2016.[14]

Organic conditions refers to the longer-term structural arrangements that the political forces are attempting to 'restore' to health or fundamentally change. They are the basis of the conjunctures which are in turn the basis of deciding which direction those organic conditions are going to take as the result of the outcome of the struggle to forge new historic blocs. This language of conjunctures and organic conditions or movements was Gramsci's rethinking of Marx's base-superstructure metaphor. '[I]n studying a structure', Gramsci wrote:

> it is necessary to distinguish organic movements (relatively permanent) from movements which may be termed 'conjunctural' (and which appear as occasional, immediate, almost accidental). Conjunctural phenomena too depend on organic movements to be sure, but they do not have any very far-reaching historical significance; they give rise to political criticism of a minor, day-to-day character, which has as its subject small ruling groups and personalities with direct governmental responsibilities. Organic phenomena on the other hand give rise to socio-historical criticism, whose subject is wider social groupings – beyond the people with immediate responsibilities and beyond the ruling personnel. When a historical period comes to be studied, the great importance of this distinction becomes clear. A crisis occurs, sometimes lasting decades. This exceptional duration means that incurable structural contradictions have revealed themselves (reached maturity), and that, despite this, the political forces which are struggling to conserve and defend the existing structure itself are making every effort to cure them, within certain limits, and to overcome them. These incessant and persistent efforts (since no social formation will ever admit that it has been superseded) form the terrain of the 'conjunctural', and it is upon this terrain that the forces of opposition organize.[15]

Gramsci's initial line about conjunctural phenomena not having 'very far-reaching historical significance' needs to be read carefully in the context of the passage as a whole. Conjunctural phenomena *appear* 'occasional, immediate, almost accidental' when they are separated from or considered in isolation from the organic dynamics of the social order (i.e. the dynamics that are essential to the social order and therefore 'relatively permanent'). There is a genre of news reportage familiar to Gramsci and us that does exactly that, hence: 'political criticism of a minor, day-to-day character, which has as its subject small ruling groups …' and so forth. But when we relate conjunctural phenomena to the 'incurable structural contradictions' of an organic crisis, then the former is transformed in our optic. We now see them as 'incessant and persistent efforts' to 'conserve and defend the existing structure' and the conjunctural as the 'terrain that the forces of opposition organize' themselves on to combat this conservation effort. Thus the development of political cultures and their capacities to defend and conserve or oppose and change the organic structure of a society in crisis, raise the historical stakes considerably. Here analysis of the terrain of the conjuncture and its relationship to the structure is imperative in order to intervene effectively for progressive change. Gramsci goes on to make a further methodological point on this score:

> A common error in historico-political analysis consists in an inability to find the correct relation between what is organic and what is conjunctural. This leads to presenting causes as immediately operative which in fact operate only indirectly, or to asserting that the immediate causes are the only effective ones. In the first case there is an excess of 'economism'…in the second, an excess of 'ideologism'.[16]

The complexity of the issues at stake in thinking through conjunctural analysis in relation to organic conditions is usefully illustrated by the debate around Stuart Hall's work on Thatcherism in the 1980s. It was precisely 'ideologism' that Hall was accused of by Jessop, Bonnett, Bromley and Ling in an exchange of essays originally published in *New Left Review* and reproduced in Jessop et al.'s book *Thatcherism*. They argued that Hall had over-emphasised the power to win political struggles and advance political and with it, social-class interests, by winning the battle of hearts and minds, or the ideological struggle. They suggested that whatever advances Thatcherism had made could be explained by its ability to command the State apparatus and with it the juridical field (for example in the form of anti-trade union legislation). This is an example of apparatus power being exercised with or without broader consent. Many laws and policies in-between General Elections are developed with very little public discussion, debate, participation or consent, but are the result of powerful corporate lobbyists. The danger of overstressing the need for consent is that it assumes that bourgeois democracy is rather more responsive to popular will than the evidence suggests.[17]

Jessop et al. also argued that Hall made little reference to 'the material rewards accruing to those sections of society who have supported the Thatcher camp'[18] (and in electoral terms that was around 42 per cent of those who voted in General Elections). In other words, it is not discourse alone that wins hearts and minds but a perceptible sense that has to have some (even if threadbare) reality to support it; that they stand to gain something important from Thatcherism, and the thing which Thatcherism valued above all else was monetary gain. Given that support for Thatcherism outside the 'power bloc' amongst the wider population depended on material rewards (such as the council house sell-offs) Jessop et al. also wondered how secure as well as deep Thatcherism's hold over hearts and minds was. For Thatcherism could not resolve the deep and systemic problems of British capitalism and this raised the prospect that Thatcherism's successes, such as they were, could be short lived once economic conditions worsened. On the other hand, perhaps all this sounded exactly like the optimistic leftist tendency to think that eventually economic reality will drive the working class back towards socialism?

Evaluating the extent and depth of Thatcherism's victory was certainly difficult. Jessop et al. contended that Hall's analysis of the efficacy of Thatcherism conflated the discourse with its effects. What they took to be the lack of substantive analysis of public opinion and reception meant that 'the danger remains of assuming that the "message" as emitted is identical to the message as received and understood.'[19] A similar argument was made by David Miller in relation to Hall's work on the mass media. He argued that Hall's definition of ideology as drawn from Louis Althusser had problematic assumptions. The earlier definition I gave of ideology from Hall makes it virtually equivalent to an anthropological definition of culture derived from Whorf and Sapir and Levi Strauss.[20] Yet we also saw that Hall had a tacit need of another definition of ideology when discussing Marx's critique of the 'bourgeois sciences': namely that they were systematically limited in ways that connected with their subtle and unconscious rationalisations of the given social order. Instead of rigorously distinguishing between culture and ideology, Hall ran them together and found in the work of Althusser a theory of ideology that made it the single most important variable to explain the reproduction of a social order as unequal as capitalism. When the anthropological and negative critique definitions of ideology are combined or conflated as routinely happens, ideology as the values of the bourgeoisie spreads throughout the cultural sites and practices of society as a whole in an untrammelled way. The power to win consent to a rationalisation and defence of unequal social relationships gets conflated with the power to produce intelligible definitions of society through culture. The Althusserian concept of interpellation positioned addressees of discourse as subjects *of* and *in* ideology. Like Althusser, Hall was charged with conflating the intelligibility of a discourse or system of representation, with our inevitable subordination to it. To look, to read, to decode or understand as a *participant in a cultural practice*, was seen as the same thing as agreeing with what it is we look at, read or decode. In terms of the circuit of communication and action, Miller noted the various conflations this model then produces:

> Hall's model blurs together, under the heading of ideology, the distinct moments of propagation and promotion of particular ideologies by the dominant class, the work done on them to transform them into media products, the understanding and response to them of audiences and the impact of this in societal outcomes.[21]

In his media analysis Hall often slid towards a view of ideology as a seamless deep structure unconscious of value systems that speaks through individual agents regardless of their conscious beliefs and powers of critical reflection.[22] In a similar vein to Miller's critique, and in relation to Thatcherism, Jessop et al. thought that Hall's discourse analysis approach 'tends to homogenize the impact and universalize the appeal of Thatcherism'.[23]

In his reply to Jessop et al., Hall argued that the Left has historically neglected the importance of ideological struggle for both itself and for its opponents. The latter understood the importance of constructing 'popular consent' so as to: 'harness to its support some popular discontents, neutralize the opposing forces, disaggregate the opposition and really incorporate *some* strategic elements of popular opinion into its own hegemonic project'.[24]

For example, layers of the skilled working class repeatedly voted for Thatcher in the 1980s. By the end of the 1980s Hall thought that his analysis of Thatcherism as a hegemonic project – one that sought to rewrite the rules of the game on its terms, establish the new parameters for politics and policy – had been borne out.

> The fact is that Thatcherism has succeeded in reversing or putting into reverse gear many of the historic postwar trends. It has begun to dismantle and erode the terms of the unwritten social contract on which the social forces settled after the war. It has changed the currency of political thought and argument. Where previously social need had begun to establish its own imperatives against the laws of market forces, now questions of 'value for money', the private right to dispose of one's wealth, the equation between freedom and the free market, have become the terms of trade, not just of political debate in parliament, the press, the journals', and policy circles, but in the thought and language of everyday calculation.[25]

However, in his reply to Jessop et al. Hall clarifies the distinction between saying that Thatcherism has 'achieved hegemony' and saying that it is a hegemonic project, that is to say it operates with the *intention* of reconstructing the status quo and stamping its own authority and philosophy as the new dispensation.[26] But despite its successes, Hall did not believe that Thatcherism had achieved hegemony. 'I do *not* believe and have nowhere advanced the claim that the project has been delivered.'[27] In particular Hall notes, like Jessop et al., that Thatcherism has been an economic failure in many ways. This is a significant shift in fact and despite disclaimers somewhat at odds with Hall's argument that Thatcherism had successfully changed the terms of political debate. 'It has shifted', he argued elsewhere, 'the parameters of common sense.'[28] But if shifting the parameters of common sense is too limited to qualify as the full hegemonic package, what would count as 'hegemony achieved'? Both Jessop et al. and Hall seem to assume that because Thatcherism cannot solve the deep structural weaknesses of British capitalism, this means that hegemony has fallen short. But is this really the case? This is a surprising argument for Hall to concede in fact, given his critique of economism. Hegemony for the dominant classes is less about really solving the economic structural problems, than managing them on terms that are most beneficial to the dominant classes and in ways that do not provoke responses – especially joined up responses across a series of struggles – that might endanger the system. As Gramsci wrote, the conjuncture is the terrain of the 'incessant and persistent efforts' by the dominant classes to 'conserve and defend the existing structure' not actually to resolve what are in fact 'incurable structural contradictions'. The exhaustion of Thatcherism due to weaknesses in its ability to deliver the economic goods to a wide enough base by no means leads to a rolling back of economic liberalism, but a shift in its repertoire of alliances. In the 1980s hegemony meant making economic liberalism the new common sense. How wide and deep did that common sense go? Indisputably it won hegemony in politics, in parliament, in the civil service, in the national press and the policy circles or burgeoning think tanks. As it advanced into the 1990s and 2000s, it also achieved hegemony in the upper echelons of other big institutions, such as education and health. Economic liberalism was readily embraced by big business and the City as a matter of course early on since they were pushing for a change. But did Thatcherism extend deeply beyond this power bloc? Did it even need to?

In their critique of what they called the 'dominant-ideology thesis', Abercrombie, Hill and Turner argued that the notion that a unified dominant ideology secures the consent of the masses and that *this* explained the reproduction of the capitalist system, was flawed. Instead they argued that in late capitalism at least, dominant ideologies within dominant groups were internally differentiated and inconsistent with each other. They pointed to the tension between meritocracy versus the right to inherit wealth which I have associated with the liberal and conservative poles of political culture respectively. They also pointed to welfare-state value systems coming into conflict with private property and market systems, although that was a conflict which was soon to be weakened in policy terms by the renewed validation of economic liberalism in the decade after their book was published.[29]

Yet the key to the dominant-ideology thesis is the presumed effect it has on the subordinate classes. Here they argued that the further one goes down the social ladder, the more the sociological evidence suggests that value systems that act as a rationalisation of capitalist property relations and interests, becomes hybridised by contact with popular ideologies or rejected altogether.[30] There was no need to depend on ideological explanations for system integration and reproduction, Abercrombie et al. suggested. There were a range of other factors that could explain why capitalism had not faced more consistent threats to its existence than it had. They pointed to the 'dull compulsion of economics' (a phrase they took from Marx) as a powerful disciplining factor on workers who have to work to survive,[31] as well as the lack of apparent alternatives and the high risks that attempts at massive social change raises.

Abercrombie el al. offer a useful correction to 'ideologism', but some of their alternative explanations for the stability of capitalist societies are not unconnected with the question of ideological struggle and hegemony. The dull compulsion of economics for example has an in-built 'ideological' dimension as we saw above with the atomisation of market relations falsely universalising itself as the true substance of society. Indeed liberalism has always seen the coercive force of market relations as enforcing classed norms around being a rational, individualistic agent deploying whatever resources one has to hand. Then there is the question of the perceived lack of alternatives. Hegemony also includes disorganising opponents and dispersing the coherence, clarity and confidence of contesting ideological forces. If hegemony does not necessarily equal affirmation then it is still significant if it succeeds in negating the plausibility of alternatives, for that is likely to enhance the security of the hegemonic bloc. It gives the bloc wider room for manoeuvre and makes tactical mistakes less likely to lead to a breach in its ramparts. Disorganising the opposition requires at the least, hegemonic ambition and if effective presumably some perceived success that demoralises the opposition. Gramsci knew that it was possible to be *dominant* without being hegemonic, but that is certainly a more vulnerable position. When a group or class is dominant without being the leading moral and intellectual force, tactical mistakes can lead very quickly to a loss of apparatus control. When, for example, Ed Miliband very narrowly won the leadership of the Labour Party against his more New Labour brother, David Miliband, in 2010, he did so with the support of the unions. New Labour MPs were outraged at this interruption in their dominance and subsequently forced a change in the rules of selecting the next leader, shifting the vote away from the trade unions and over to 'one person, one vote' amongst the Labour Party membership. Here apparatus control, dominance without hegemony, had led New Labour to believe its own propaganda. They were sure that their intellectual and moral dominance amongst the membership was such that they would triumph next time. Yet this proved a colossal blunder and what they thought was their own tactical triumph turned into their nightmare after Jeremy Corbyn was elected Labour Party leader in 2015 as the party membership shifted substantially to the left. And in a microcosm, this is the situation now of the historic bloc as a whole. Dominance without hegemony, the substantial exhaustion of neo-liberalism as a moral and intellectual project, now makes the bloc more vulnerable than it has been since the early 1980s. It faces the prospect of losing *political* power, although of course business control over the economic apparatus would still be untouched by elections alone as would various parts of the State apparatus.

All this suggests that ideology does indeed matter, now as it did during the Thatcher years. Across the upper echelons of the major institutions, economic liberalism certainly achieved hegemonic leadership. Thatcherism installed a new 'realism', one that was quite enthusiastically embraced by New Labour in its leadership cadres and one that was, to varying degrees of reluctance or resignation, accepted as the new reality by many outside the power bloc. The paradox of Thatcherism was that it helped bring a new historic bloc into formation, but it could not fill out that historic bloc by itself. It was *the bloc* that was hegemonic, Thatcherism turned out to be *one* repertoire at the disposal of the new historic bloc. In his last work before his death in 2014, Hall recognised this in his survey of the long march of neo-liberalism: 'it is a dangerous error to assume that, because both neo-liberalism and conservatism derive from and politically represent the dominant power-system, they are the same. Both have deep roots in British history and mentalities. But they are two quite different ideological repertoires'.[32]

But while in Hall's model there are two repertoires to the current historic bloc, in my mapping of the conjuncture, I have clearly distinguished between economic liberalism, conservatism and social liberalism. With this tripartite model we can better map how the dynamics between different political–cultural projects, different political–cultural 'caps' attached to economic liberalism, played out.

As we have seen, economic liberalism, which Thatcherism successfully installed as the hegemonic political economy, unleashed economic changes that led to Thatcherism being outflanked on key political and cultural issues. The very geographically uneven spread of economic liberalism, its dependence on a southern base that is substantially a traditional 'rentier' economy based on finance, property assets and servicing the elites, gradually opened up on its 'northern' flank legitimacy questions concerning conservatism's powerbase in the British State vis-à-vis the subaltern nation of Scotland. Economic individualism had many other contradictory impacts on conservatism. One boom – helped by North Sea oil revenues – sandwiched between two recessions was enough to give the Conservative Party an undeserved reputation as the party of new social mobility. Yet its aggressive meritocracy could be claimed by a whole range of subjects who on class, ethnic and gender grounds disrupted traditional Tory hierarchies. Thatcherism for example had a very traditional image and role for women and Hall showed how the image of 'women' that Thatcherism mobilised was connected to a host of themes in the Thatcherite armoury. The woman as shopper who knows the evil of inflation, the parent who wants traditional values taught in school, the woman concerned about safety on the streets or the wife who tells her wayward militant trade union husband on strike to put the family first.[33] Yet economic liberalism accelerated the trend of larger numbers of women entering the labour-market thus breaking down at least some of the bases for conservatism's ideological image of women and traditional gender roles.[34]

Meritocracy could also be claimed by conservatism's social liberal competitor for leadership of economic liberalism. Meritocracy remains one of the obsessions of the elites, both at the liberal end of conservatism and for social liberals: how to increase social mobility and tap into *just enough* new ideas and talents to replenish the stock of social leadership without seriously changing a deeply stratified order. In 2014 the Blairite New Labour MP Alan Milburn wrote a forward to a report from the Commission on Social Mobility and Child Poverty Commission called *Elitist Britain?*, which would have been better retitled without the question-mark. The report found that the small percentage of people attending fee-paying independent schools (7 per cent) and going to Oxbridge were massively overly represented at the top of the professions. Seventy-five per cent of senior judges, 59 per cent of the Cabinet, 50 per cent of diplomats, 47 per cent of leading newspaper columnists, 33 per cent of BBC executives, and 24 per cent of MPs had gone to Cambridge or Oxford. Only 0.8 per cent of the population make it to those hallowed halls.[35]

In the same year as the report was released, so too was the film *The Kingsman: The Secret Service* (2014) with a narrative that turns very largely around the issue of recruiting and integrating a young working-class boy living a stereotypical 'chav' life, into an aristocratic/upper-middle class, iconically British, James Bond-style secret service organisation. This assimilation story revivifies a traditional image of the dominant classes with new energy, loyalty, commitment and initiative and at the same time this allegory of a wider social process, means that the working class are robbed of the 'leadership' material they need to improve their lives. The whole film is precisely about bridging and reconciling the class divide on the terms of the conservative–liberal elite, championing both tradition and meritocracy and leaving the working-class majority (carefully framed as thuggish) deservedly behind.

If economic liberalism opened up a space for social liberalism to take territory from conservatism on the question of meritocracy, so too did the international dimension of economic liberalism which, in the shape of supranational developments on the European continent, divided and weakened the Conservative Party throughout the nineties and into the turn of the century. Relatively more unified on Europe, New Labour could offer itself to both electors and capital as the party political vehicle that could 'manage' the question of Europe.

At the immediate cultural level, economic liberalism also proved an ambiguous partner for conservatism as it disrupted traditional hierarchies and helped pluralise culture with its internal disruptions of the national terrain and its international currents and flows. Social liberalism laid claim to the political capital to be had from this cultural diversity against conservatism. It has even attempted to win back from conservatism its dominance over Britishness and stake a claim that this supranational identity has mitigated the excesses that any of the nationalisms (particularly Englishness) that are its component parts, may be prone to. On this reading, Britishness facilitates the nations that make it up to embrace non-essentialised and diverse identities pooled from many different currents. Yet the deepening imbalances and inequalities of economic liberalism have tugged the differing cultural and political-constitutional visions of conservatism and social liberalism in increasingly contrary directions. Just as conservatism's eighteen-year-long electoral dominance from 1979 laid the ground for its own subsequent marginalisation, social liberalism's electoral hegemony in New Labour and then the Conservative–Liberal coalition government of 2010–15, sowed the seeds for a come-back for a culturally Thatcherite political project around the geopolitics of Europe and (conservative-style) Brexit.

Conservatism and social liberalism try to utilise the contradictions which each political culture has with economic liberalism to outflank each other in their competition for leadership of economic liberalism. Objective trends such as capitalist internationalism work both for liberalism (undermining national insularity) and for conservatism (which is best placed thanks to its hegemony of 'the national question' to mobilise grievances as inequality bites). Each advance by one may help mobilise in time the constituency for a counter-strike by the other. The traditional conservatism that powered anti-EU feeling was very much cast as in opposition to the Conservative Party front bench and the alliance with the Liberal Democrats between 2010 and 2015 in the coalition government. This too enabled this reactionary conservatism to downplay its commitments to economic liberalism and cast instead the problems in terms of a Westminster elite wedded to EU internationalism. Yet conservatism's ability to revive its traditional cultural-political reflexes and downplay its commitments to economic liberalism also betrays how weak that latter model has become, especially after the 2007–8 crash. There could be no return to the buoyant celebration of economic liberalism that characterised Thatcherism and here the 'incurable structural contradictions' are indeed powerfully limiting for a political philosophy that cannot contemplate a redistribution of wealth from the minority to the majority. This was economic liberalism without any uplifting narrative, not even a gesture towards individual social mobility. All that conservatism could offer was more austerity and personal debt. With its social base contracting, it was relying more and more on 'pure' ideology to win the day.

In the 2017 General Election the Conservatives did not even bother to pretend that there would be anything more on offer than a continual redistribution of wealth towards the wealthy, even hitting, in a quite extraordinary way, their traditional bedrock support of elderly homeowners with their plans to support social care by stripping these voters of their property values and transferring assets to banks and private social care contractors. Conservative strategists hoped that 'delivering Brexit' would be sufficient compensation in exchange for increasing material impoverishment. Not for the first time they hoped that 'culture' or ideology would trump 'economics'. Had the Labour Party continued its New Labour trajectory, this might have paid off. But Conservative Party hopes were partially blocked by the Corbyn leadership within the Labour Party that shifted the conversation back to the domestic agenda and offered a real prospect of material improvement through social provision, modest wealth redistribution and a hesitantly articulated return to social democracy that nevertheless caught people's imagination.

Labourism and social democracy

In his *Marxism Today* writings, Hall critiqued the economism of Labourism and its conservative version of social democracy in ways that are surprisingly combative. The terms of the critique do not seem to me to be an invitation to dump social democracy and open the door for a New Labour-type oscillation back to economic liberalism. Instead they raise some very profound and difficult questions about social democracy in the context of capitalism in crisis. That he was interested in this is also an indication that he was unimpressed with some of the more ritualistically invoked solutions to the capitalist crisis that the radical Left sometimes pose, such as 'the long wished-for "Winter-Palace" showdown'.[36] Hall was, it turns out, well aware of the contradiction between social democracy and capitalism. Since this is the only practical institutional form the west has yet had as a modification of capitalism's 'natural laws', the incompatibility between them is a historical lesson which it is very difficult to absorb and even more difficult to come up with solutions to. Our historical impasse and tragedy – and here of course I am taking a more global view of the situation – is that the models we have had either for reform or revolution have fallen short, leaving us stuck inside an unviable mode of production.

Hall was highly critical of the Labour Party's model of reform for its fetishisation of parliamentarianism to the exclusion of any political space or practice outside the 'parliamentary mould'. He was clear that Labour has always been 'deeply suspicious of the self-activation of the working class' as a result.[37] Channelling Marx's famous rebuke concerning 'parliamentary cretinism'[38] Hall noted that political practice not emanating from or directed to the House of Commons produces in the leadership of the Labour Party 'the deepest traumas and the most sycophantic poems of praise for parliamentarianism.'[39]

Labourism is defined by its attempt to monopolise all legitimate political activity on the Left and yoke it to electoral and parliamentary outcomes. Had the SNP taken the same electoral attitude, it would have given up on Scottish independence many decades ago. Labour's fetishisation of parliament ultimately makes Labour safe for the establishment because it dries up its roots in an activist base facilitating co-option of the MPs by powerful State and economic actors opposed to change. Hall wanted the Labour Party to make itself 'the focal point of popular aspirations, the leading popular political force'[40] but it looked like it had no idea how to do that and was instead pulled along in the slipstream of Thatcherism.

While not blind to the historical advances it represented, Hall was very critical of the version of social democracy that Labourism produced. He saw *this* version of social democracy at least as a means 'to discipline the class struggle' on behalf of capital.[41] Social democracy and Labourism suffers from the 'illusion' that 'through the mediation of "Labour in power" it could win "concessions" for the working class (without mobilizing the class)'.[42] Labourism's fetishisation of parliamentarianism helped define social democracy in the most paternalistic and top-down manner. It was this nexus of institutional power that had congealed into a frozen form at the birth of social democracy that was powerless to respond at the moment of crisis in the 1970s.

Social democracy as Labour interpreted it was thus very conservative. Wary of mobilising the working class, it offered no leadership of a critical and combative kind but only reinforcement of 'the most traditionalist and conservative elements in popular morality.'[43] It had no sense of the educative role of parties in relation to classes or that classes, as Marx noted, must exist not only *in* themselves but, crucially, *for themselves.*

Together, Labourism and social democracy helped redefine socialism within a 'statist' paradigm that, Hall reminds us, was only one strand of the many socialist currents in play at the beginning of the twentieth century.

Hall identifies the period between 1880 and 1920 as the key moment in which the statist conception of socialism became ascendant and hegemonic and that this was a conception 'in which the ruling classes played a key, educative role'[44] Here Hall cites the Fabian tradition within the Labour Party as crucial. 'In the Fabian conception of social engineering, the people are … the objects not the subjects of political practice.'[45] One problem with this paternalistic politics is that the forces that might defend social democracy, let alone advance it towards socialism, are underdeveloped when the goals of social democracy begin to clash with capitalism's ability to make concessions. Once again, sounding the alarm, and at some distance from the future New Labour philosophy, Hall noted:

> The central illusion – the social-democratic illusion, Mark I – to which Labour leaders good, bad and indifferent were attached was that the social-democratic bandwagon could be hitched to the star of a reformed capitalism: and the latter would prove capable of infinite expansion so that all the political constituencies could be 'paid off' at once: the TUC and the CBI, labour and capital, public housing and the private landlord, the miners and the bank of England.[46]

When that circle could not be squared, Labour governments in the 1970s began to bear down on wages and living standards in order to restore profitability. 'If you are inside a declining capitalism, there are no extra funds in the kitty to pay off the working class.'[47] With the economic crisis and the more disciplinary functions of the State increasing as a result – Thatcherism was able to present itself as the only political philosophy 'committed to oppose the exponential growth of the state, its penetration into every corner of life.'[48]

Where by contrast, Hall wondered, had the Left's commitment to the self-organisation of social and community life gone? On the one hand the Left had forgotten its critique of the State, thus allowing Thatcherism

234 · ENGLAND'S DISCONTENTS

to win political and moral leadership on the question of what to do with the State (Thatcherism's answer was *less* social State and *more* coercive State to patrol the negative outcomes from *more* free markets). On the other hand, lurking somewhere unarticulated within the Left's socialist imaginary was an embarrassed half memory that the Left and the Right shared some common ground in terms of a dissatisfaction with the State, even if the analysis of why and what to do about the State were radically different:

> what the left urgently needs is to reappropriate the concept of freedom and give it an alternative articulation within the context of a deepening of democratic life as a whole. The problem is that this socialist conception of freedom is not compatible with – is in fact deeply undermined by – the idea of a state which takes over everything, which absorbs all social life, all popular energies, all democratic initiatives, and which however benevolently – governs society *in place of the people.*[49]

Recognising that the role of the State is 'to organize and orchestrate the space of capital accumulation' Hall concluded that 'the state has to be dismantled, and another conception of the state put in its place'.[50] Hall suggested that 'choice', the concept which Thatcherism linked to the free market and capitalism, and which powerfully constructed socialism as 'the drab lack of diversity' and 'planed sameness' was not necessarily fixed in its 'articulation' to capitalism. Socialists, in taking some critical distance from the statist conception of their philosophy, ought not to let the devil have the rather good tune of 'choice' all to itself. Indeed, given that choice becomes both stratified according to ability to pay and standardised and rationalised according to the ability of capitalists to make sufficient profit from a good or service, 'choice' is indeed far from being irrecoverable as a motif from capitalist ideology.

The dilemmas and contradictions of the State – which on the one hand is the only feasible model we have historically at hand as the mechanism that could begin to unlock the resources and provide the legal framework for the development of property held in common, and on the other, has an inbuilt tendency to supplant and displace the project to absorb the various functions of the State back into the community as a whole – has to be confronted in a serious and substantive way. While critical of the statist conception of socialism, Hall was also clear that it was the indispensable organ available to begin to open up a different future. If the State is a problematic but necessary instrument, Hall is convinced that a concept of *the public*, which he distinguishes from the State, lies somewhere central to socialism.

> The idea of 'public space' signifies a construction of space not bounded by the rights of private property, a space for activities in common, the holding of space in trust as a social good. In each case the adjective *public* represents an advance in conception on the limits of possessive individualism … of liberal thought itself. In this conception of the public and the social, socialism is still ahead. And the public can only be carved out of market space, capital's space, by the engine of state action.[51]

The State may carve out and provide the legal and financial guarantees for public space and public action but the latter must be the development of popular initiatives that will facilitate agency and a real range of choices, a real unleashing of repressed creativity and collective intelligence. The partnership, if there is one, should be with the State supporting but transferring power to society (not hoarding it for itself or transferring it to capital).[52] Of course this is easier said than done – but the principle is right or at least better than a merely statist conception in which initiatives come 'to a dead halt with the state elite.'[53]

The development of a democratic conception of numerous public spheres in civil society and in the economy depends crucially on persuading large numbers of people to participate in the reconstruction of social relations on terms that challenge the accumulated sedimentation of divisions and inequalities, all the muck of ages, which capitalism has deposited in the culture and consciousness of us all. This means, Hall argues, challenging the conservatism of working-class political culture. Such conservatism may come from two rather different sources: either from a need to conserve gains already won (as with social democracy as a whole) or from an uncritical internalisation of the political culture of conservatism, especially its displacement strategies around 'nation' and 'race'. This means doing more than 'merely translating' lived experience, it also means a more challenging project, one that involves 'qualifying, criticising and interrogating working-class "experience". It means, often, breaking the mould of working-class common sense.'[54]

Hall does write of the need to overcome the crippling intellectual division of labour that affects both the working and middle class but he only alludes to what this might mean for the latter. Although in any complex society, one cannot wish away social divisions of labour, many people who now think of themselves as middle class, as 'professionals' with a monopoly of specialist knowledge that cements social esteem and underpins higher than average earnings, also need to have their class assumptions challenged. So the process of qualifying, criticising and breaking the mould would also need to be directed at the middle class themselves. Hall's own critique of Fabian-style top-down statist socialism absolutely demands a critique of precisely the role this political culture allotted for the intelligentsia as technocratic leaders of a passive working class. And one may also say that the 'vanguardist' revolutionary politics that flowed from Leninism also demands a similarly self-critical 'education of the educators' which I think even Gramsci himself did not stress enough.[55] In short, 'organic intellectuals' from the working class and organic intellectuals from the middle class must engage in mutual critiques of the crippling tendencies that the social division of labour has constructed.[56]

The one-sidedness of Hall's conception of where the energies for the reconstruction of popular habits and perceptions would be directed, perhaps also surface in his broader conception of the working class.

While for Hall *capital* remains an indispensable category for analysis and the working class remains a substantial social presence, the latter appears to be framed as *residual*, politically and culturally. All the more exciting, progressive, emergent and prefigurative political battles seem, for Hall, to be coming from the 'democratic' struggles around gender, race, sexuality, environmentalism and so forth and when he does talk about class and strikes he often implies that it is the middle class public sector professions that are now leading the way.[57] This is very much a subtext in the discourse rather than an explicitly stated position but it is I think there.[58] These hints and cues threatened to saw away at the causal connections between critical political economy and the politics of 'recognition' or anti-discrimination or oppression, when what is needed is precisely to develop awareness of those causal connections on all sides.

One reason why Hall may have implied that the working class was a residual category was because getting the balance between change and continuity is a significantly difficult epistemological enterprise when confronted with a phenomenon like capitalism, which sustains its fundamentals even as it furiously transforms itself, which as we have seen causes problems for conservatism as well as Labourism. Hall pointed to 'the decline of certain traditional sectors and the growth of new sectors; the shift in patterns of skill; radical recomposition as a result of the new gender and ethnic character of labour; the new divisions of labour resulting from changing technologies …'[59] and how new industries, new technologies, new types of work, new methods of work, new processes of work were all eroding the 'socialist imagery' once based on industrialism of the old mass-Fordist kind.[60]

The difficulty is tracing the changes but resisting the inference that either capitalism itself as a mode of production has fundamentally changed or that the recomposition of the working class has in some way *irretrievably* blocked class agency from transforming capitalism. Here a distinction that Manuel Castells made is useful. He distinguished between a mode of development, which refers in the first instance to the technical changes in the economic relations, and the mode of production, which refers to the fundamental social relations of ownership and control. Although Castells himself failed to always properly *embed* the mode of development back into the mode of production and thus secure a dialectical understanding of change and continuity, the conceptual differentiation helps us think about the shift from industrialism to what is now sometimes referred to as an information economy.[61] While there is much rhetoric around the latter that is mystificatory and designed to uncouple changes from the persistent features of the capitalist mode of production, there have been significant changes of a technical and hence also social kind, without thereby changing the dynamics of the most fundamental social relations of capitalism.

Along with the transformations in class relations there has been an expansion of political issues that begin at the point of production, at the point of ownership and control, but which in their implications, ripple out to raise complex questions of democratic accountability across a social terrain marked by great interdependence and complexity. For example, what is the point of workers acquiring control of the means of agricultural and food production if the barbarous meat industry is not radically reformed and if the production process of agriculture and meat is not thoroughly reconstructed to address the escalating health and environmental damage that intensive capitalist production methods are causing? If there is going to be a socialist politics of food production, then it is going to have to be informed by a very wide range of struggles, interest constituencies and issues that include workers, consumers, citizens and a range of health and environmental stakeholders. The same is true of 'big pharma', which perhaps because it cloaks itself in the legitimacy of the natural sciences, many socialists have an inordinately uncritical perspective on, typically regarding any criticism of orthodox medicine as the province of cranks. All of this suggests the centrality of the means of communication, information, dialogue and debate and therefore democracy to any future socialist project. This reminds us of one of Hall's central arguments, namely that a socialist politics does not issue automatically from questions of economy, ownership and class. It is a politics that has to be constructed.

Hall was under no illusions about how dangerous the democratic erosion of the prerogatives of private ownership and the imperatives of the accumulation logic might be: 'The problem is that the positive commitment to the serious, dangerous and difficult task of unpacking the oldest capitalist system in the world, and beginning to construct some other system – without triggering off "barbarism" – will require a great deal of popular will, mobilisation, commitment and nerve'.[62]

Here is a very substantive reason for being concerned to engage in and win the ideological struggle. For although it may be said that the dominant social order only requires consent patchily in order for *it* to reproduce itself, a genuine transformation away from capitalism will need to mobilise popular participation against the continuing control over powerful economic, political and State apparatuses that will be leveraged by the dominant classes against any democratic change.

8

Going forwards, facing backwards

With all the usual caveats regarding reductionism, I have tried to present in a diagrammatic form some of the key dynamics of political cultures that have formed the three hegemonic blocs discussed in the course of this book (see Figure 8.1). Historic blocs are forged out of alliances between political cultures and the class constituencies they assemble. The nineteenth-century historic bloc was forged out of an alliance between conservatism and liberalism. The material base of conservatism was in the coercive State and civil society; it left the market free to do as it wished by default. Liberalism was identical with its economic base in the market (economic liberalism) and explicitly propounded the market (as opposed to the State) as the source of progressive norms, but it still nevertheless needed and had a subordinate role in the State apparatus. This was the terms of the balance of power and division of labour within the ruling power bloc between conservatism and liberalism with the coercive State and the coercions of the market both providing the necessary force to seal degrees of consent. The vertical arrows indicate the original and persisting basis that shapes and defines the respective political cultures (i.e. its relationship with either the State or the free market). However, we have also seen in the formation of the second historic bloc (social democracy) and the third historic bloc (neo-liberalism) conservatism and liberalism make a 'knight's move' towards combining the material base of other political cultures directly into their repertoire. By the end of the nineteenth century, liberalism had separated itself from economic liberalism and developed into a new liberalism in which reform requires a social State. This liberalism combined with the labour movement was the basis of social democracy, although the conservative version of social democracy that Stuart Hall was rightly very critical of. The third historic bloc saw conservatism make a knight's move towards the territory of the market as an explicit programme to mobilise a normative project around what had once been the basis of late eighteenth and early-to-mid-nineteenth-century liberalism. And we saw that social liberalism in time oscillated back from social democracy to make its peace with this new settlement, this new suture of social forces around economic liberalism. Now this third historic bloc is facing its own midnight hour. We must remember that the competitive tensions *between* political cultures interact with the *contradictions* between them and the mode of production. But the current historic bloc will not dismantle itself and given time and space it could find once more temporary solutions to its 'incurable structural contradictions' (Gramsci) most likely around the kind of populist and nationalist right wing politics that Trump and his coalition – which includes fascists – represent.

Given the current starting point of the Left, whose recent revival is actually quite shallow in the UK and whose culture has been badly deformed by four decades of defeat, the only realistic prospect available in the short to middle term, of exiting the current conjuncture in a progressive direction, is to forge a new historic bloc around social democracy. However, this must be a social democracy that has learned some of the lessons of recent history to guard against future iterations of economic liberalism. The main historical lesson we must absorb is, unfortunately, extremely difficult: namely that social democracy cannot be a stable end-destination within the dynamics of capitalism. For capitalism, every boundary to its accumulation dynamic, such as political regulation of the profit motive, or public services, is an obstacle that must be surmounted. This is the *essential* and *remorseless* characteristic of capital.[1] Such dynamics are intensified as capital declines into long-term stagnation with low or no growth.[2] As capital hordes wealth it drains effective demand out of the economy while its global mobility facilitates avoidance of national jurisdictions that impose social obligations. Therefore we need a different version of social democracy from the one

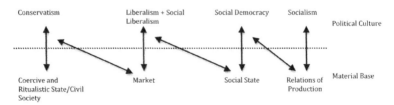

8.1 Material bases for political cultures.

that was in place before. We need a radical model of social democracy that empowers a knight's move from social democracy to socialism, a move from a historic bloc based on the social State to a historic bloc where the dominant forms of productive property are held, through a diversity of forms, in common. The international dimension of capital means that this cannot succeed in one country alone, but we can only be responsible for our own national terrain. In closing then I want to look at what we have learned through a Gramscian lens about the formation of Britishness over the last two hundred odd years so that we can remind ourselves of where the bases for a new historic bloc could be formed.

The formation of a new historic bloc requires a continual struggle with the economic, political, cultural and ideological bases of the dominant power bloc. The battle of hearts and minds is particularly important in the period leading up to and immediately after the taking of political (governmental) power, as the rise of Thatcherism shows us. We can also look at the history of the dominant power bloc and learn something else – namely what Gramsci I believe was asking us to learn: the need to build alliances (a complex business in any modern society) to broaden and mobilise the popular support necessary to counter the counter-offensive when it comes. The battle for hearts and minds is important because of its capacity to mobilise 'people power' against the medium-term persistence of economic, political and State power continuing to reside with the privileged minority both within the nation-state and outside and 'above' it.

Firstly, a new historic bloc built around a new model of social democracy must have as its material and political cultural basis *the public.* This itself will require a complex and ongoing struggle on many fronts. We saw that the concept of the public developed from its most anti-democratic version, around an aristocratic/bourgeois elite dominance of the coercive apparatus and ritualistic-ideological State apparatus. It was challenged and partly democratised by the professional and commercial middle classes, especially in connection with industry in which a more dynamic, scientific and transformative sense of work and society emerged. But the most radical and democratic concept of the public came out of working class struggles and demands to socialise wealth and uncouple use value from exchange value.

In our present moment, the public as a concept and value has been subjected to four decades of de-legitimation and lack of investment by economic liberalism.[3] We cannot doubt the extent to which that has sunk deep roots into popular consciousness. Hall noted that the public sector, public services and public intervention have been devastatingly de-legitimated by Thatcherism. Economically it has been associated with spending money that the nation does not have; it is a form of profligacy that ends in tears – as if the capitalist economy functioned without borrowing and debt. Indeed so persistent has this ideological discourse been that the Conservative Party and the media successfully managed to fix in the public mind during 2010–15 that it was Labour's public spending that caused the global financial crash of 2007–8 rather than out of control banks and financial speculators.

As Grierson's political communications project shows (see Chapter 5), we have to find ways of making a democratic and participatory civic identity vivid for people; we have to find ways of dramatising the connection between private lives and experiences and their public environment and involvement. We have had four decades of experiments in neo-liberal governance which has left a mountain of evidence of many failures and negative consequences stemming from the privatisation of public assets, the marketisation of what are formally public services, the penetration of State services by private contractors and the substantial weakening of the regulatory responsibilities that once imposed some public, social duties on the profit motive. There is plenty of space here to make tactical interventions to begin to organise popular resentments about rising energy and rail prices (as well as shareholder returns) into alternative policy programmes that revalidate the public sphere and ethos. Market failure is everywhere about us but mainstream political discourse sees it not.

The public is a crucial concept, as Hall argued, because it directly attacks the very foundation of capitalism: the profit motive and the capturing of surpluses by undemocratic and unaccountable organisations. This is why the political culture of economic liberalism has expended so much effort in attempting to erode popular support and identification for the public as a concept and mode of practice. The public as concept makes use and need rather than exchange value its priority and therefore, against stratified access to resources, it is a much better basis for providing universal access for fundamental services.

The public sector and the public services provides the material underpinning for an alliance between the working and middle classes, precisely the alliance which has frayed as economic liberalism has dismantled social democracy and made the financial resources people have in their pockets an increasingly determining factor in satisfying their needs. Yet the social base of economic liberalism is contracting and the trend is towards oligarchical rule in which a large middle class will also struggle to find jobs, housing, healthcare and other opportunities. Indeed there is probably only one or two more generations of accumulated assets available to the middle class to be used up or expropriated by 'big capital' and a housing crash could consume those assets even more quickly. Yet despite there being a strong material interest at stake that might prise at least some of the middle class away from economic liberalism, we know from Hall, that it will not happen automatically, because the 'logics of ideological inference turn out to be … multivariate'.[4] In Latin America for example, oligarchies keep a fairly impoverished middle class in line by stoking their fears of the poor, the rabble, or the mob, who are all made synonymous with crime and violence. On present trends, there is nothing to stop Britain converging with Latin American levels of inequality and authoritarianism in the decades to come. The gated communities springing up in the cities are perhaps a foretaste of things to come in that regard.

So, at least some strata of the middle classes will need to be won around with more than just the promise of being material beneficiaries of a reinvigorated public sphere. One of the historic attractions of public service to the middle classes was the idea, as Weber argued, of work as a moral duty, with a wider social purpose. The fullest possibilities of developing a work ethic with a wider social purpose are only realised when work is uncoupled from exchange value, as it is with public services. Four decades of economic liberalism has been an object lesson in how the profit motive corrupts and corrodes trust, reciprocity, professional autonomy, meaningful activity and the virtues of forward planning. Market rationality turns out to be deeply irrational time and time again. The dogma that competition produces 'efficiency' stands exposed as a cruel lie as bureaucracy expands to monetise every transaction, as marketing budgets balloon to conceal cutbacks in the most precious resources (such as workers) and as legal departments expand to ward off litigation from increasingly ill-served 'customers'. This is to say nothing of the corruption of public service and public officials by commercial forces in such areas as housing by predatory property developers. There is plenty of opportunity here to make a reconstructed public sphere morally attractive once more as a source of pride and satisfaction, for both workers and users of those services. While this may be particularly appealing to the middle classes, it is certainly not exclusively a middle-class value to feel an ethical pride in work performed. The values of skilled, craft and artisanal labour have long had similar ethical underpinnings. Less individualistic than middle-class investments in work, this cluster of values has often been about achieving a compensatory sense of respect that is withheld elsewhere in society. The appeal of a 'good job' that is skilled and meaningful has been stubbornly adhered to by many working class people resentful and unimpressed by the low-wage and low-skill economy that the employers have prepared for them.

Thus far I have framed the concept of the public in ways that are familiar from the historic bloc of social democracy past. But we have seen that this was a top down version of social democracy which in party-political terms meant monopolising political participation and legitimate politics around the Labour Party and parliament, where the great and the good assemble and electoral politics. In political terms, the working classes were conceived of as passive recipients of the benefits of the system. In broader social terms, the middle class ran the institutions as benevolent but unaccountable leaders. When Hall wrote of 'breaking the mould of working class common sense' I think he was, not untypically, blind to an even greater blockage in the development of a radical social democracy: breaking the mould of middle-class common sense. The old model of the public had middle class buy in because it protected and reinforced middle-class investments in status, esteem, and hierarchy. Visitors from other capitalist countries are immediately struck by just how embedded these features of British class divisions are. Perhaps here we do see the enduring marks of Britain's peculiar historic development and the very long alliance between a traditional conservatism (with its aristocratic colouration) and liberalism. Difficult as it is, the educator must be educated, and a critical self-reflexivity that has been rare among the British middle classes concerning their class subjectivity, with its entrenched sense of self-entitlement, would need to be nurtured. This can only be done by the development of friendly but critical interlocutors in the form of organic intellectuals from the working classes. This itself is now a huge and urgent task. The scale of the repair needed on the political consciousness, confidence and articulacy of the working classes after decades of assault by economic liberalism, is immense. Yet there can be no real progressive change in Britain unless the social base for political and cultural participation on equal terms is widened in class terms – a widening that will necessarily include the heterogeneous ethnicities to be found at the 'base' of society. What is needed today is a shift in the middle-class intelligentsia on a par with that which took place in the 1930s, itself premised on a longer and slower shift which the new liberalism of the previous half-century or so had prepared. If political and cultural participation on equal terms can happen then perhaps a dialogue that can cut across existing inequalities and divisions of labour can begin that would foster non-antagonistic social development. That 'dialogue' would need an immensely transformed public sphere, in politics, in the media (including, crucially, the development of a non-corporate media) in education, and in the trade unions. Needless to say, trade unions must be unshackled from the legal framework that has rendered them powerless against employer offensives. Again, a major public relations battle should be fought to reframe the role of the trade unions as at present small islands of democratic counterweight to unaccountable management power. A new radical multi-cultural plebeian identity based in communities as much as in the workplace, needs to make its way into the heart of British identity.

The concept of the public, Hall reminded us, ought to be distinct from the concept of the State, although the latter is the necessary guarantor of the former. Diverse strands on the left became from the 1990s onwards, disengaged with State apparatuses, in a move towards 'horizontalism', social movements, anti-party structures, and neo-anarchist and syndicalist currents, amid a desire to carve out niche spaces within capitalism that tacitly gave up trying to transform it. The positive side of this development is precisely the percolation into civil society of the kind of small-scale 'molecular' experiments that can seed innovations in local and community ventures. Such libertarian yet community orientated impulses are important assets and Gramsci was clear that both the normative historic justification of capitalism and its strength in depth, lay in the relatively autonomous initiatives which civil society, mirroring economic life, had developed. Currently dominated by the tactical multiplicity and autonomy of the dominant classes, Gramsci's conception of civil society looks forward to enlarging civil society for the subaltern classes – and thereby deepening democracy.[5] Yet without an engagement with the State, these molecular experiments, if they are truly antithetical to capital, will remain tiny and vulnerable. One of the transformations of the public that a radical form of social democracy would have to develop is to find ways of encouraging and resourcing the local and/or small-scale experiments in democratic participation that develop the talents that our current society wastes, the initiative and individual and collective intelligence that is left idle. The particularly interesting and successful experiments could then be rolled out in more widely available forms as social-public 'franchises'. We could do worse than start with the democratic transformation of football clubs as an intervention into a popular leisure time activity that already has mass working class involvement and widespread simmering resentments among fans against corporate owners.

Another area that the State remains the indispensable guarantor of, financially and legally, in the development of non-State power and participation, is the whole terrain of collective, common and community ownership of productive resources. Again, this would require the development of experiments in civil society and the development in the skills and capacities to work collectively, collaboratively and with accountable forms of decision-making in the allocation of resources and the strategic development of plans both inside collectively owned organisations and in conjunction with wider community involvement. Existing successful cooperatives, surviving against all the odds in a hostile environment, are the obvious place to start to look for models that could be developed and supported by strategic thinking about supply chains for these worker controlled collectives. A network that begins to establish a commons would begin to redefine wealth and produce, just as the universalisation of the market in labour-power now does, its own 'spontaneous' forms of social consciousness that can then be elaborated by civil society organs. The material and ideological complexes which capitalism's 'dull compulsion of economics' currently produces can only be contracted by developing more choices for labour so that it has greater leverage against employers and the market in labour-power.

The small-scale and the local is also a good way of driving a wedge between big capital and small businesses. The latter has often provided an important and influential layer of support for what are essentially the aims and interests of monopoly capital. Crucial here is the conflation that is often made between capital and the market. Looked at historically, we can see this is an ideological strategy, for markets have long pre-existed capitalism. What capital did was to turn markets into a accumulation model by commodifying labour on a universal basis and capturing the surplus value of that labour-power. By differentiating between big capital and small businesses, between capital and the market as a form of trade and exchange in goods (but not labour-power) a very potent ideological weapon (the market) can be partly neutralised. Small businesses, which are often only sole traders or employing a handful of people, are not part of that accumulation imperative by definition. They are, however, extremely vulnerable to the power of big capital and the resources it can mobilise to squeeze small businesses out of markets and communities. If hegemony means building alliances and reconciling tensions between different interests in order to weaken the power of capital, then prising a chunk of small businesses away from monopoly capital would be a smart tactical move to achieve the strategic goal of weakening the power of capital to mobilise support from outside the power bloc.

The differentiations between big capital and small businesses would provide a way of exposing the unaccountable power of big capital to lobby local and national governments or hoard desperately needed investment that has been expropriated from society. We need political leadership that blows the whistle on how big capital operates and amplifies the anti-corporate campaigns of the late 1990s and early 2000s. By contrast, many small business start-ups are motivated by social and cultural purposes that can also be better guaranteed by the development of public service frameworks within which to work. As Hall noted, 'most of the innovatory trends in everyday life with which younger people spontaneously identify – in music, clothes, styles …' operate on this artisanal basis.[6] Small businesses desperately need loans that the private sector is notoriously reluctant to advance. Public investment can provide extra leverage to bind businesses into public and cultural purposes while legal tools could both prevent automatic take-overs by big capital without substantial compensation to the public purse and triggers that would convert small businesses to collective ownership models if they grow to a certain size.

In the period of social-democratic formation, industry was the basis for the political imaginary of industrialism. It represented a fusion between the labour movement and liberalism (the working class and sections of the intelligentsia of the middle class) and its limited success represented a short-term accommodation of it by industrial capital and the other key sectors. At the cultural level industrialism had a significant impact on British national identity, making the working class a legitimate, important and even respected component of the national imaginary in a way that had not been the case in the nineteenth century. In time, the social-democratic historic bloc led to material improvements in the lifeworld of the working class and some redressing of economic inequalities through the growth of the social State or public provision as well as a more regulated labour market. Industrialism had a number of strengths as the core part of this political culture. It allied the workers' movement with modernity – always a powerful if ambiguous cultural resource. It gave this cultural project a clearly defined agency in the form of the industrial worker who was now imbued with a powerful normative justification as at the very least necessary to the economic wealth of the country or even, in more Marxist versions, the source of economic wealth. The production of useful things that give identity to cities (Sheffield steel for example) and regions (Lancashire cotton) or the nation (the British car industry with its specific models such as the Rolls Royce and the Mini) and that find their way into everyday use, helped make industry a tangible, durable and enriching part of people's lives. The contrast here is with banking and finance, which is seen as fickle, mobile, or rather not seen at all, part of 'invisible earnings' that benefit a tiny elite. This contrast became acute during the Reagan and Thatcher years as the City of London and Wall Street boomed once more and domestic manufacturing in Britain and the United States declined, exposed as they were to international competition and global capital flows moving in and out of countries to maximise the advantages of local conditions (which get progressively worse for the majority in a race to the bottom to attract capital investment). Even in this period of contraction for industry (at least in the advanced Western countries) popular culture often articulated a critique of capitalism by making a distinction between finance and banking and industrial, manufacturing or artisanal work where 'real people' made things that are useful and enjoyable for other people.[7] Today, banking scandals and revelations about British-connected tax havens provide ample opportunities to throw British finance and service sector capital on the defensive and repatriate private offshore wealth for national public purposes.

Although there is an ongoing debate about how large British manufacturing remains (depending on what is included in the statistics), what is indisputable is that the political culture that was once attached to it, has been very largely dismantled. Yet this history continues as popular memory as we try to make sense of where we are now. Films such as *Made in Dagenham* (2010) about the strike for equal pay by women workers on Ford's production line, and *Pride* (2014) about the alliance between striking miners and the Gay and Lesbian community in the 1984–5 conflict, continue to resonate with the wider public. It is as if a hole has been torn in our symbolic cultural order and we are trying to figure out what it means, what has been lost and how to go forward on the different terrain we now find ourselves in.

Despite its rhetorical power, industrialism had a number of weaknesses, of course. While it had a clear agent that could be seen to underpin the social-democratic historic bloc, that agent was very sector specific, i.e. it was grounded in a few extractive and manufacturing industries although there was some crossover with some of the services in the public sector. Yet the romance of the male worker in what were seen as the key industrial sectors dominated the political imaginary, potentially narrowing the social base for social democracy or at least opening up routes of recruitment to the economic liberal project when social democracy clashed with and declined in relation to capitalist imperatives. One indicator of how powerfully the identification between the industrial worker and social democracy or socialism was, is that with the contraction of industry in the west and the expansion of the service sector, it became common to think that there was no longer such a social subject as 'the working class' or that we had moved into a qualitatively different era in which wealth production no longer revolved around an inherently antagonistic relationship.

The other major weakness of industrialism is that it often lacked sufficient clarity of the different economic-class interests at play within industry. Politically this could lead to illusions about alliances with industrial capital against finance capital and its powerhouse the City. At a policy making level it underestimated how difficult it is to work out the institutional mechanisms for making privately held wealth that is subject to competitive accumulation dynamics, democratically accountable to the demos. Industry was always embedded into and part-and-parcel of wider capitalist social relationships that make reform or 'modernisation' very difficult to implement, to implement successfully and to implement successfully over the long term.

A very important dimension to the current state of the British national-popular is the divide between the north and the south, and especially and increasingly between London and the other major cities. The value of goods and services that London has monopolised per head of the population is seven times that of its nearest 'rival' Greater Manchester.[8] These distorting asymmetries of growth are making both London and the north increasingly unviable in the long term. People feel and know this – but once again, it requires political will to crystallise these sentiments and articulate them into popular images and policy proposals that will do more than tinker at the edges. The north continues to suffer disproportionately from the planned de-industrialisation Thatcherism initiated in the 1980s. Discussing the Miners' Strike of 1984–5, Stuart Hall was critical of the terms in which it was fought. Instead of a conservative defence of coal, a more offensive 'Gramscian' stance would have been to pose both the question of a necessary shift away from fossil fuels and how that long transition could be managed and planned for in a way that it was not 'borne by the sectors of the society who are most vulnerable to technological change, who are simply then thrown on the scrapheap of history, their communities and cultures offered up on the alter of efficiency and "modernization"'.[9] Such a position would have struck at the heart of capital and the market as a morally justifiable allocation of resource mechanism. A different version of the national-popular can mobilise sentiments of national identity against the dominant mobilisers of national identity by exposing the gap between their rhetoric and the reality of national divisions and exploiting the contradiction between conservative nationalism and British capitalism's continuing and historic overseas orientation (and hence national underinvestment).

The question of democratic accountability over what Habermas once called the unaccountable steering mechanisms of money and political power is most starkly posed in relation to the existential threat of climate change. One suspects that what worries capital most here is that deep down, in order to address this major threat to humanity, capital's representatives know that it will require the kind of extensive coordination and planning that curbs the freedom of private property to do as it pleases. But it is not only climate change but all the negative costs which capitalist production externalises into the environment and into the bodies of human beings which must be confronted. With cancer now affecting one in two people in the west, we can truly say that capitalism's toxicity has reached unprecedented levels.[10] Socialism can recover modernity as a powerful resource to think the future by shifting the concept away from the temporal dimension (merely the old/new) and versions of technological determinism and articulating it to public service, common forms of property, democratic accountability and ecologically sustainable and life-enhancing production.

Engaging with the British State and mobilising it against its own dominant interests is of course a highly contradictory prospect. We have seen that conservatism has long dominated the coercive and ritualistic departments of the State and that these have been formidable shapers of a reactionary British national-popular identity. However in my assessment of the Nairn/Anderson thesis I also argued that conservatism has always had to have competitive partnerships with other political cultures within any of the three historic blocs that have shaped Britishness in the period we have been studying. By eclipsing the presence and role of liberalism within the British historical experience, Nairn and Anderson deployed an overly functionalist version of Gramsci's concept of hegemony. While dominant in the State apparatus, within the first historic bloc, laissez-faire principles were dominant in the economy and liberalism was the political culture that best articulated them. Conservatism's social, spatial and temporal distantiation from production at the cultural level was perfectly compatible with letting the market operate with less and less in the way of impediments of custom and habit. Cultural norms dualistically opposed to the economy were all the more necessary precisely because the latter was legitimised by an abstract rationality, scientism and positivism that evacuated any notion of the moral good. Yet civil society was not seamlessly dominated by conservatism but by a partnership between conservatism and liberalism that was not without tensions. Those tensions intensified with the rise of the labour movement and the emergence of social liberalism (the new liberalism) as distinct from economic liberalism. These conflicts *between* political cultures have also interacted with the *contradictions* between conservatism and economic liberalism, even as they fused together in a new configuration after the rise of Thatcherism. The old dualistic model between conservative culture and free market that characterised conservatism in the nineteenth century has become harder to sustain. The tendency for economic liberalism to liquidate the moral-cultural universe of its conservative partner has become more pronounced.

For this reason, even the State institutions that conservatism has made its own are not impregnable. Indeed the unleashing of economic liberalism has hollowed out both the institutions of conservative Britain and the deferential attachments to those institutions, while at the same time, the motor of economic liberalism has come to a spluttering near-stop. Simultaneously the main party-political vehicle of conservatism – the Conservative Party – is in turmoil – as is the alliance between conservatism and social liberalism – over Britain's future relationship with the EU. In such circumstances the remaining conservative institutions look dangerously exposed. There is little popular feeling for the House of Lords, stuffed as it is with politicians who have been rejected

252 · ENGLAND'S DISCONTENTS

by the public at the ballot box, while the political class in the Commons is widely seen as in need of a major change in composition. The powerful nexus between the Treasury and the City needs to be made visible to the public and then broken up as part of a campaign to 'clean up' the City. The monarchy meanwhile has been engaging in a very long-term public relations plan to recover the public affection which it catastrophically lost over the messy divorce between Charles and Diana and the latter's subsequent death in a car accident while being madly chased by the paparazzi. Both the divorce and the circumstances of the death (hounded by a celebrity-obsessed press) seem to illuminate some of the dynamics unleashed by conservatism that rebounded on conservative institutions. More seriously and substantively, anti-militarism after the 2003 Iraq War debacle has not receded and lies as a reservoir of popular feeling that could be mobilised to re-imagine British involvement in the world and shift it away from a morally and financially irresponsible nuclear deterrent – something which the Scottish referendum of 2014 already put on the agenda.

In Chapter 3 I also argued that the core proposition of the Nairn/Anderson thesis reversed the true causalities shaping the formation of British capitalism. According to them, a backward, reactionary ruling class whose social base was firstly in agriculture and then in the City, developed a political culture and set of institutions that thwarted the development of industrial capitalism and with it the development of a social base that could have supported a more democratic political culture within which working class ascendency could be constructed. I argued instead that the political and cultural superstructure that we have could be consolidated because the historical development of British capitalism meant that it made sense to exploit its comparative advantage as an imperial and trading world power, within which industry took up a subaltern role in which it was indeed a beneficiary for a very long time. We should avoid evaluative assessments of British capitalism that rely on ahistorical teleological models of growth paths (i.e. to develop the forces of production), uncritical normative investments in 'good' capital, plans based on strategic alliances with industrial capital and avoidance of the historical record that British capitalism has been very profitable for the power bloc and a wider layer of middle-class retainers. Its decline in economic terms has been relative. Of more interest, has been the amassing of wealth at the top. An economy that is still among the top ten biggest in the world has a lot of wealth it can redistribute.

But my reassessment of the Nairn/Anderson thesis does not mean cultural and political cultural battles are 'secondary'. A differentiated but integrated economic base set the conditions for a differentiated but integrated repertoire of political cultures (conservatism and liberalism) that represented, organised and strategised (sometimes in conflicting ways) on behalf of that differentiated but integrated economic base. We also saw that the *culture* of industrialism eventually mobilised widespread sentiments against the dominant political cultures and helped seed social democracy as a significant section of liberalism oscillated away from economic liberalism into an alliance with the labour movement. Likewise today we must mobilise sentiments against the superstructures that have so badly served the demos (the centralised political system, the 'first past the post' electoral system, the patronage-stuffed Lords, the monarchy, the elite civil service, etc). A bold constitutional revolution – as was envisaged following a successful vote for Scottish independence – could act as a catalyst for energising political conversations and imaginaries about future change and would be an opportunity to embed the rights of common ownership and public rights, access and accountability as part of a new popular-national identity, one in which the historic exclusions in public life, along the lines of class, gender and race, are acknowledged and addressed. Undoubtedly, the hegemonic struggle requires winning over at least some groups and individuals who would today identify themselves within the liberal tradition, by pushing that tradition closer to the kind of radical liberalism and rapprochement with socialism that we saw in such figures as Hobson or Grierson, at their best.

There is clearly now a deep desire for an alternative to economic liberalism, to capitalism unleashed. Historically, that alternative, short of socialism, was social democracy. We must remember that the institutionalisation of social democracy did not happen in the context of peace and good will. Social democracy was born out of war, revolution, economic collapse and counter-revolution (fascism and Stalinism) and desperate struggles between 1914 and 1945. No one wants to go back to that but the contradiction between the very modest goals that many people would like to see right now and the resistance to implementing those very modest goals by the dominant power bloc can lead either to paralysis and demoralisation or, with the help of a Gramscian strategy, a deepening of political consciousness and an awakening to the historical options and responsibilities we have before us.

Notes

Introduction

1 Antonio Gramsci, *Selections from the Prison Notebooks*, (eds) Quentin Hoare and Geoffrey Nowell Smith, Lawrence and Wishart, London, 1971, pp. 323–4.
2 Ibid., p. 324.

Chapter 1

1 Linda Colley, *Britons, Forging the Nation, 1707–1837*, Bath Press, Bath, 1992, pp. 56–60.
2 Ibid., p. 69.
3 Antonio Gramsci, *Antonio Gramsci, Prison Notebooks, Vol. 1* (ed.) Joseph A. Butigieg, Columbia University Press, New York, 2011, p. 126.
4 Michael Billig, *Banal Nationalism*, Thousand Oaks, CA, Sage, p. 74.
5 Craig Lindsay, 'A Century of Labour Market Change: 1900–2000' *Labour Market Trends*, March 2003, Office of National Statistics, p. 137.
6 Stuart Hall, 'The State in Question' in *The Idea of the Modern State*, (eds) Gregor McLennan, David Held and Stuart Hall, Oxford University Press, Oxford, 1984, p. 14.
7 Karl Marx, *The Thought of Karl Marx*, (ed.) David McLellan, Macmillan Press, Basingstoke, 1980, p. 216.
8 Colley, *Britons*, p. 68.
9 Benedict Anderson, *Imagined Communities, Reflections on the Origin and Spread of Nationalism*, Verso, London, 2006, p. 7.
10 Karl Marx and Friedrich Engels, *The Communist Manifesto*, Penguin Books, 1985, p. 84.
11 Neil Davidson, 'Neoliberal Politics in a Devolved Scotland', *Neoliberal Scotland, Class and Society in a Stateless Nation*, (eds) Neil Davidson, Patricia McCafferty and David Miller, Cambridge Scholars, Newcastle Upon Tyne, 2010, p. 317.
12 Karl Marx and Friedrich Engels, *The Communist Manifesto*, Penguin Books, London, 1985, p. 82.
13 Karl Marx, *The Thought of Karl Marx*, p. 219.
14 Antonio Gramsci, *A Gramsci Reader*, (ed.) David Forgacs, Lawrence and Wishart, London, 1988, p. 261.
15 Karl Marx, *Capital, Vol. One*, Lawrence and Wishart, London, 1983, p. 266.

16 See Engels's letter to J. Bloch in *Selected Works Volume One*, Karl Marx and Frederick Engels, Lawrence and Wishart, London, 1968, p. 682.

17 See Engels's letter to C. Schmidt in *Selected Works Volume One*, Karl Marx and Frederick Engels, Lawrence and Wishart, London, 1968, p. 679–680.

18 Antonio Gramsci, *The Modern Prince and Other Writings*, Lawrence and Wishart, London, 1967, p. 153.

19 Ibid., p. 69.

20 Antonio Gramsci, *A Gramsci Reader*, (ed.) David Forgacs, p. 208.

21 Ibid, p. 205.

22 Ibid.

23 Antonio Gramsci, *The Modern Prince*, p. 155.

24 Ibid., p. 155.

25 Ibid., pp. 137–8.

26 Ibid., p. 147.

27 Ibid., p. 126.

28 Antonio Gramsci, *Selections From the Prison Notebooks*, (eds) Quintin Hoare and Geoffrey Nowell-Smith, Lawrence and Wishart, 1998, p. 247.

29 Ibid., p. 238.

30 Antonio Gramsci *Prison Notebooks*, edited by Jospeh A. Buttigeg, 2011, p. 153.

31 Antonio Gramsci, *A Gramsci Reader*, p. 250.

32 Antonio Gramsci, *Prison Notebooks*, (eds) Quintin Hoare and Geoffrey Nowell-Smith, p. 12. From this point on, the Gramscian conceptualisation of civil society, as opposed to Marx's early usage of the term (as private economic interests) will be used.

33 For a very comprehensive discussion of the complex debates around Gramsci's work, and in particular on the way different writers have interpreted Gramsci's conception of State, civil society and political economy, see Peter D. Thomas, *The Gramscian Moment, Philosophy, Hegemony and Marxism*, Brill, Leiden/London, 2009.

34 Noel O'Sullivan 'Conservatism' in *The Oxford Handbook of Political Ideologies*, (eds) Michael Freeden, Lyman Tower Sargent and Marc Stears, Oxford University Press, Oxford, 2013.

35 Antonio Gramsci, *Selections from the Prison Notebooks*, p. 155.

36 John Medhurst, *That Option No Longer Exists: Britain 1974–1976*, Zero Books, Alresford, Hants., 2014.

37 Antonio Gramsci, *The Modern Prince*, p. 91.

38 Antonio Gramsci, *Selections from the Prison Notebooks*, p. 194.

39 V.N. Volosinov, *Marxism and the Philosophy of Language* (translated by Ladislav Matejka and I.R. Titunik, Seminar Press, New York/London, 1973, p. 23.

40 Raymond Williams, 'Base and Superstructure in Marxist Cultural Theory' in *New Left Review I*, 82, 1973, p. 12.

41 Gramsci, *A Gramsci Reader*, p. 365.

42 Ibid., p. 369.

43 See Gramsci's English language interpreter, Geoffrey Nowell-Smith's complaint about British cinema in 'But Do We Need It?' in *British Cinema Now*, BFI, London, 1985, p. 152.

44 We should also note that outside the more respectable genres of British cinema, with its literary, heritage and 'realist' modes, genuinely popular 'low' culture examples of British cinema have been produced.

45 Michael Wayne, 'Working Title Mark II: A Critique of the Atlanticist Paradigm for British Cinema' in *International Journal of Media and Cultural Politics*, 2 (1), 2006, pp. 59–73.

46 Joel Windle, "Anyone can make it, but there can only be one winner": Modelling Neoliberal Learning and Work on Reality Television' in *Critical Studies in Education*, 51 (3), 2010, p. 256.

47 Raymond Boyle and Maggie Magor, 'A Nation of Entrepreneurs? Television, Social Change and the Rise of the Entrepreneur' in *International Journal of Media and Cultural Politics*, 4 (2), 2008, pp. 126–9.

48 Nick Couldry and Jo Littler, 'The Work of Work: Reality TV and the Negotiation of Neo-liberal Labour in *The Apprentice*' in *Rethinking Documentary, New Perspectives, New Practices*, (eds) Thomas Austin and Wilma de Jong, Open University Press, Maidenhead, 2008, p. 264.

49 Although an analysis informed by Slavoj Žižek's notion that cynical self-reflexivity is today part of the dominant ideology, would suggest that this 'knowing' distance from the entrepreneurial ideal could help sell it to the viewer even more effectively. The subject believes 'I am not stupid enough to take this seriously, but as a result, I will perform a neo-liberal subjectivity even better than those who really believe in this nonsense, because I do it without illusions.' See Slavoj Žižek, *The Sublime Object of Ideology*, Verso, 1989, pp. 28–30.

50 Antonio Gramsci, 'The Southern Question' in *The Modern Prince*.

51 Krishan Kumar, 'English and British National Identity' *History Compass* 4(3), 2006, pp. 428–47.

52 This geographical unevenness in the density of the middle class is historic. Rubinstein finds that in 1860, at the height of the industrial revolution, London's middle classes were approximately three times the size of Lancashire and Yorkshire combined. See W.D. Rubinstein, *Capitalism Culture and Decline in Britain*, Routledge, 1994, pp. 30–1. Certainly as a Londoner, I am always amazed whenever I travel north, how the middle class 'thin out', both in the institutions they usually have an overwhelming presence in and just visibly in the public streets themselves.

53 Danny Dorling, 'Class Segregation' in *Considering Class, Theory, Culture and the Media in the 21st Century*, (eds) Deirdre O'Neill and Mike Wayne, Brill, Leiden/Boston 2018, p. 78.

Chapter 2

1 See Peter D. Thomas, *The Gramscian Moment, Philosophy, Hegemony and Marxism*, Brill, Leiden/Boston, 2009, pp. 95–102.

2 Antonio Gramsci, *A Gramsci Reader* (ed.) David Forgacs, Lawrence and Wishart, London, 1988, p. 201.

3 Ibid.

4 Perry Anderson, 'The Figures of Descent' in *English Questions*, Verso, London, 1992, p. 179.

5 Andrew Gamble, 'The Free Economy and The Strong State: The Rise of the Social Market Economy', *Socialist Register*, 1979, p. 6.

6 Michael Freeden cites the Earl of Balfour and Conservative Party Prime Minister between 1902–5, arguing that what 'a man possess' he 'earns' and that 'no greater injury can be done to the working classes of this country than to spread [a] feeling of insecurity about private property', in *Ideologies and Political Theory: A Conceptual Approach*, Clarendon Press, Oxford, 1996 p. 355.

7 Karl Marx and Friedrich Engels, *The Communist Manifesto*, Penguin Books, London, p. 83.

8 Max Weber, 'Selections' in *Classes, Power and Conflict, Classical and Contemporary Debates*, (eds) Anthony Giddens and David Held, University of California Press, California, 1982, p. 67.

9 Antonio Gramsci, *Selections from the Prison Notebooks*, (eds) Quintin Hoare and Geoffrey Nowell Smith, Lawrence and Wishart, London, 1988, pp. 119–20.

10 Johann Gottfried Herder, *Another Philosophy of History and Selected Political Writings*, translated by Ionnis D. Evrigenis and Daniel Pellerin, Hackett Publishing Company, Indianapolis/Cambridge, 2004, pp. 29–30.

11 Reidar Maliks, *Kant's Politics in Context*, Oxford University Press, Oxford, 2014, p. 29–32.

12 Perry Anderson, *Lineages of the Absolutist State*, Verso, London, 1979.

13 Michael Skey, *National Belonging and Everyday Life*, Palgrave/Macmillan, 2011.

14 Noel Sullivan, 'Conservatism' in *The Oxford Handbook of Political Ideologies*, (eds) Michael Freedman, Lyman Tower Sargent and Marc Stears, Oxford University Press, Oxford, 2013, p. 299.

15 Michael Freeden is sceptical that there is a deep dualism between conservative defence of authority and investment in individualism. Critics of conservatism he suggests are wasting their time 'referring to tensions, contradictions, and double standards', see *Ideologies and Political Theory: A Conceptual Approach*, Clarendon Press, Oxford, 1996, p. 385. I think this underestimates how 1980s Conservatism did exhaust itself precisely around these tensions in the 1990s.

16 As Perry Anderson famously wrote: 'The two great chemical elements of this blanketing English fog are "traditionalism" and "empiricism": in it, visibility – of any social or historical reality – is always zero … A comprehensive, coagulated conservatism is the result, covering the whole of society with a thick pall of simultaneous philistinism (towards ideas) and mystagogy (towards institutions), for which England has justly won an international reputation.' 'Origins of the Present Crisis' in *English Questions*, p. 31.

17 Michael Freeden, *Ideologies and Political Theory: A Conceptual Approach*, Clarendon Press, Oxford 1996, p. 322.

18 Perry Anderson, 'Components of the National Culture', in *English Questions*, p. 57. The category of the 'totality' refers to the Marxist critique of the way capitalism fosters partial and fragmented knowledge of social processes that are inexplicable unless they are related as parts of a differentiated totality of unequally weighted forces.

19 Margaret Thatcher, *Women's Own*, 23 September, 1987.

20 'As the 1983 Conservative manifesto indicates, the family and the individual – frequently mentioned in the same breath, so that individualism is underpinned by and interpreted through a 'natural' group framework which is institutionally constraining and morally directive – are the two complementary units of society.' Michael Freeden, *Ideologies and Political Theory*, p. 390.

21 Raphael Samuel, 'Mrs Thatcher's Return to Victorian Values' *Proceedings of the British Academy*, 78 (9), 1992, p. 23.

22 William H. Beveridge, *Voluntary Action: A Report on Methods of Social Advance*, Macmillan, New York, 1948.

23 Peter Kennard's iconic photomontage *Maggie Regina* (1983) which transposed Thatcher's head onto a well-known painting of Queen Victoria from 1883, plays with the temporal fusing (past and present) of Thatcherism, its relationship with the traditional conservative establishment (reinforcement/displacement) and its highly selective Victoriana.

24 This points to a limitation in Michael Freeden's analysis of the morphological rearrangements within a political discourse. While logically economic individualism and an authoritarian social and moral order can be reconciled, in practice, the former tends to end up transgressing the latter. When this starts to register within the public sphere, a fairly rapid de-legitimisation can take place together with the de-moralisation of conservatism. This happened to the Conservative Party in the 1990s.

25 www.margaretthatcher.org/document/105147

26 Neil Davidson, 'What Was Neoliberalism?' in *Neoliberal Scotland, Class and Society in a Stateless Nation*, (eds) Neil Davidson, Patricia McCafferty and David Miller, Cambridge Scholars, Newcastle Upon Tyne, 2010, pp. 4–5.

27 P. J. Cain and A.G. Hopkins, 'Gentlemanly Capitalism and British Expansion Overseas II: New Imperialism, 1850–1945' in *Economic History Review*, 1987, p. 6.

28 Graham John Taylor, *State Regulation and the Politics of Public Service*, Mansell, London, 1999, pp. 34–5.

29 John Gray, *False Dawn: The Delusions of Global Capitalism*, Granta Books, London 2002, p. 13.

30 Ibid., p. 5.

31 The classic example here is J.A Hobson's liberal critique *Imperialism: A Study*, James Pott & Company, New York, 1902.

32 In *The Battle of Algiers* (Gillo Pontecorvo, 1966) the liberal assumption that certain means of killing people are morally superior to uncivilised means of killing people is effectively skewed. In one scene a French journalist questioning a captured militant from the FLN asks whether it is cowardly to use women's baskets to transport and conceal bombs that have killed people. The FLN militant notes that napalming defenceless villages that kills many thousands more is hardly morally superior. 'Give us your bombers and you can keep our baskets'.

33 See the alternate Nick Cohen's *Cruel Britannia: Reports on the Sinister and the Preposterous*, Verso, London, 1999.

34 Michael Kenny, *The Politics of English Nationhood*, Oxford University Press, Oxford, 2014, p. 113.
35 As the horrified response of the majority of the Parliamentary Labour Party to the election of Jeremy Corbyn to the leadership by the membership shows.
36 John Gray, *After Social Democracy*, DEMOS, London, 1996, p. 25.
37 Raymond Williams, *Marxism and Literature*, Oxford University Press, Oxford, 1988, p. 122.
38 John Gray, *After Social Democracy*, p. 13.
39 Kelvin MacKenzie, 'It's time for a Southern Party', www.cityam.com/211584/conservatives-have-outlived-their-usefulness-it-s-time-southern-party
40 Michael Kenny, *The Politics of English Nationhood*, p. 107.
41 Carl Boggs, *The End of Politics: Corporate Power and the Decline of the Public Sphere*, The Guilford Press, New York, 2000, p. 115.
42 Ibid., p. 98.
43 Peter Mair, 'Ruling The Void', *New Left Review*, 42 Nov/Dec 2006.
44 Friedrich Engels, *The Condition of the Working Class in England*, Penguin, London, 2005, p. 112.
45 Andrew Glyn, *Capitalism Unleashed: Finance, Globalization, and Welfare*, Oxford University Press, Oxford, 2006, pp. 26–8.
46 Tony Benn and Andrew Hood, *Common Sense: A New Constitution for Britain*, Hutchinson, London 1993, pp. 4–5.
47 Tony Benn and Andrew Hood, ibid, p. 86.
48 Will Hutton, *The State We're In*, Jonathan Cape, London, 1995, p. 35.
49 Christina Beatty, Steve Fothergill and Tony Gore, 'The Real Level of Unemployment', September 2012, www.shu.ac.uk/research/cresr/sites/shu.ac.uk/files/real-level-of-unemployment-2012.pdf
50 Fredric Jameson, *Representing Capital: A Reading of Volume One*, Verso, London, 2014.
51 Randall Collins, 'The End of Middle Class Work: No More Escapes' in *Does Capitalism Have a Future?* I. Wallerstein, Randall Collins, Michael Mann, Georgi Derlugian and Craig Calhoun, Oxford University Press, Oxford, 2013.
52 Friedrich Engels, *The Condition of the Working Class*, p. 234.
53 E.P. Thompson, 'The Peculiarities of the English', *Socialist Register 1965*, pp. 343–4.
54 John Saville, 'Labourism and the Labour Government', *The Socialist Register*, 1967, pp. 43–71.
55 Gregory Elliot, *Labourism and the English Genius: The Strange Death of Labour England?* Verso, London, 1993.
56 Raymond Williams, 'Culture is Ordinary', *Raymond Williams On Culture and Society*, (ed.) Jim McGuigan, Sage, London, p. 3.
57 Ibid., p. 11.
58 Ibid., p. 12.
59 Ibid., p. 6.
60 Tony Garnett 'Working in the Field' in *Looking at Class, Film, Television and the Working Class in Britain*, (eds) Sheila Rowbotham and Huw Beynon, Rivers Oram Press, London, 2001, p. 74.

61 John McGrath, *A Good Night Out: Popular Theatre – Audience, Class and Form*, Methuen, London, p. 24.
62 Ibid., p. 25.
63 Ibid., p. 28.
64 John Schwarzmantel, *Gramsci's Prison Notebooks*, Routledge, London, 2015, p. 75.
65 Antonio Gramsci *The Modern Prince*, p. 58.

Chapter 3

1 Stuart Hall, 'Gramsci and Us', *Marxism Today*, June 1987, p. 17 and 19.
2 Tom Nairn, *The Break-Up of Britain*, Verso, London, 1981, pp. 13–14.
3 Ibid., p. 23.
4 Ibid., p. 22.
5 Ibid., p. 23.
6 Perry Anderson, 'Origins of the Present Crisis' in *English Questions*, Verso, London, 1992 p. 43.
7 Ibid., p. 17.
8 Ibid.
9 Tom Nairn, *The Break-Up*, p. 22.
10 Ibid., pp. 64–5.
11 Perry Anderson, 'Origins', p. 44. The cult of the amateur dabbling in this or that fits snugly with established patronage networks in which elite connections rather than expertise is decisive.
12 Ibid., p. 43.
13 Ibid., p. 30.
14 Ibid., p. 20 and p. 31.
15 Ibid., p. 24.
16 Ibid., p. 27.
17 Antonio Gramsci, *Selections From The Prison Notebooks*, (eds) Quintin Hoare and Geoffrey Nowell Smith, Lawrence and Wishart, London, 1998, p. 18.
18 Perry Anderson, *English Questions*, Verso, London, 1992, p. 5.
19 P. J. Cain and A.G. Hopkins, 'Gentlemanly Capitalism and British Expansion Overseas I: The Old Colonial System, 1688–1850', *The Economic History Review*, 39 (4), 1986, p. 503.
20 E.P. Thompson, 'The Peculiarities of the English', *Socialist Register*, 1965, p. 316.
21 Ibid., p. 317–18.
22 Perry Anderson, 'The Figures of Descent' in *English Questions*, pp. 122–8.
23 Ibid., p. 139.
24 Richard Johnson, 'Barrington Moore, Perry Anderson and English Social Development' in *Culture, Media, Language*, (eds) Stuart Hall, Dorothy Hobson, Andrew Lowe and Paul Willis, Routledge, London, 1980, pp. 69–70.
25 Ellen Meiksins Wood, *The Pristine Culture of Capitalism*, Verso, London, 1991, p. 17.
26 EP. Thompson, 'The Peculiarities of the English', p. 315.

27 Ibid., p. 317.
28 David Canadine, *The Decline and Fall of the British Aristocracy*, Vintage Books, New York, 1999, pp. 9–12.
29 John Rose, *Thatcher and Friends: The Anatomy of the Tory Party*, Pluto Press, London, 1983, p. 48.
30 Raymond Williams, *The Country and the City*, Spokesman, Nottingham, 2011, p. 39.
31 John Berger, *Ways of Seeing*, Penguin, 2008, pp. 100–1.
32 Raymond Williams, *The Country*, p. 46.
33 E.P. Thompson, 'The Peculiarities of the English', p. 316.
34 Gillian Rose, *Feminism and Geography: The Limits of Geographical Knowledge*, Polity Press, Cambridge, pp. 91–2.
35 Perry Anderson, 'Origins', p. 19.
36 Paul Langford, *Public Life and the Propertied Englishman, 1689–1798*, Clarendon Press, Oxford, 2003, p. 61.
37 Raymond Williams, *The Country*, p. 48.
38 Ellen Meiksins Wood, *Democracy Against Capitalism*, Cambridge University Press, Cambridge, 2000, p. 31.
39 E.P. Thompson, 'The Moral Economy of the English Crowd in the Eighteenth Century' in *Past and Present*, 50 (1), 1971, p. 90.
40 E.P. Thompson, 'Eighteenth-century English Society: Class Struggle without Class?' in *Social History*, 3 (2), 1978, p. 154.
41 EP Thompson, 'The Moral Economy'.
42 Peter Coss, *The Origins of the English Gentry*, Cambridge University Press, Cambridge, 2003, p. 6.
43 Thorstein Veblen, *Conspicuous Consumption*, Penguin, London, 2005, p. 2.
44 Ibid., p. 26.
45 Ibid., p. 21.
46 The dualism (and interdependence) of business and culture is represented respectively by the Wilcox and Schlegel families in E.M. Forster's *Howard's End* (1910). The same antithesis is given a geographical dimension in Elizabeth Gaskell's *North and South* (1855).
47 P. J. Cain and A.G. Hopkins, 'Gentlemanly Capitalism and British Expansion Overseas I: The Old Colonial System, 1688–1850', *The Economic History Review*, Vol. 39, (4) 1986, p. 504.
48 Ibid., p. 505.
49 Paul Langford, *Public Life and Propertied Englishmen, 1689–1798*, Oxford University Press, Oxford, p. 59.
50 Sanchez Manning, 'Britain's Colonial Shame: Slave-owners Given Huge Payouts after Abolition' www.independent.co.uk/news/uk/home-news/britains-colonial-shame-slave-owners-given-huge-payouts-after-abolition-8508358.html
51 Guy Adams, 'How Benedict Cumberbatch's Family Made a Fortune from Slavery', www.dailymail.co.uk/news/article-2549773/How-Benedict-Cumberbatchs-family-fortune-slavery-And-roles-films-like-12-Years-A-Slave-bid-atone-sins.html

52 K. Pavid, 'Were These Your Family', www.bristolpost.co.uk/family/story-26892102-detail/story.html

53 *Accounts and Papers: Railway Subscription Contracts, 31 January-17 July 1837,* no. 28, p. i. House of Commons, 1837.

54 Takeshi Abe, 'Organizational Changes in the Japanese Cotton Industry during the Inter-War Period' in *The Fibre That Changed the World, The Cotton Industry in International Perspective, 1600–1900s,* (eds) Douglas A. Farnie and David J. Jeremy, Oxford University Press, Oxford, pp. 461–94.

55 Eric Hobsbawm, *Industry and Empire,* Penguin Books, London, p. 166.

56 Perry Anderson, 'Figures of Descent', in *English Questions,* writes: 'The City did not raise venture capital for investment in provincial manufacturing. Its strictly banking functions were effectively divorced from the accumulation of industrial capital, whose firms typically remained small in size and met their financial needs from internal savings or local banks,' p. 138.

57 Martin Weiner *English Culture and the Decline of the Industrial Spirit,* Cambridge University Press, Cambridge, p. 13.

58 Ibid., p. 28–9.

59 Erik Olin Wright, *Understanding Class,* Verso, London, 2015, pp. 28–31.

60 V. I. Lenin, *On Imperialism and Imperialists,* Progress Publishers, Moscow, 1973, p. 50.

61 John Rose, *Thatcher and Friends,* p. 47.

62 Michael Barratt Brown, 'Away With All Great Arches', *New Left Review I,* 167, 1988, p. 27 and p. 44.

63 V. I. Lenin, *On Imperialism,* p. 59.

64 Colin Leys, *Politics in Britain: From Labourism to Thatcherism,* Verso, London 1989, p. 43.

65 Perry Anderson, 'Figures of Descent', in *English Questions,* p. 149.

66 Eric Hobsbawn, *Industry and Empire,* p. 169.

67 Colin Leys, *Politics in Britain,* p. 19.

68 P. J Cain and A.G. Hopkins, 'Gentlemanly Capitalism and British Expansion Overseas II: New Imperialism, 1850–1945' in *The Economic History Review,* vol. 40 (1), 1987, p. 2.

69 W.D. Rubinstein, *Capitalism Culture and Decline in Britain,* Routledge, London, 1994.

70 P. J Cain and A.G. Hopkins 'Gentlemanly Capitalism', p. 11.

71 Rosa Luxemburg, *The Accumulation of Capital,* Routledge and Kegan Paul Ltd, London, 1951, p. 422.

72 Ibid., p. 429.

73 David Harvey, *The New Imperialism,* Oxford University Press, Oxford, 2005, pp. 138–41.

74 Karl Marx, *Grundrisse,* Penguin Books, London, 1993, pp. 415–16.

75 David Harvey, 'Globalization and the "Spatial Fix"' in *Geographische Revue,* 2, 2001, p. 25.

76 Ellen Meiksins Wood, *Empire of Capital,* Verso, London, 2003, p. 111.

77 Perry Anderson, 'Figures of Descent' in *English Questions,* p. 168.

78 J.A. Hobson, *Imperialism: A Study*, James Pott & Company, New York, 1902, p. 59.
79 Michael Barratt Brown, 'Commercial and Industrial Capital in England: A Reply to Geoffrey Ingham', *New Left Review I*, 178, Nov–Dec 1989 and 'Away With All Great Arches', pp. 29–30.
80 David Smith, *Something Will Turn Up: Britain's Economy, Past, Present and Future*, Profile Books, London, 2015.
81 V. I. Lenin, *On Imperialism*, p. 65.
82 Antonio Gramsci, *Selections from the Prison Notebooks*, p. 281.
83 Ibid.
84 Ibid., p. 285.
85 J.A. Hobson, *Imperialism: A Study*, p. 60.
86 Ibid., p. 32.
87 John Rose, *Thatcher and Friends*, p. 66.
88 F. Engels, 'Engels to K. Kautsky in Vienna' in *Karl Marx and Frederick Engels: Selected Works*, Volume One, Lawrence and Wishart, London, 1977, p. 678.
89 J.A. Hobson, *Imperialism: A Study*, p. 67.
90 James Curran, *Media and Power*, Routledge, London, 2002, pp. 27–8.
91 Perry Anderson, 'Origins' in *English Questions*, p. 25.
92 Patrick Wright, *On Living in an Old Country*, Oxford University Press, Oxford, 2009, p. 51.
93 Alan Howkins, 'The Discovery of Rural England' in *Englishness, Politics and Culture, 1880–1920*, (eds) Robert Colls and Philip Dodd, Bloomsbury, London, 2014, p. 87–8.
94 See Katherine Tyler's essay on the construction of a village identity in a suburban area close to Leicester in 'The English Village, Whiteness, Coloniality and Social Class' in *Ethnicities*, 12 (4), pp. 427–44, 2012.
95 Terry Eagleton, *Criticism and Ideology*, Verso, London, 1986, pp. 102–161.
96 Mike Wayne, 'Utopianism and Film' in *Historical Materialism*, 10 (4), pp. 135–54.
97 Fredric Jameson, 'Cognitive Mapping' in *Marxism and the Interpretation of Culture*, (eds) Cary Nelson and Lawrence Grossberg, University of Illinois Press, 1988, p. 349.
98 Tom Nairn, *The Break-Up*, Verso, London, 1981, p. 69.
99 Ben Harker, "The Manchester Rambler': Ewan MacColl and the 1932 Mass Trespass' in *History Workshop Journal*, 59 (1), 2005, pp. 219–28.
100 Ingrid Pollard, *Postcards Home: Photographs by Ingrid Pollard*, Chris Boot Publishers, New York, 2004.
101 Andrew Glyn, *Capitalism Unleashed: Finance, Globalization and Welfare*, Oxford University Press, Oxford, 2006, p. 111.
102 Robert C. Hine and Peter W. Wright, 'Trade with Low Wage Economies, Employment and Productivity in UK Manufacturing', *The Economic Journal*, 108 (450), 1998, p. 1500.
103 Colin Leys, 'Thatcherism and British Manufacturing: A Question of Hegemony' *New Left Review I*, no.151, May–June 1985, p. 16.
104 Nicholas Shaxson, *Treasure Island: Tax Havens and the Men Who Stole the World*, Vintage, London, 2012.

105 Will Hutton, *The State We're In*, Jonathan Cape, 1995, p. 43.
106 Ibid., p. 44.
107 Ibid., p. 45.
108 Tony Benn and Andrew Hood, *Common Sense: A New Constitution for Britain*, Hutchinson, London 1993, p. 28.
109 John Rose, *Thatcher and Friends*, p. 27.
110 There is a broader context to all this of course that was at that time called postmodernism – which Fredric Jameson diagnosed as a major extension of commodity relations into culture and nature, one which collapsed former distinctions between the economy and the superstructure and high and popular culture. See 'Postmodernism, or the Cultural Logic of Late Capitalism', *New Left Review* I, 146, July–August, 1984.
111 See, for example, Mike Wayne, 'Crisis and Opportunity: Class, Gender and Allegory in *The Grand*' in *Dissident Voices: The Politics of Television and Cultural Change*, (ed.) Mike Wayne, Pluto Press, 1998.
112 Rupert Murdoch, 'Freedom in Broadcasting' in *Television Policy, The MacTaggart Lectures*, (ed.) Bob Franklin, Edinburgh University Press, Edinburgh, 2005, p. 132.
113 Ibid., p. 137.
114 Bob Franklin (ed.), *Television Policy: The MacTaggart Lectures*, Edinburgh University Press, 2005, p. 164.
115 See James Curran's critique of these liberal narratives in part one of *Media and Power*.
116 See Anita Biressi and Heather Nunn, *Class and Contemporary British Culture*, Palgrave, 2013, pp. 29–43.
117 See Doreen Massey's analysis of Thatcher's 1987 General Election victory, 'Heartlands of Defeat' in *Marxism Today*, July 1987, pp. 18–23.
118 Susan Watkins, 'A Weightless Hegemony, New Labour's Role in the Neoliberal Order' in *New Left Review* II, 25, Jan–Feb 2004, p. 26.

Chapter 4

1 Robert St George, 'Study Reveals Higher Proportion of FTSE Revenues Derived Overseas', Citywire, 12 Nov, 2013, at: http://citywire.co.uk/money/study-reveals-higher-proportion-of-ftse-revenues-derived-overseas/a716388. Of course not all the companies listed in the FTSE 100 are 'British', but many of them are. Who is in and who is out of the FTSE 100 does change over time.
2 *Naked Attraction* is Channel Four's find-a-date show which has participants displaying full-frontal nudity. According to *The Sun* it featured an average of five penises and two vaginas every minute: www.thesun.co.uk/tvandshowbiz/2152152/naked-attraction-will-return-for-a-second-series-on-channel-4-despite-dozens-of-complaints-about-its-nudity
3 Michael Freeden, *Ideologies and Political Theory: A Conceptual Approach*, Clarendon Press, Oxford, 1996, p. 363.
4 Edmund Burke, *Reflections on the Revolution in France*, J. Dodsley, London, 1793, pp. 48–9.

5 Paul Gilroy, *After Empire: Melancholia or Convivial Culture*, Routledge, London, 2004.

6 Donald Read, *Peterloo: The Massacre and Its background*, Manchester University, 1958, p. 85.

7 John Medhurst, *That Option No Longer Exists: Britain 1974–76*, Zero Books, Alresford, Hants., 2014.

8 James Kirkup, 'Russia Mocks Britain, the Little Island', *The Telegraph*, 5 September 2013. www.telegraph.co.uk/news/worldnews/europe/russia/10290243/Russia-mocks-Britain-the-little-island.html. Accessed 18 January 2017.

9 Stuart Hall, 'New Ethnicities', *Stuart Hall, Critical Dialogues in Cultural Studies*, (ed) David Morley and Kuan-Hsing Chen, New York, Routledge, 1996, p. 445.

10 Philip Schlesinger, 'The Nation and Communicative Space' in *Media Power, Professionals and Policies*, Routledge, London, 2000, p. 107.

11 E.T. MacDermot and C.R. Clinker, *History of the Great Western Railway* Vol. 1, Ian Allan Publishing, Birmingham, 1973.

12 Geoffrey Channon, *Railways in Britain and the United States, 1830–1940*, Ashgate, Farnham, Surrey, 2001, p. 301–2.

13 Nick Robins, *The Corporation That Changed The World*, Pluto Press, London, 2006.

14 The recent television series *Taboo* (2017) starring Tom Hardy has, unusually, identified the East India Company as an early form of rapacious corporate power.

15 I recall watching an episode of the BBC discussion programme *Question Time*. The panel was discussing the long delayed Chilcot enquiry into the political manoeuvring that went on in the run up to the 2003 Iraq War. A member of the audience makes a contribution. A well-built rugged man announces that he is a member of the armed forces. He suggests that while he is prepared to die for 'Queen and Country' he is not so enthusiastic to die for 'corporations'. This alludes to the western economic interests that critics of the war in Iraq argued had most to gain from it: not only oil interests such as Halliburton, but military hardware companies, security contractors, construction companies, and other large-scale corporations with close links to the US and British state. It was the anti-war movement that had succeeded in de-legitimising the invasion and its neo-imperialist basis (to bring 'democracy' to Iraq), to the extent that a member of the armed forces could articulate this critique. Yet dying for 'Queen or Country' has in fact always been tied up with dying for corporations, and this indicates the success with which a conservative political culture has in general rewritten the history books using State institutions like the monarchy to establish an apparent distance from such pecuniary forces. That the economic interests alone of business are not sufficient motivation to stir the sinews and suspend the critical faculties, alerts us to the important role these State institutions play.

16 Peter Linebaugh, *The London Hanged: Crime and Civil Society in the Eighteenth Century*, Verso, London, p. 17.

17 Colin Jones and Alan Murie, *The Right to Buy: Analysis and Evaluation of a Housing Policy*, Blackwell, Oxford, 2006.

18 Andrew Glyn, *British Capitalism, Workers and the Profits Squeeze*, Penguin Books, London, 1972.

19 Andrew Gamble, 'Thatcher – Make or Break', *Marxism Today*, November 1980, pp. 14–19.

20 Stuart Hall, Chas Critcher, Tony Jefferson, John Clarke and Brian Roberts, *Policing the Crisis: Mugging, the State and Law and Order*, Macmillan Press, London, 1978.

21 Stuart Hall, *The Hard Road to Renewal: Thatcherism and the Crisis of the Left*, Verso, London, p. 137.

22 Hall, 'The Great Moving Right Show', *Marxism Today*, January 1979, p. 19.

23 Stuart Hall, 'Authoritarian Populism: A reply' in *Thatcherism*, (eds) Bob Jessop, Kevin Bonnett, Simon Bromley and Tom Ling, Polity Press, Oxford, 1988, p. 100.

24 Hall did not, for example, clearly articulate this shift in the applicability of the concept of populism in reply to his critics who argued that the term was more useful for understanding the rise of Thatcherism in the 1970s than its policy programme once it got into power. See Jessop et al., *Thatcherism*.

25 Michael Freeden, *Ideologies and Political Theory*, p. 384.

26 Stuart Hall, 'The Toad in the Garden: Thatcherism among the Theorists' in *Marxism and the Interpretation of Culture*. University of Illinois Press, Chicago, p. 42.

27 Ibid., p. 37.

28 Ibid., p. 39.

29 Stuart Hall, 'The Great Moving Right Show', p. 18.

30 Michael P. Devereux, Rachel Griffith and Alexander Klemm, 'Why Has the UK Corporation Tax Raised So Much Revenue?' *Institute For Fiscal Studies*, 2004, p. 3.

31 Tom Clark and Andrew Dilnot, 'Long-term Trends in British Taxation and Spending' *Institute for Fiscal Studies*, 2002, pp. 7–8.

32 Jessop et al., *Thatcherism*, p. 88.

33 Zygmunt Bauman, 'Now Way Back to Bliss', *Times Literary Supplement*, 24 January 1997, pp. 4–5.

34 David Canadine, *The Decline and Fall of the British Aristocracy*, Vintage Books, New York, 1999, p. 24.

35 Perry Anderson, 'Origins of the Present Crisis' in *English Questions*, Verso, London, 1992 p. 28.

36 David Canadine, *The Decline and Fall*, p. 238.

37 Ibid., p. 457.

38 Ibid., p. 603.

39 Polly Toynbee, 'What if Downton Abbey Told the Truth about Britain?', see www.theguardian.com/commentisfree/2014/dec/22/downton-abbey-truth-about-britain

40 Matthew d'Ancona, 'Politicians Come and Go but the Queen Gives Us a Sense of Continuity' in *Evening Standard*, Wednesday, April 20, 2016, p. 14.

41 Tom Nairn, *The Enchanted Glass: Britain and Its Monarchy*, Radius, Santa Fe New Mexico, 1988, p. 135.

42 Ibid., p. 118.

43 'A modern Prime Minister controls government like a feudal monarch, exercising Crown powers …', Tony Benn and Andrew Hood, *Common Sense: A New Constitution For Britain*, Hutchinson, London 1993, p. 46.
44 In this instance it was Prime Minister Tony Blair who blocked a criminal investigation on the grounds that it was against the 'national interest'.
45 Benn and Hood, *Common Sense*, p. 37.
46 Benn was critical of those who argued for constitutional change to be limited to procedural rights such as free speech, free association, the right to vote, habeus corpus and so forth. For Benn, these were not 'neutral' rights but had themselves been won by political struggle, and so there was no strong dividing line between them and social and economic rights, which Benn argued, should also be part of a new written constitution. As he witheringly observed, '[a]rguments against social and economic rights usually reflect prejudice or opportunist pragmatism', ibid., p. 78.
47 Ibid., p. 2.
48 Alex Callinicos, 'Exception or Symptom? The British Crisis and the World System', *New Left Review* I, 169, May–June 1988, p. 101.
49 Susan Buck-Morss, *Walter Benjamin and the Arcades Project*, MIT Press, Massachusetts, 1989.
50 Tom Nairn, *The Break-Up*, Verso, London, 1981, pp. 96–8.
51 Krishnan Kumar, 'Englishness and the English National Identity', in *British Cultural Studies: Geography, Nationality, and Identity*, (eds) David Morley and Kevin Robbins, Oxford University Press, Oxford, 2001, p. 43–5.
52 Krishnan Kumar, 'Negotiating English Identity: Englishness, Britishness and the Future of the United Kingdom' in *Nations and Nationalism*, 16 (3), 2010, p. 475.
53 I leave aside Ireland and Northern Ireland which suffered an 'inclusion' into the United Kingdom that was much closer to a conventional colonialist dynamic.
54 Tom Nairn, *The Break-Up*, p. 73.
55 Tony Benn and Andrew Hood, *Common Sense*, p. 98.
56 See Richard Dyer's book *White* for a discussion of the way certain 'ethnicities' (the Irish, the Italians, etc.) create a hierarchy of whiteness judged against the 'norm' of Anglo Saxon whiteness. See also Alastair Bonnett who argues that whiteness was also very largely equated with the middle class in Victorian Britain, and that the working class 'were positioned as marginal to this construction.' 'How the British Working Class Became White: the Symbolic (Re)formation of Racialized Capitalism' in *Journal of Historical Sociology*, 11 (3), 1998, p. 318.
57 Robert C. Young *The Idea of English Ethnicity* Blackwell, Oxford, 2000.
58 Michael Kenny, *The Politics of English Nationhood*, Oxford University Press, Oxford, 2014, p. 60.
59 Krishnan Kumar 'Negotiating English Identity: Englishness, Britishness and the Future of the United Kingdom' *Nations and Nationalism*, 16 (3), 2010, p. 479.
60 Ibid., p. 471.
61 Tom Nairn, *The Break-Up*, pp. 74–8.

62 Paul Gilroy, *There Ain't No Black in the Union Jack: The Cultural Politics of Race and Nation*, Routledge, London, 1993, p. 46.

63 Stuart Hall, 'Political Belonging in a World of Multiple Identities' in *Conceiving Cosmopolitanism, Theory, Context, and Practice*, (eds) Steven Vertovec and Robin Cohen, Oxford University Press, 2002, p. 28.

64 Stuart Hall, 'The Whites of Their Eyes: Racist Ideologies and the Media' in *Silver Linings, Some Strategies for the Eighties*, (eds) George Bridges and Rosalind Brunt, Lawrence and Wishart, London, 1981.

65 Stuart Hall, 'Gramsci and Us', *Marxism Today*, June 1987, p. 19.

66 Robert Eccleshall, 'The Doing of Conservatism', in *Political Ideologies: The Durability of Dissent*, (ed) Michael Freeden, Routledge, London, 2001, p. 68.

67 Kevin Davey, *English Imaginaries*, Lawrence and Wishart, London, 1999, p. 15.

68 Arjun Apparadurai, 'Disjuncture and Difference in the Global Cultural Economy', *Theroy, Culture and Society*, vol. 7, 1990, pp. 295–310.

69 See, for example: www.ons.gov.uk/peoplepopulationandcommunity/culturalidentity/ethnicity/articles/ethnicityandthelabourmarket2011census englandandwales/2014-11-13

70 See, for example: www.poverty.org.uk/06/index.shtml

71 See, for example: www.irr.org.uk/research/statistics/poverty/

72 Steve Fenton, 'Resentment, Class and Social Sentiments about the Nation: The Ethnic Majority in England' in *Ethnicities*, 12 (4), 2012.

73 'Lenny Henry Racism Row Candidate Quits UKIP', www.bbc.co.uk/news/uk-politics-27202753

Chapter 5

1 Perry Anderson, 'Figures of Descent' in *English Questions*, Verso, London, 1992, p. 145.

2 David Ricardo, 'The Principles of Political Economy and Taxation' in *The Liberal Tradition: From Fox to Keynes*, eds) Alan Bullock and Maurice Shock, Clarendon Press, Oxford, 1956, p. 32.

3 Robert Eccleshall, 'The Identity of English Liberalism' *Politics and Society*, 9 (1), 1979, pp. 13–17.

4 Earl Grey, 'Speech in the House of Lords' in *The Liberal Tradition*, p. 6.

5 Thomas Macauley, 'Speech in the House of Commons' *The Liberal Tradition*, p. 23.

6 Jeremy Bentham, 'Plan of Parliamentary Reform', in *The Liberal Tradition*, p. 40.

7 Robert Eccleshall, 'The Identity of English Liberalism', *Politics and Society*, p. 9.

8 Ibid., pp. 11–12.

9 Edmund Burke, *Reflections on the Revolution in France*, J. Dodsley, London, 1793, pp. 64–5.

10 James Curran and Jean Seaton, *Power without Responsibility: The Press and Broadcasting in Britain*, Routledge, London, 1997, p. 11.

11 Friedrich Engels, *The Condition of the Working Class in England*, Penguin Press, London, 2005, p. 139.

12 Jean K. Chalaby, *The Invention of Journalism*, Palgrave/Macmillan, Basingstoke, 1998, p. 14.
13 James Curran and Jean Seaton, *Power without Responsibility*, p. 12.
14 J. A. Epstein 'Feargus O'Connor and The Northern Star', *International Review of Social History*, 21 (1), 1976, p. 53.
15 Ellen Meiksins Wood, *The Pristine Culture of Capitalism*, Verso, London, 1991, p. 74.
16 Curran and Seaton, *Power without Responsibility*, p. 15.
17 Graham Murdock, 'Money Talks: Broadcasting, Finance and Public Culture' in *Behind the Screens, the Structure of British Television in the Nineties*, (ed) Stuart Hood, Pluto Press, London, 1994, pp. 158–9.
18 J.A. Epstein, 'Feargus O'Connor and The Northern Star', p. 51.
19 James Curran and Jean Seaton, *Power without Responsibility*, p. 19.
20 Perry Anderson, 'Origins of the Present Crisis' in *English Questions*, p. 23.
21 'Friends, Brethren, and Fellow-Countrymen', *The Poor Man's Guardian*, May 5, 1832, issue 47.
22 Richard Cobden, 'Speech in London' in *The Liberal Tradition*, p. 48.
23 'Agricultural and Commercial "Vampires": Obligation of Capitalists in Olden Times to Provide Labour for the People', *The Northern Star*, March 9, 1839, Issue 69.
24 Richard Ashcraft, 'Liberal Political Theory and Working–Class Radicalism in Nineteenth-Century England' in *Political Theory*, 21 (2) 1993.
25 Ibid., p. 253.
26 Isambard Kingdom Brunel, 'The New Machine' in *Industrialisation and Culture 1830–1914*, (eds) Christopher Harvie, Graham Martin and Aaron Scharf, Macmillan/Open University Press, London and Basingstoke, 1976, p. 48.
27 Ibid., p. 49.
28 Ibid., pp. 49–50.
29 Martin Weiner, *English Culture and the Decline of the Industrial Spirit*, Cambridge University Press, Cambridge, 2004, p. 18.
30 Antonio Gramsci, *Selections From the Prison Notebooks*, (eds) Quintin Hoare and Geoffrey Nowell Smith, Lawrence and Wishart, London, 1998, p. 302.
31 Michael Freeden, *The New Liberalism, An Ideology of Social Reform*, Clarendon Press, Oxford, 1986, p. 51.
32 Ibid., p. 45.
33 Ibid., p. 121.
34 David Powell, 'The New Liberalism and the Rise of Labour 1886–1906', *The Historical Journal*, 29 (2), 1986, pp. 369–93.
35 Graham John Taylor, *State Regulation and the Politics of Public Service*, Mansell, London, 1999, p. 34.
36 Ibid., pp. 41–2.
37 Robert Eccleshall, 'The Identity of English Liberalism', *Politics and Society*, p. 23.
38 T.H. Green, 'Liberal Legislation or Freedom of Contract' in *The Liberal Tradition*, p. 182.
39 L.T. Hobhouse, 'Liberalism' in *The Liberal Tradition*, p. 192.

40 Ibid., p. 194.

41 Ibid., p. 214.

42 Mark Johnson and Georg Lakoff, *Philosophy in the Flesh: The Embodied Mind and Its Challenge to Western Thought*, Basic Books, New York, 1999, p. 91.

43 Michael Freeden, *The New Liberalism*, pp. 102–3.

44 Robert Eccleshall, 'The Identity of English Liberalism', *Politics and Society*, p. 19.

45 Ibid., p. 30.

46 J.A Hobson, 'The General Election: A Sociological Interpretation', *The Sociological Review*, 3 (2) 1910, p. 108.

47 Ibid., p. 109.

48 Ibid., p. 114.

49 Ibid., p. 113.

50 J.A. Hobson, *Imperialism: A Study*, James Pott & Company, New York, 1902, p. 381.

51 Selina Todd, *The People: The Rise and Fall of the Working Class*, John Murray, London, 2014, p. 14.

52 J.A.Hobson, 'The General Election: A Sociological Interpretation', *The Sociological Review*, 3 (2), 1910, p. 117.

53 For a critique of the politics of Tressell's book, see James D. Young, 'Militancy, English Socialism and the Ragged-Trousered Philanthropists' in *Journal of Contemporary History*, 20 (2), 1985, pp. 283–303.

54 John Ross, *Thatcher and Friends: The Anatomy of the Tory Party*, Pluto Press, London, 1983, p. 48.

55 Martin Weiner, *English Culture*, p. 144.

56 It also means he was probably disappointed by the advent of Thatcherism, since while Thatcherism reinstalled the profit motive as the most important incentive in society, it also rapidly advanced deindustrialisation, combining a more typical version of conservatism: economic liberalism and its various rentier and service sector capital formations.

57 Martin Weiner, *English Culture and the Decline of the Industrial Spirit*, Cambridge University Press, Cambridge, 2004, p. 128.

58 John Grierson, *Grierson on Documentary*. Edited by Forsyth Hardy, Collins, London, 1946, p. 98–9.

59 Ibid., 86.

60 Ibid., p. 138.

61 Ibid., pp. 139–40.

62 Ibid., p. 139.

63 Ibid., p. 198.

64 Jack C. Ellis, *John Grierson: Life, Contributions, Influence*, Southern Illinois Press, 2000, p. 47.

65 Ibid., p. 139.

66 John Grierson, *Grierson on Documentary*, p. 126.

67 See Edward Bernays, *Propaganda*, G Publishing, Brooklyn New York, 2005.

68 John Grierson, *Grierson on Documentary*, p. 140–1.

69 Colin Leys, *Politics in Britain*, Verso, London, 1989, p. 50.

70 John Grierson, *Grierson on Documentary*, p. 171.

71 Ibid., p. 141.

72 Ibid., pp. 184–5.

73 Ibid., p. 185.

74 Ibid., p. 144.

75 Ibid., p. 195.

76 Ibid., p. 196.

77 Jeremy Paxman, *The English: A Portrait of a People*, Penguin, London, 1999, p. 163.

78 Bob Franklin, '"A Good Day to Bury Bad News?": Journalists, Sources and the Packaging of Politics.' In *News, Public Relations and Power*, (ed.) Simon Cottle, Sage, London, 2003.

79 Tom Nairn, *The Break-Up of Britain*, Verso, London, 1981, p. 44.

80 Will Hutton, *The State We're In*, Jonathan Cape, London, 1995.

81 Robert Hewison, *Cultural Capital: The Rise and Fall of Creative Britain*, Verso, London, 2014, p. 35.

82 Tony Blair, 'Britain Is on a Roll Whatever the Pop Stars Say' reprinted in *Contemporary Britain, A Survey with texts*, (ed.) John Oakland, Routledge, London, 2001, p. 53.

83 Toby Miller, 'From Creative to Cultural Industries: Not All Industries Are Cultural and No Industries Are Creative' in *Cultural Studies*, 23 (1), 2009, p. 95.

84 Nicholas Garnham. 'From Cultural to Creative Industries', *International Journal of Cultural Policy*, 11 (1), 2005, pp. 20–1.

85 Department for Culture Media and Sport, 'Creative Industries Economic Estimates', January 2016, p. 11.

86 Don Redding, 'The Non-democratic Regulator: A Response to Sylvia Harvey' in *Screen*, 47 (1), Spring, 2006.

87 Larry Elliott and Dan Atkinson, *Fantasy Island: Waking Up to the Incredible Economic, Political and Social Illusions of the Blair Legacy*, Constable and Robinson, London 2007.

88 Ibid., p. 76.

89 Mark Banks and David Hesmondhalgh, 'Looking for Work in Creative Industries Policy' in *International Journal of Cultural Policy*, 15 (4), 2009.

90 Nick Srnicek, *Platform Capitalism*, Polity, Cambridge, 2017.

91 Luc Boltanksi and Eve Chiapello, *The New Spirit of Capitalism*, Verso, London, 2007.

92 Andrew Ross, *Nice Work If You Can Get It: Life and Labour in Precarious Times*, New York University Press, New York, 2010, p. 16.

93 Jim McGuigan, *Cool Capitalism*, Pluto Press, London, 2009, p. 124.

94 Blair, 'Britain Is on a Roll Whatever the Pop Stars Say', p. 55.

95 The class inequalities structuring access and opportunities in the acting profession has attracted scholarly research and goes some way to evidencing how little meritocracy there actually is in the cultural industries. See Sam Friedman, Dave O'Brien and Daniel Laurison, '"Like Skydiving without a Parachute": How class origin shapes occupational trajectories in British acting.' *Sociology*, February 2016. The feature documentary *The Acting Class* (dir Deirdre O'Neill and Michael Wayne 2017) also explores these issues.

96 David Graeber, 'Despair Fatigue' *The Baffler*, No.30 March 2016, https://
    thebaffler.com/salvos/despair-fatigue-david-graeber

Chapter 6

1   Tom Devine, *The Scottish Nation, 1700–2007*, Penguin Books, London, 2006.
2   Kevin Bonnett, Simon Bromley, Bob Jessop and Tom Ling, 'Popular
    Capitalism, Flexible Accumulation and Left Strategy' in *New Left Review I*
    165, Sept–Oct 1987.
3   A.E. Green, 'The North-South Divide in Great Britain: An Examination of
    the Evidence' *Transactions of the Institute of British Geographers* vol. 13 (2)
    p. 191.
4   David Smith, *North and South: Britain's Growing Divide*, Penguin Books,
    London, 1989, p. 31.
5   Graham Gudgin and Andrew Schofield, 'The Emergence of the North-
    South Divide and Its Projected Future' in *Spatial Policy in a Divided Nation*,
    (eds) Richard T.Harrison and Mark Hart, Jessica Kingsley Publishers,
    London and Philadelphia, 1993, p. 24.
6   Andrew Gamble, 'The Great Divide' in *Marxism Today*, March 1987, p. 13.
7   A.E. Green, 'The North-South Divide', p. 182.
8   Graham Gudgin and Andrew Schofield, 'The Emergence', p. 28.
9   Neil Davidson, 'Neoliberal Politics in a Devolved Scotland', *Neoliberal
    Scotland, Class and Society in a Stateless Nation*, (eds) Neil Davidson,
    Patricia McCafferty and David Miller, Cambridge Scholars, Newcastle
    Upon Tyne, 2010, p. 333.
10 See David Torrance, *The Battle for Britain and the Independence Referendum*,
    Biteback, London, 2013, p. 73–4 and Neil Davidson, 'Neoliberal Politics in a
    Devolved Scotland', ibid., p. 352.
11 'Johann Lamont Raises Questions over Free Tuition Policy', available at:
    www.bbc.co.uk/news/uk-scotland-scotland-politics-20755329
12 Tom Nairn, *The Break-Up of Britain*, Verso, London, 1981, p. 73.
13 Ibid., p. 48.
14 Ibid., p. 51.
15 Ibid., p. 22.
16 Scottish Government, *Scotland's Future*, Edinburgh, 2013, p. 5.
17 Ibid., p. 351.
18 Ibid., p. 353.
19 David Torrance cites one Downing Street advisor thus: 'The Nationalists I'm
    used to are blood-and-soil types; "we were wronged historically and need
    to correct it", explained one advisor. "But the SNP aren't like that, they talk
    about values, social justice and the economy".' See *The Battle For Britain,
    Scotland and the Independence Referendum*, Biteback Publishing, London,
    p. 183.
20 Ibid., p. 185.
21 Jan-Werner Müller, *Constitutional Patriotism*, Princeton University Press,
    2009.
22 Étienne Balibar, *Politics and the Other Scene*, Verso, London, 2002, p. 61.

23 'Scotland at Crossroads ahead of Referendum', *Manchester Evening News*, 26 August 2014 p. 10.
24 Martin Kettle, *The Guardian*, 17 September, 2014, 'Don't let Salmond blind you to the yes campaign's dark side: The referendum has energised Scotland but also divided its people. That's what nationalism does', p. 35.
25 Douglas Alexander, *The Daily Telegraph*, Sep, 18, 2014, p. 22. Alexander forgot about the sizeable proportion of Scots who were also hoping for a Yes vote, but he was to be reminded of that in the General Election the following year when he lost his seat to the SNP's Mhairi Black, who became the youngest MP elected to the House of Commons since 1832.
26 Tom Nairn, *The Break-Up*, p. 78.
27 Editorial, *London Evening Standard*, 26 August, 2014, p. 14.
28 *Scotland Decides: The Dimbleby Interviews*, BBC One, 16 September 2014, 21:00–22.00.
29 David Torrance, *The Battle for Britain*, p. 181.
30 'As It Happened: Scottish Independence Campaign', *The Daily Telegraph*, Monday 15 September, www.telegraph.co.uk/news/uknews/scottish-independence/11098097/As-it-happened-Scottish-independence-campaign-Monday-September-15-2014.html
31 Tom McTague, ''Why Are We Paying Them to Eat Deep-fried Mars Bars When We Can't Even Get Decent Health Care in this Country?', *Mail Online*, 15 September 2014, www.dailymail.co.uk/news/article-2756338/Why-paying-eat-deep-fried-Mars-Bars-t-decent-health-care-Tory-MPs-demand-English-Parliament.html
32 Richard Littlejohn, 'Stop the Referendum – I Am Declaring Myself Independent', *Scottish Daily Mail*, 9 September 2014, p. 17.
33 Despite his rehabilitation by post-structuralism, Nietzsche's *On the Genealogy of Morality* is a truly chilling vision of power seeking to free itself from any moral inhibitions. For Nietzsche, *ressentiment* is a category that reveals the 'cunning' of the subaltern. No doubt the subaltern must be cunning in their subversion of the master's power, but the way Nietzsche himself uses *ressentiment*, makes it a category of the way things look to those in power.
34 Nancy Fraser et al., *Transnationalizing The Public Sphere*, Polity Press, Cambridge, 2014.
35 Philip Schlesinger, 'Scottish Devolution and the Media', *Politics and the Media: Harlots and Prerogatives at the Turn of the Millenium*, Blackwell, Oxford, 1998, p. 56.
36 It would be a mistake to exaggerate or essentialise the political differences between Scotland and the rest of the UK. Research on social attitudes, which itself must be treated cautiously as a snapshot of where opinion is at any one time, not as a timeless 'truth' impervious to political change, suggests that the differences are modest. See for example John Curtice and Rachel Ormston 'Is Scotland More Left-wing than England?' *British Social Attitudes* 28, no. 42, 5 December 2011.
37 Philip Schlesinger, David Miller and William Dinan, *Open Scotland? Journalists, Spin Doctors and Lobbyists*, Polygon, Edinburgh, 2001, p. 40–1.
38 Ibid., p. 261.

39 Philip Schlesinger, 'Communication Policy' in *The Media in Scotland*, (eds) Neil Blain and David Hutchison, Edinburgh University Press, Edinburgh, 2008, p. 38.

40 Philip Schlesinger et al., *Open Scotland?*, p. 34.

41 John Robertson, *Fairness in the First Year? BBC and ITV Coverage of the Scottish Referendum Campaign from September 2012 to September 2013.* http://issuu.com/creative_futur/docs/robertson2014fairnessinthefirstyear

42 Peter Geoghegan, *The People's Referendum: Why Scotland Will Never Be the Same Again*, Luath Press Limited, Edinburgh, 2015, p. 149.

43 www.dailyrecord.co.uk/news/politics/latest-survation-poll-shows-england-6015818

44 Pat Anderson, *Fear and Smear: The Campaign Against Scottish Independence*, Snowy Publications, Edinburgh, 2015.

45 See a more extended discussion of this in Michael Wayne, 'Beneath the Bias, the Crisis: The Press, the Independent Media and the Scottish Referendum' in *International Journal of Media and Cultural Politics*, 12 (3), 2016.

46 David Hutcheon, 'The History of the Press' in *The Media in Scotland*, (eds) Neil Blain and David Hutcheon, Edinburgh University Press, Edinburgh, 2008, p. 67.

47 Iain MacWhirter, *Disunited Kingdom: How Westminster Won a Referendum but Lost Scotland*, Cargo Press, Glasgow, 2014, p. 73.

48 Michael Wayne, Julian Petley, Craig Murray, Lesley Henderson, *Television News, Politics and Young People: Generation Disconnected?* Palgrave, 2010.

49 Iain MacWhirter, *Disunited Kingdom*, p. 88.

50 Paolo Gerbaudo, *Tweets and the Streets: Social Media and Contemporary Activism*, Pluto Press, London, 2012, p. 135.

51 Antonio Gramsci, *A Gramsci Reader*, (ed.) David Forgacs, Lawrence and Wishart, London, 1988, p. 250.

52 Iain MacWhirter, *Disunited Kingdom*, p. 55.

53 Ibid., p. 88.

54 Antonio Gramsci, *The Modern Prince and Other Writings*, Lawrence and Wishart, London, 1967, p. 58.

55 Dominic Ponsford, 'Survey Reveals Importance of Media in Helping Scots Make Referendum Decision'. www.pressgazette.co.uk/survey-reveals-importance-media-helping-scots-make-referendum-decision

56 Angela Haggerty, Social Media More Influential Information Source than Newspapers in Scottish Independence Referendum', www.thedrum.com/news/2014/10/17/social-media-more-influential-information-source-newspapers-scottish-independence

57 Vivien A. Schmidt, 'Britain-out and Trump-in: A Discursive Institutional Analysis of the British Referendum on the EU and the US Presidential Election' in *Review of International Political Economy*, 24 (2), 2017, p. 255.

58 George Monbiot, 'Neoliberalism – the Ideology at the Root of All Our Problems' in *The Guardian*. www.theguardian.com/books/2016/apr/15/neoliberalism-ideology-problem-george-monbiot

59 Stephen Cusion and Justin Lewis, 'Impartiality, Statistical Tit-for-tats and the Construction of Balance: UK Television New Reporting of the 2016 EU Referendum Campaign' in *European Journal of Communication*, 32 (3), 2017,

pp. 213–15. The authors found that 71 per cent of all politicians appearing on TV nightly news bulletins over the campaign were from the Conservative Party, another extraordinary failure of diversity of political opinion.

60 Socialist Resistance, http://socialistresistance.org/brexit-vote-is-a-disaster-but-the-struggle-goes-on/8534

61 John Pilger, http://johnpilger.com/articles/why-the-british-said-no-to-europe

62 BrendanO'Neill,www.spectator.co.uk/2016/07/brexit-voters-are-not-thick-not-racist-just-poor

63 Christakis Georgiou, 'British Capitalism and European Unification, from Ottawa to the Brexit Referendum' in *Historical Materialism*, 25 (1), 2017, pp. 90–129.

64 Although in 2017, the Conservative trade secretary Liam Fox triggered a row about US chlorinated-washed chicken being imported into the UK in early exploratory talks about a trade deal with the US authorities. See 'The UK Cabinet Flap over Chlorinated Chicken' in the *Financial Times*, 24 July, 2017: www.ft.com/content/f17e1e64-7063-11e7-93ff-99f383b09ff9. It seems that conservative hopes that everyone will sign up for the free-market deregulated utopia of the future may fall short.

65 Mark I. Vail, 'Between One-Nation Toryism and Neoliberalism: The Dilemmas of British Conservatism and Britain's Evolving Place in Europe.' *Journal of Common Market Studies*, 53 (1), 2015, p. 106.

66 Margaret Thatcher, 'Speech to the College of Europe', 20 September 1988, www.margaretthatcher.org/document/107332

67 Wolfgang Streeck, *How Will Capitalism End?* Verso, London, 2016, pp. 151–63.

68 Imogen Tyler, *Revolting Subjects: Social Abjection and Resistance in Neoliberal Britain*, Zed Books, London, 2013.

69 Simon Winlow, Steve Hall, James Treadwell, *The Rise of the Right: English Nationalism and the Transformation of Working-class Politics*, Policy Press, Bristol, 2017, p. 72.

70 Gramsci, *The Modern Prince*, p. 147.

71 Nathaniel Copsey and Tim Haughton, 'Farewell Britannia? "Issue Capture" and the Politics of David Cameron's 2013 Referendum Pledge' *Journal of Common Market Studies*, 52, June 2014, pp. 78–9.

72 Benjamin Hawkins, 'Nation, Separation and Threat: An analysis of British media Discourses on the European Union Treaty Reform Process' in *Journal of Common Market Studies*, 50 (4), 2012, pp. 561–77.

73 According to Anthony Hilton, he once asked Rupert Murdoch why he was so hostile to the EU. '"That's easy" he replied. "When I go into Downing Street they do what I say; when I go to Brussels they take no notice."' See www.standard.co.uk/comment/comment/anthony-hilton-stay-or-go-the-lack-of-solid-facts-means-it-s-all-a-leap-of-faith-a3189151.html

74 Copsey and Haughton, 'Farewell Britannia?', p. 85.

75 Kevin Davey, *English Imaginaries*, Lawrence and Wishart, London, 1999, p. 9.

76 Peter Ives, *Language and Hegemony in Gramsci*, Pluto Press, London, 2004, p. 60.

77 Antonio Gramsci, *Prison Notebooks*, (ed.) Jospeh A. Buttigieg, Columbia University Press, New York, p. 273.

78 Karl Heinz Roth, *Greece: What Is to Be Done?*, Zero Books, Alresford, 2013.

Chapter 7

1 Stuart Hall, *The Hard Road to Renewal: Thatcherism and the Crisis of the Left*, Verso, London, 1988, p. 177.
2 Ibid., p. 178.
3 Stuart Hall, 'The Toad in the Garden: Thatcherism among the Theorists' in *Marxism and the Interpretation of Culture*, University of Illinois Press, Chicago, p. 43.
4 A.K. Voronsky, *Art as the Cognition of Life*, Mehring Books, Michigan, 1998, pp. 147–8.
5 Stuart Hall, *The Hard Road*, p. 179.
6 Stuart Hall, 'The Problem of Ideology, Marxism without Guarantees' in *Stuart Hall: Critical Dialogues in Cultural Studies*, (eds) David Morley and Kuan-Hsing Chen Routledge, London, 1996, p. 38.
7 Stuart Hall, *The Hard Road*, p. 179.
8 Stuart Hall, 'The Problem of Ideology', p. 29.
9 Aeron Davis, 'Mediation, Financialization, and the Global Financial Crisis: An Inverted Political Economy Perspective' in *The Political Economies of Media*, (eds) Dwayne Winseck and Dal Yong Jin, Bloomsbury, London, 2012.
10 Stuart Hall, 'The Problem of Ideology', p. 32.
11 Ibid., p. 26.
12 Ernesto Laclau, 'Metaphor and Social Antagonism' in *Marxism and the Interpretation of Culture*, p. 254.
13 Stuart Hall, 'The Rediscovery of "Ideology": Return of the Repressed in Media Studies' in *Cultural Theory and Popular Culture*, (ed.) John Storey, Routledge, London, 2009, p. 131.
14 Stuart Hall, *The Hard Road*, p. 130.
15 Antonio Gramsci, *A Gramsci Reader*, (ed.) David Forgacs, Lawrence and Wishart, 1988, p. 201.
16 Ibid., pp. 201–2.
17 David Miller, 'Media Power and Class Power: Overplaying Ideology' in *Socialist Register*, 2002, p. 254.
18 'Authoritarian Populism, Two Nations and Thatcherism' in *Thatcherism*, Bob Jessop, Kevin Bonnett, Simon Bromley and Tom Ling, Polity Press, Cambridge, 1988, p. 73.
19 Ibid., p. 73.
20 Stuart Hall, 'The Rediscovery of "Ideology": Return of the Repressed in Media Studies' in *Cultural Theory*, pp. 120–2.
21 David Miller, 'Media Power and Class Power: Overplaying Ideology' in *Socialist Register*, 2002, p. 248.
22 Stuart Hall, 'The Rediscovery of "Ideology"', p. 140.
23 'Authoritarian Populism', p. 74.
24 Stuart Hall, 'Authoritarian Populism: A Reply' in *Thatcherism*, pp. 100–1.
25 Stuart Hall, 'The Toad in the Garden', p. 40.
26 Stuart Hall, 'Authoritarian Populism: A Reply', p. 103.
27 Ibid., p. 104.

28 Stuart Hall, *The Hard Road*, p. 188.

29 Nicholas Abercrombie, Stephen Hill, Bryan S. Turner, *The Dominant Ideology Thesis*, George Allen & Unwin, London, 1980, pp. 128–40.

30 Ibid., pp. 140–51. For example, the rights of private property to do as it pleases or the profit motive itself, did not command universal assent on the sociological evidence the authors considered in the 1970s.

31 Ibid., p. 163.

32 Stuart Hall, 'The Neo-Liberal Revolution' in *Cultural Studies*, 25 (6), 2011, p. 711.

33 Stuart Hall, *The Hard Road*, p. 145.

34 In 1971, 52.8 per cent of women were in the labour market in some capacity. In 1979 it was 56.9 per cent: a 4 per cent increase. By 1990 this had increased to 63.3 per cent: a 6 per cent rise, and by 1997 when the Conservatives lost power it had increased again to 64.3 per cent. By 2013 the percentage of women in employed had only gained a further 2 per cent. The biggest increase in women's employment occurred, then, during the Conservative Party's years in office. See Labour Force Survey, Office for National Statistics, 25 September 2013.

35 *Elitist Britain?* 2014, pp. 11–14. www.gov.uk/government/publications/elitist-britain

36 Stuart Hall, *The Hard Road*, p. 127.

37 Ibid., p. 207.

38 Karl Marx, *The Eighteenth Brumaire of Louis Bonaparte*, Lawrence and Wishart, London, 1984, p. 79. Marx meant by this term the way the spectacle of bourgeois politics seems to transfix its protagonists as if they were at the centre of the universe, instead of very often the last place to ratify and catch up with movements and forces that are happening elsewhere.

39 Stuart Hall, *The Hard Road*, p. 207.

40 Ibid.

41 Ibid., p. 134.

42 Ibid., p. 135.

43 Ibid., p. 143.

44 Ibid., p. 223.

45 Ibid., p. 248.

46 Ibid., p. 186.

47 Ibid., p. 187.

48 Ibid., p. 227.

49 Ibid., p. 228.

50 Ibid., p. 230.

51 Ibid.

52 Ibid., p. 231.

53 Ibid.

54 Ibid., p. 180.

55 Carl Boggs argues that both liberalism and Marxism have common roots in a Jacobin ideology susceptible to a 'technocratic elitism'. See *Intellectuals and the Crisis of Modernity*, State University of New York Press, New York, 1993, p. 24.

56 See Deirdre O'Neill and Mike Wayne, 'On Intellectuals' in *Considering Class, Theory, Culture and the Media in the 21st Century*, (eds) Deirdre O'Neill and Mike Wayne, Brill, 2017.
57 Stuart Hall, *The Hard Road*, p. 208.
58 See, for example, Hall's discussion of the Miners' Strike, *The Hard Road*, pp. 203–5.
59 Ibid., p. 200.
60 Ibid., p. 245.
61 See my discussion of this in *Marxism and Media Studies: Key Concepts and Contemporary Trends*, Pluto Press, 2003, pp. 44–6.
62 Stuart Hall, *The Hard Road*, p. 187.

Chapter 8

1 Karl Marx, *Grundrisse*, Penguin Books, London, p. 334.
2 Wolfgang Streeck, *How Will Capitalism End?* Verso, London, 2016, p. 48.
3 One measure of the defunding of the Social state has been the decline of public investment in fixed assets. Total public investment as a percentage of GDP declined from 8.9 per cent in 1975 to 1.7 per cent in 2000. See Tom Clark, Mike Elsby and Sarah Love, 'Twenty-Five Years of Falling Investment?', Institute of Fiscal Studies, Briefing Note 20, www.ifs.org.uk/bns/bn20.pdf
4 Start Hall, 'The Toad in the Garden: Thatcherism among the Theorists' in *Marxism and the Interpretation of Culture*, University of Illinois Press, Chicago, p. 43.
5 John Sanbonmatsu, *The Postmodern Prince*, Monthly Review Press, New York, 2004, pp. 157–202.
6 Stuart Hall, *The Hard Road to Renewal: Thatcherism and the Crisis of the Left*, Verso, London, 1988, p. 229.
7 See Judith Williamson, '"Up Where You Belong": Hollywood Images of Big Business in the 1980s' in *Enterprise and Heritage: Crosscurrents of National Culture*, (eds) John Corner and Sylvia Harvey, Routledge, 1991.
8 Mike Savage, *Social Class in the 21st Century*, Pelican, London, 2015, pp. 265–7.
9 Stuart Hall, *The Hard Road*, pp. 204–5.
10 See John McMurray, *The Cancer Stage of Capitalism: From Crisis to Cure*, Pluto Press and Fernwood, London, 2013.

Index

Printed and bound by CPI Group (UK) Ltd, Croydon, CR0 4YY

23/04/2025

14661019-0004